First World War
and Army of Occupation
War Diary
France, Belgium and Germany

7 DIVISION
Headquarters, Branches and Services
Adjutant and Quarter-Master General
31 August 1914 - 31 December 1914

WO95/1635

Published by

The Naval & Military Press Ltd

Unit 10 Ridgewood Industrial Park,

Uckfield, East Sussex,

TN22 5QE England

Tel: +44 (0) 1825 749494

www.naval-military-press.com

www.nmarchive.com

This diary has been reprinted in facsimile from the original. Any imperfections are inevitably reproduced and the quality may fall short of modern type and cartographic standards.

© **Crown Copyright**
Images reproduced by permission of The National Archives, London, England, 2015.

Contents

Document type	Place/Title	Date From	Date To
Heading	7th Division 'A' & 'Q' Branch Aug 1914-Dec 1914		
Heading	Headquarters (AA & QMG) 7th Division Vol I 31.8-30.11.14		
Miscellaneous	A.G. Base.	14/12/1914	14/12/1914
War Diary		31/08/1914	06/10/1914
War Diary	Bruges	07/10/1914	08/10/1914
War Diary	Ostend	08/10/1914	10/10/1914
War Diary	Bruges	10/10/1914	10/10/1914
War Diary	Beernem	10/10/1914	11/10/1914
War Diary	Ghent	11/10/1914	11/10/1914
War Diary	Beernem	12/10/1914	12/10/1914
War Diary	Roulers	13/10/1914	14/10/1914
War Diary	Hooge	16/10/1914	31/10/1914
War Diary	Halte	01/11/1914	02/11/1914
War Diary	Ypres	03/11/1914	10/11/1914
War Diary	Bailleul	11/11/1914	17/11/1914
War Diary	Sailly	18/11/1914	30/11/1914
Miscellaneous	Reinforcements Received 7th Division		
Miscellaneous	Appendix-3		
Miscellaneous	Appendix-B		
Miscellaneous	Appendix-B 7th Division 6th Division	30/11/1914	30/11/1914
Miscellaneous	Casualties, 7th Division. 18th October 1914 To 13th November 1914	18/10/1914	18/10/1914
Miscellaneous			
Heading	A & Q 7th Div Dec 1914		
War Diary	Sailly	01/12/1914	31/12/1914
Miscellaneous	Detail Of Re-inforcements Received By 7th Division On December 2nd 1914	02/12/1914	02/12/1914
Miscellaneous	Detail Of Re-inforcements Received By 7th Division On December 13th 1914	13/12/1914	13/12/1914
Miscellaneous	Detail Of Re-inforcements Received By 7th Division On December 17th 1914	17/12/1914	17/12/1914
Miscellaneous	7th Division Casualties Operation 18th/19th December 1914 Appendix D	18/12/1914	18/12/1914
Miscellaneous	1st Bn. S. Staffordshire Regiment	15/12/1914	15/12/1914
Operation(al) Order(s)	7th Divisional Routine Order No. 70 Appendix V (a)	15/12/1914	15/12/1914
Miscellaneous	Nominal Roll Officer Departing to Front	16/12/1914	16/12/1914
Operation(al) Order(s)	7th Divisional Routine Orders. No. 60 Appendix VIII	22/12/1914	22/12/1914
Miscellaneous	7th D. O. No. 80 Dated 22/12/14 Administrative Staff	22/12/1914	22/12/1914
Miscellaneous	Nominal Roll Offers To Font	22/12/1914	22/12/1914
Miscellaneous	Detail Of Re-inforcements Received By 7th Division On December 23rd 1914 Appendix E	23/12/1914	23/12/1914
Miscellaneous	Order To Proceed Appendix F	24/12/1914	24/12/1914
Miscellaneous	Order To Proceed	24/12/1914	24/12/1914
Miscellaneous	Qrs 22nd Bde Hd	26/12/1914	26/12/1914
Miscellaneous	B Form Messages And Signals.		
Miscellaneous	2nd Battn Border Regiment	29/11/1914	29/11/1914
Miscellaneous	6th Battalion Gordon Highlanders Nominal Roll Of Officer		
Miscellaneous			

Miscellaneous	2nd Battn Scots Guards		
Miscellaneous	Daily Report	12/10/1914	12/10/1914
Miscellaneous	2/h War H	30/12/1914	30/12/1914
Miscellaneous	Daily Return	30/12/1914	30/12/1914
Miscellaneous	2nd Bn The Return Rgt	30/12/1914	30/12/1914
Miscellaneous	1st Bn R.W. Fus.	30/12/1914	30/12/1914
Miscellaneous	Cavalry, Artillery And Infantry Only	29/11/1914	29/11/1914
Miscellaneous	Officers Absent On Duty		
Miscellaneous	Cavalry, Artillery And Infantry Only	30/11/1914	30/11/1914
Miscellaneous	Officers Absent On Duty		
Miscellaneous	Cavalry, Artillery And Infantry Only.	30/11/1914	30/11/1914
Miscellaneous	Officers Absent On Duty		
Miscellaneous	Cavalry, Artillery And Infantry Only	30/11/1914	30/11/1914
Miscellaneous	Officers Absent On Duty		
Miscellaneous	Nominal Roll Of Officers	30/11/1914	30/11/1914
Miscellaneous	2nd Bn The Gordon Highlanders	30/11/1914	30/11/1914
Miscellaneous			
Miscellaneous	2 Bn. Wiltshire Regt	30/11/1914	30/11/1914
Miscellaneous	Cavalry, Artillery And Infantry Only	30/11/1914	30/11/1914
Miscellaneous	Officers Absent On Duty		
Miscellaneous	Cavalry, Artillery And Infantry Only	01/12/1914	01/12/1914
Miscellaneous	Officers Absent On Duty		
Miscellaneous	Cavalry, Artillery And Infantry Only	30/11/1914	30/11/1914
Miscellaneous	Officers Absent On Duty		
Miscellaneous	Cavalry, Artillery And Infantry Only	30/11/1914	30/11/1914
Miscellaneous	Officers Absent On Duty		
Miscellaneous	10th Bn R W Fus	30/11/1914	30/11/1914
Miscellaneous	Nominal Roll Of Officers R. A. M. Corps		
Miscellaneous		12/12/1914	12/12/1914
Miscellaneous	7th Divisional Train Nominal Roll Of Offeceir Of The Above Formation	11/12/1914	11/12/1914
Miscellaneous	3 Infantry Brigade	01/12/1914	01/12/1914
Miscellaneous	22nd Infantry Brigade	01/12/1914	01/12/1914
Miscellaneous	Work On Support And Communication	02/12/1914	02/12/1914
Miscellaneous	7th Division		
Miscellaneous	Daily Routine In Trenches For A Company 2nd Battn Border Regiment	09/12/1914	09/12/1914
Miscellaneous	20th Doc	06/12/1914	06/12/1914
Miscellaneous	A Form Messages And Signals.		
Miscellaneous	Daily Routine In The Trenches 1st Battn		
Miscellaneous	20th Inf Bde		
Miscellaneous	Battalion Order	27/11/1914	27/11/1914
Miscellaneous	Battalion Orders	27/11/1914	27/11/1914
Miscellaneous	Daily Routine In The Frenches		
Miscellaneous	7th Division Routine Orders 1914		
Operation(al) Order(s)	7th Division Routine Orders No 1	03/09/1914	03/09/1914
Miscellaneous	G.S.O 1		
Operation(al) Order(s)	7th Division Routine Orders No. 2	05/09/1914	05/09/1914
Miscellaneous	G.S.O 1		
Operation(al) Order(s)	7th Division Routine Orders No. 3	04/09/1914	04/09/1914
Miscellaneous	G.S.O 1		
Operation(al) Order(s)	7th Division Routine Orders No. 4	09/09/1914	09/09/1914
Operation(al) Order(s)	7th Division Routine Orders No. 5	11/09/1914	11/09/1914
Operation(al) Order(s)	7th Division Routine Orders No. 6	12/09/1914	12/09/1914
Miscellaneous	Administrative Staff		
Operation(al) Order(s)	7th Divisional Routine Orders. No. 7	14/09/1914	14/09/1914

Type	Title	Date 1	Date 2
Operation(al) Order(s)	7th Divisional Routine Orders. No. 8	15/09/1914	15/09/1914
Miscellaneous	7th division evening conference	15/09/1914	15/09/1914
Operation(al) Order(s)	7th division routine orders no. 9	16/09/1914	16/09/1914
Miscellaneous	7th division evening conference	16/09/1914	16/09/1914
Operation(al) Order(s)	7th divisional routine orders. no. 10	17/09/1914	17/09/1914
Operation(al) Order(s)	7th divisional routine orders. no. 11	18/09/1914	18/09/1914
Operation(al) Order(s)	7th divisional routine orders. no. 12	14/09/1914	14/09/1914
Operation(al) Order(s)	7th Division Routine Orders no. 13	21/09/1914	21/09/1914
Operation(al) Order(s)	7th Division Routine Orders no. 14	21/09/1914	21/09/1914
Operation(al) Order(s)	7th Division Routine Orders no. 15	22/09/1914	22/09/1914
Operation(al) Order(s)	7th Division Routine Orders no. 15	21/09/1914	21/09/1914
Operation(al) Order(s)	7th Division Routine Orders no. 16	23/09/1914	23/09/1914
Miscellaneous	Shoot 2 Of Routine Order No. 16		
Operation(al) Order(s)	7th Division Routine Orders no. 17	24/09/1914	24/09/1914
Miscellaneous	March Discipline		
Operation(al) Order(s)	7th Division Routine Orders No. 18	25/09/1914	25/09/1914
Operation(al) Order(s)	7th Division Routine Orders No. 18	26/09/1914	26/09/1914
Operation(al) Order(s)	7th Division Routine Orders No. 20	27/09/1914	27/09/1914
Operation(al) Order(s)	7th Division Routine Orders No. 21	28/09/1914	28/09/1914
Operation(al) Order(s)	7th Division Routine Orders No. 22	29/09/1914	29/09/1914
Operation(al) Order(s)	7th Division Routine Orders No. 23	30/09/1914	30/09/1914
Miscellaneous	Deficiencies		
Operation(al) Order(s)	7th Division Routine Orders. No. 23	30/09/1914	30/09/1914
Miscellaneous	Special 7th Divisional Order	01/10/1914	01/10/1914
Operation(al) Order(s)	7th Division Routine Orders No. 24	01/10/1914	01/10/1914
Operation(al) Order(s)	7th Division Routine Orders No. 25	02/10/1914	02/10/1914
Miscellaneous	Preliminary Orders For Evacuation Of Lyndhurst And Ashurst Camps	01/10/1914	01/10/1914
Operation(al) Order(s)	7th Divisional Routine Orders No. 26	03/10/1914	03/10/1914
Operation(al) Order(s)	7th Divisional Routine Orders No. 27	04/10/1914	04/10/1914
Operation(al) Order(s)	7th Divisional Routine Orders No. 29	16/09/1914	16/09/1914
Operation(al) Order(s)	7th Divisional Routine Orders No. 28	14/10/1914	14/10/1914
Operation(al) Order(s)	7th Divisional Routine Orders No. 50	17/10/1914	17/10/1914
Operation(al) Order(s)	7th Divisional Routine Orders No. 31	18/10/1914	18/10/1914
Miscellaneous	Instructions Regarding The Services Of Maintenance For The Guidance Of The 3rd Cavalry Division And 4th Corps	14/10/1914	14/10/1914
Operation(al) Order(s)	7th Divisional Routine Orders No. 33	23/10/1914	23/10/1914
Operation(al) Order(s)	7th Divisional Routine Orders No. 34	27/10/1914	27/10/1914
Operation(al) Order(s)	7th Divisional Routine Orders No. 35	28/10/1914	28/10/1914
Operation(al) Order(s)	7th Divisional Routine Orders No. 36	04/11/1914	04/11/1914
Operation(al) Order(s)	7th Divisional Routine Orders No. 37	07/11/1914	07/11/1914
Operation(al) Order(s)	7th Divisional Routine Orders No. 38	08/11/1914	08/11/1914
Operation(al) Order(s)	7th Divisional Routine Orders No. 30	09/11/1914	09/11/1914
Operation(al) Order(s)	7th Divisional Routine Orders No. 40	10/11/1914	10/11/1914
Operation(al) Order(s)	7th Divisional Routine Orders No. 41	11/11/1914	11/11/1914
Operation(al) Order(s)	7th Divisional Routine Orders No. 42	12/11/1914	12/11/1914
Operation(al) Order(s)	7th Divisional Routine Orders No. 45	15/11/1914	15/11/1914
Operation(al) Order(s)	7th Divisional Routine Orders No. 44	16/11/1914	16/11/1914
Operation(al) Order(s)	7th Divisional Routine Orders No. 45	17/11/1914	17/11/1914
Operation(al) Order(s)	7th Divisional Routine Orders No. 46	18/11/1914	18/11/1914
Miscellaneous	Care Of Horses And Stable Management In The Field	18/11/1914	18/11/1914
Operation(al) Order(s)	7th Divisional Routine Orders No. 47	19/11/1914	19/11/1914
Operation(al) Order(s)	7th Divisional Routine Orders No. 48	20/11/1914	20/11/1914
Operation(al) Order(s)	7th Divisional Routine Orders No. 49	21/11/1914	21/11/1914
Operation(al) Order(s)	7th Divisional Routine Orders No. 50	22/11/1914	22/11/1914

Type	Description	Date 1	Date 2
Miscellaneous	Issued With 7th Divl Routine Orders Of 22/11/14 Clearing Areas Of Inhabitants	22/11/1914	22/11/1914
Miscellaneous	Issued With 7th Divl Routine Orders Of 22/11/14 Sanitation	22/11/1914	22/11/1914
Operation(al) Order(s)	7th Divisional Routine Orders No. 50	22/11/1914	22/11/1914
Operation(al) Order(s)	7th Divisional Routine Orders No. 51	23/11/1914	23/11/1914
Operation(al) Order(s)	7th Divisional Routine Orders No. 52	24/11/1914	24/11/1914
Miscellaneous	7th Division Return Of Horse Casualties For Week Ending 21st November 1914	21/11/1914	21/11/1914
Operation(al) Order(s)	7th Divisional Routine Orders No. 53	25/11/1914	25/11/1914
Operation(al) Order(s)	7th Divisional Routine Orders No. 54	26/11/1914	26/11/1914
Operation(al) Order(s)	7th Divisional Routine Orders No. 55	27/11/1914	27/11/1914
Operation(al) Order(s)	7th Divisional Routine Orders No. 56	28/11/1914	28/11/1914
Operation(al) Order(s)	7th Divisional Routine Orders No. 57	29/11/1914	29/11/1914
Operation(al) Order(s)	7th Divisional Routine Orders No. 58	30/11/1914	30/11/1914
Miscellaneous	7th Divisional Routine Orders.	01/12/1914	01/12/1914
Operation(al) Order(s)	7th Divisional Routine Orders No. 59	01/12/1914	01/12/1914
Miscellaneous	7th Division		
Operation(al) Order(s)	7th Divisional Routine Orders No 60	02/12/1914	02/12/1914
Operation(al) Order(s)	7th Divisional Routine Orders No 61	03/12/1914	03/12/1914
Operation(al) Order(s)	7th Divisional Routine Orders No 62	04/12/1914	04/12/1914
Operation(al) Order(s)	7th Divisional Routine Orders No 63	05/12/1914	05/12/1914
Operation(al) Order(s)	7th Divisional Routine Orders No 64	06/12/1914	06/12/1914
Miscellaneous	Issued With 7th Divl Routine Orders D/4 S/12/1914	05/12/1914	05/12/1914
Operation(al) Order(s)	7th Divisional Routine Orders No. 65	07/12/1914	07/12/1914
Operation(al) Order(s)	7th Divisional Routine Orders No. 66	08/12/1914	08/12/1914
Operation(al) Order(s)	7th Divisional Routine Orders No. 67	09/12/1914	09/12/1914
Operation(al) Order(s)	7th Divisional Routine Orders No. 68	10/12/1914	10/12/1914
Operation(al) Order(s)	7th Divisional Routine Orders No. 69	11/12/1914	11/12/1914
Operation(al) Order(s)	7th Divisional Routine Orders No. 70	12/12/1914	12/12/1914
Operation(al) Order(s)	7th Divisional Routine Orders No. 71	15/12/1914	15/12/1914
Miscellaneous	Return Of Horse Casualties In 7th Division During Week Ended 12th Dec. 1914.	12/12/1914	12/12/1914
Operation(al) Order(s)	7th Divisional Routine Orders No. 72	14/12/1914	14/12/1914
Operation(al) Order(s)	7th Divisional Routine Orders No. 72	15/12/1914	15/12/1914
Operation(al) Order(s)	7th Divisional Routine Orders No. 74	16/12/1914	16/12/1914
Operation(al) Order(s)	7th Divisional Routine Orders No. 75	17/12/1914	17/12/1914
Operation(al) Order(s)	7th Divisional Routine Orders No. 76	18/12/1914	18/12/1914
Operation(al) Order(s)	7th Divisional Routine Orders No. 77	19/12/1914	19/12/1914
Miscellaneous	Return Of Horse Casualties For Week Ending 19th December 1914	20/12/1914	20/12/1914
Operation(al) Order(s)	7th Divisional Routine Orders No 78	20/12/1914	20/12/1914
Operation(al) Order(s)	7th Divisional Routine Orders No 79	21/12/1914	21/12/1914
Operation(al) Order(s)	7th Divisional Routine Orders No 80	22/12/1914	22/12/1914
Operation(al) Order(s)	7th Divisional Routine Orders No 81	23/12/1914	23/12/1914
Operation(al) Order(s)	7th Divisional Routine Orders No 82	24/12/1914	24/12/1914
Operation(al) Order(s)	7th Divisional Routine Orders No 83	25/12/1914	25/12/1914
Operation(al) Order(s)	7th Divisional Routine Orders No 85	27/12/1914	27/12/1914
Miscellaneous	Return Of Horse Casualties For Week Ending 26th December 1914	27/12/1914	27/12/1914
Operation(al) Order(s)	7th Divisional Routine Orders No. 86	28/12/1914	28/12/1914
Operation(al) Order(s)	7th Divisional Routine Orders No. 87	29/12/1914	29/12/1914
Operation(al) Order(s)	7th Divisional Routine Orders No. 88	30/12/1914	30/12/1914
Operation(al) Order(s)	7th Divisional Routine Orders No. 89	31/12/1914	31/12/1914
Heading	A & Q 7th Division Nominal Rolls Casualties 1914		
Miscellaneous	State of Infty Bdes		

Miscellaneous	Casualties, 7th Division, 18th October 1914 To November 1914	18/12/1914	18/12/1914
Miscellaneous	7th Division List Of Casualties-Officers From 18th October 1914	18/10/1914	18/10/1914
Miscellaneous	Reinforcements Received 7th Division		
Miscellaneous	1st Battalion, Grenadier Guards	25/11/1914	25/11/1914
Miscellaneous	2nd Battalion, Grenadier Guards	18/11/1914	18/11/1914
Miscellaneous	8th Battalion, Royal Scots.	18/11/1914	18/11/1914
Miscellaneous	2nd Battalion, Border Regiment.	18/11/1914	18/11/1914
Miscellaneous	2nd Battalion, Gordon Highlanders,	18/11/1914	18/11/1914
Miscellaneous	2nd Battalion, Bedfordshire Regiment.	18/11/1914	18/11/1914
Miscellaneous	2nd Battalion, Yorkshire Regiment.	18/11/1914	18/11/1914
Miscellaneous	2nd Battalion, Royal scots Fusiliers	18/11/1914	18/11/1914
Miscellaneous	2nd Battalion, Wilts Regiment.	18/11/1914	18/11/1914
Miscellaneous	2nd Battalion "Queens"	18/11/1914	18/11/1914
Miscellaneous	2nd Battalion, Royal Warwickshire Regiment.	18/11/1914	18/11/1914
Miscellaneous	1st Battalion, Royal Welsh Fusiliers.	18/11/1914	18/11/1914
Miscellaneous	7th Division Cammissions Artist's Rifles		
Miscellaneous	M. S. To C-In-No. 1878	27/02/1918	27/02/1918
Miscellaneous	Headquarters 22nd Infantry Brigade.	28/02/1915	28/02/1915
Miscellaneous	Headquarters 20th Infantry Brigade.	17/02/1915	17/02/1915
Miscellaneous			
Miscellaneous	7th Division	24/12/1914	24/12/1914
Miscellaneous	Head Quarters, 4th Army Corps	24/12/1914	24/12/1914
Miscellaneous	Headquarters, 4th Army Corps	10/12/1914	10/12/1914
Miscellaneous	Statement Shewing Distribution And Probationary Officers From Artists Rifles		
Miscellaneous	Headquarters, 4th Army Corps.	17/12/1914	17/12/1914
Miscellaneous	Headquarters, Infantry Brigade.	26/02/1915	26/02/1915
Miscellaneous	List Of Man Of Artists Rifles For Commissions As Second Lieut.		

7TH DIVISION

'A' & 'Q' BRANCH
AUG 1914- DEC 1914

121/2751

Headquarters (AA & QMG) 7th Division.

Vol I. 31.8 — 30.11.14

A. G. Base.

    Herewith war diary of the A & Q.M.G's branch of the Head Quarter Staff of the 7th division for the period August 31st - November 30th with 3 appendices:-

    A.   Total casualties October 18th - November 13th.
    B.   Officers' Casualties.
    C.   Reinforcements received.

                                            Major

14/12/14   A. A. & Q. M. G., 7th Division

G. O. C. 7th Division.

War Diary & Appendices received.

Crawford Atkins
Major for D.A.G.

Army Form C. 2118.

A. A. & Q. M. G's Branch 7th Division

WAR DIARY
or
INTELLIGENCE SUMMARY.
(Erase heading not required.)

Instructions regarding War Diaries and Intelligence Summaries are contained in F.S. Regs, Part II. and the Staff Manual respectively. Title pages will be prepared in manuscript.

Hour, Date, Place	Summary of Events and Information	Remarks and references to Appendices
31st August	The staff of the division was collected at Lyndhurst. The details connected with the formation of the division are not at present available. The mobilization was only completed on the eve of embarkation.	
4th October 3 p.m. 8 p.m.	Orders to commence embarkation at Southampton, at 8 p.m. received. Embarkation commenced. Troops arrived by "Train Loads" at ½ hour intervals although the troops were within a march and did march to the Docks. The arrangement caused considerable difficulty as Units had to be split up and did not travel in the same ship.	
5th October 6-30 p.m. 6th October 8 p.m.	Embarkation concluded. Ships having left the Dock as loaded. Disembarkation at ZEEBRUGGE commenced as troops arrived, the dismounted portions were railed to BRUGES. Mounted portion and all wheel traffic proceeded by march route (10 miles).	
BRUGES 7th October	Disembarkation continued and troops placed in billets in BRUGES and surrounding villages. The usual difficulty of finding accommodation for all horses was experienced. Troops were billetted in Brigade Areas. Only two days rations and forage for the troops and horses were placed on board for the voyage. As some ships took more than the prescribed time, 2 days, no rations or forage were available for the troops on landing.	
8th October 7 a.m.	Orders were issued over night (3 a.m.) to march to OSTEND at 7-30 a.m. A small supply depot had been formed at BRUGES from which an issue was made and all supplies were then sent by train to OSTEND.	
OSTEND 8th October OSTEND 9th October 6-30 a.m.	March to OSTEND (13 miles) was concluded by 4 p.m. An attempt was made to save time by entraining to GHENT (40 miles) 2 brigades with their transport and affiliated troops. This resulted in a long delay, owing to the inexperience of the Railway Staff. Probably all animals would have been less worn out had the distance to GHENT (40 miles) been done by broad. The delay was chiefly due to the lack of organization by the railway staff.	

2.

A. A. & Q. M. G's Branch 7th Division

Army Form C. 2118.

WAR DIARY
or
INTELLIGENCE SUMMARY.
(Erase heading not required.)

Instructions regarding War Diaries and Intelligence Summaries are contained in F.S. Regs., Part II. and the Staff Manual respectively. Title pages will be prepared in manuscript.

Hour, Date, Place	Summary of Events and Information	Remarks and references to Appendices
OSTEND 9th October 12.30 p.m.	The remainder of the division marched to BRUGES. Considerable difficulty in getting transport, etc, out of OSTEND owing to the troops which were going by train having left part of their transport.	
OSTEND 10th October 1 a.m.	Last of the transport of troops marching to BRUGES arrived.	
OSTEND 10th October 12 noon	Entraining of the 2 Brigades of division completed.	
BRUGES 10th October 5 p.m.	Remainder of Division marched to BEERNEM (6 miles).	
BEERNEM 10th October 10 p.m.	Last of transport arrived.	
BEERNEM 11th October	Remainder of Division rested at BEERNEM.	
GHENT 11th October	The 2 Brigades covering withdrawal of troops from Antwerp.	
GHENT 11th October	The 2 Brigades marched during the night to AELTRE (12 miles) men and animals very tired.	
BEERNEM 12th October	Remainder of division marched to COOLSCAMP (12 miles).	
ROULERS 13th October	The division marched to ROULERS where it was again concentrated (10 miles) during these marches the transport horses had suffered considerably owing to horses being soft, ill fitting harness, and crude drivers.	
ROULERS 14th October	The division marched to YPRES (12 miles) while some 1000 footsore men were sent by rail. Remain at YPRES on 15th.	
HOOGE 16th October	The division marched to HOOGE (4 miles) and took up a position covering YPRES, during the whole of this period the system of supply was hand to mouth. The base was shifted 3 times and considerable difficulty was experienced in rationing men and horses.	
17th October	H.Q. established in a chateau near the 5th kilo on the YPRES–MENIN road. Troops billetted from ZONNEBEKE to KRUISIK.	
18th October 19th October	Slight engagement, 1 officer 3 men killed and about 50 wounded. March out to attack MENIN but meet superior force and have to withdraw. Heavy casualties in 22nd Infantry Brigade	
20th October 21st October	Germans attack in force. Heavy artillery fire all day. Action continues.	

(D 29 6) W 4141—463 100,000 9/14 HWV   Forms/C. 2118/10

Army Form C. 2118.

A. A. & Q. M. G's Branch 7th Division

WAR DIARY
or
INTELLIGENCE SUMMARY.
(Erase heading not required.)

Instructions regarding War Diaries and Intelligence Summaries are contained in F.S. Regs., Part II. and the Staff Manual respectively. Title pages will be prepared in manuscript.

Hour, Date, Place	Summary of Events and Information	Remarks and references to Appendices
HOOGE 22nd October	Battle continued in same position. Colonel Perceval A.A. & Q.M.G., wounded in the leg and transferred to the base. Supply and ammunition arrangements working well. Supply sections refilled at YPRES and come up at dusk. Some difficulty experienced in getting wagons up to Units owing to shell fire on the roads. Supply Sections ews return to YPRES during darkness.	
HOOGE 23rd October	Action continues. Baggage wagons now all parked just S. of YPRES. Heavy casualties. Empty baggage wagons sent up to help to evacuate wounded. Large numbers of stragglers from the trenches.	
HOOGE 24th October	Action continues. 2nd Division arrives in support about 10 a.m. Supply sections up at 6 p.m.	
HOOGE 25th October	Little change in situation. Supply & baggage wagons used to evacuate wounded at night. All supplies brought up at night.	
" 26th October	Action continues. H.Q. move forward ½ mile. R.W.F. 1st reinforcements arrive.	
" 27th October	2 brigades withdrawn to rest. 3rd left in trenches	
" 28th October	return to old chateau. Col. Ryan A.S.C. appointed A.A. & Q.M.G.	
" 29th October	Action continues. 7 officers R.W.F. arrive.	
" 30th October	All baggage & spare vehicles parked well back.	
" 31st October	heavy shell fire all day. Admn Staff H.Q. move back to HALTE.	
HALTE 1st November	Ad. Staff H.Q. remain at HALTE.	
" 2nd November	Ad. Staff H.Q. move back to YPRES Capt Butler A.D.C. and Capt" Douglas G.S.O. 3 wounded.	
YPRES 3rd November	Town shelled. First reinforcements for 7 Battalions arrive.	
" 4th November	Action continues. Reinforcements for Wiltshires & Queens arrive.	
" 5th November	D.A.A. & Q.M.G. goes to G.H.Q. with A.Q.M.G. 1st Corps and sees Q.M.G. & A.G. on the subject of deficiencies in personnel & materiel.	
" 6th November	Troops withdrawn from the trenches. YPRES heavily shelled. 6 men & 7 horses of H.Q. staff killed by 1 shell. 20th & 21st Brigades move to LOORE during the night 5/6. 22nd Brigade remain at YPRES, also R.A. less 35th Brigade, Troops moved into billets in BAILLEUL and METEREN. H.Q. remain at LOORE. Roads very congested. On these narrow roads it is essential to permit traffic to move in one direction only.	

A. A. & Q. M. G's Branch 7th Division

Army Form C. 2118

WAR DIARY
or
INTELLIGENCE SUMMARY.
(Erase heading not required.)

Instructions regarding War Diaries and Intelligence Summaries are contained in F.S. Regs., Part II. and the Staff Manual respectively. Title pages will be prepared in manuscript.

Hour, Date, Place	Summary of Events and Information	Remarks and references to Appendices
7th November	H. Q. move in to BAILLEUL commence to refit and get in accurate casualty reports. Owing to continuous fighting since October 18th and heavy casualties in Brigade and regimental staffs it was quite impossible to get accurate daily casualty reports. Names of Officers casualties, often incomplete, were all that could be obtained. The only way in which units could ascertain their casualties was to make a nominal roll of the men left, deduct actual known casualties and report the balance as missing. The 2nd R.Scots Fus. had 8 officers 490 O.R. missing, 2nd Wilts 19 Officers 574 O.R. 1st R.Welch Fusiliers 15 Officers 724 O.R. and 1st S.Staffs 5 Officers 742 O.R. missing but a large proportion of these men are undoubtedly killed & wounded.	
8th November	Colonel Ryan A.S.C. took over the duties of A.A. & Q.M.G.	
9th November	The 22nd Infantry Brigade which had been left at YPRES rejoin the division and are billetted # in BAILLEUL	
10th November	Remain at BAILLEUL refitting.	
November 11th BAILLEUL	Major A.C.Daly, West Yorkshire Regt took over duties of A.A. & Q.M.G. 20th Infantry Brigade METEREN 22nd Infantry Brigade MERRIS 35th Bde R.F.A. " 21st Infantry Brigade detached at PLOEGSTRAET. Div: Hd Qrs & R.E. & Northumberland Hussars at BAILLEUL. Remainder of R.A. with 1st Corps.	)The Divisional Artillery less 35th Bde R.F.A. & heavy Brigade remained at BAILLEUL also 21st Inf: Brigade & 21st Field Ambulance.
November 12th	No change - Refitting.	Casualties
November 13th	No change - Refitting.	1 man killed
November 14th	7th Division (as above) marched to SAILLY & took over line from BRIDOUX- ROUGES-BANCS from 6th Division & 19th Infantry Brigade. 7th Division Hd Qrs at CHATEAU MAISON BLANCHE.	1 " wounded

Army Form C. 2118.

WAR DIARY
or
INTELLIGENCE SUMMARY.

A. A. & Q. M. G's Branch, 7th Division.

(Erase heading not required.)

Hour, Date, Place	Summary of Events and Information	Remarks and references to Appendices
November 15th	No change. Reinforcements 1 officer & 100 men 2/Bedford Regt.	Casualties 1 killed 9 wounded.
November 16th	Reinforcements 1 officer & 12 men 2/Queens Regt. 14th Brigade R.H.A. 22nd Brigade R.F.A. 21st Infantry Brigade, Nos 3 & 4 Companies Train A.S.C. & 21st Field Ambulance moved from BAILLEUL to SAILLY. - the Divisional Ammunition Column moved to BAILLEUL. Reinforcements 5 Officers & 510 men 2/Yorkshire Regt 4 Officers & 141 men R.F.A. Casualties 1 officer wounded (Lt. Ward, 1/Grenadier Guards)	O.R. 7 killed. 18 wounded. 2 missing.
November 17th	Weather wet & cold with showers of sleet. Infantry of 7th Division redistributed in 3 Sections - 2 Battalions of each Brigade in trenches on line BRIDOUX - ROUGES BANCS - (20th Brigade on right, 21st Centre, 22nd left). 1 Battalion each brigade billetted in Brigade reserve along RUE de QUESNES, 1 Battalion each Brigade in General Reserve billetted along RUE BATAILLE. 20th Bde H.Q. RUE du QUESNES - 21st & 22nd at FLEURBAIX. Divisional Ammunition Column moved from BAILLEUL to DOULIEU - 1 Section of 5th Siege Battery already in position in this Section placed under orders of G.O.C. 7th Division - Northumberland Hsrs at Pt de MORTIER. Weather damp & cold	Casualties 6 men killed 17 men wounded 1 missing
SAILLY November 18th	4th Corps notified 7th Division that 3rd Brigade Heavy Artillery was under orders to rejoin 7th Division.	Casualties 2 men killed Lt. Mackenzie, Grenadier Gds & 9 men wounded. Reinforcements 16 Offrs & 574 Other Ranks for details see appendix.
November 19th	Weather very cold & snow fell. Efforts made to secure supply of Coke and Braziers for use in the trenches.	Casualties 5 men killed 15 men wounded 1 man missing

Army Form C. 2118.

A. A. & Q. M. G's Branch, 7th Division.

WAR DIARY
or
INTELLIGENCE SUMMARY.
(Erase heading not required.)

Instructions regarding War Diaries and Intelligence Summaries are contained in F.S. Regs., Part II. and the Staff Manual respectively. Title pages will be prepared in manuscript.

Hour, Date, Place	Summary of Events and Information	Remarks and references to Appendices
November 20th	Hard frost & cases of frost bite occurring in trenches. 111th Battery arrived and were put into billets for night about Le Pl MORTIER. Roads very slippery & no frost nails yet arrived for horses.	Reinforcements R.A.M.C. 38 R & F. Casualties 1 man killed 10 men wounded
SAILLY November 21st	Informed by Corps Hd.Qrs that 116th Heavy Battery ordered to report at SAILLY for duty in this section. Weather continues bitterly cold and more cases of frost bite notwithstanding plenty of coke sent to trenches with good supply of braziers.	Reinforcements 54th Coy R.E. 44 R & F. 55th Coy R.E. 1 Officer 35 R & F.
November 22nd	Weather remains the same. 111th Heavy Battery arrived. First consignment of warm clothing received and a proportional issue made to troops. Frost nails arrived in the evening but no proper winter horse shoes December 1st had been fixed as commencement of winter and exceptional cold caught us unprepared.	Casualties 1 man killed. 5 wounded. Lt.Oldfield) R.F.A.) Lt,West,R.E.) Wounded. Capt Todd) 8/R.S.F.)
Nov 23rd	Weather still very cold and hard frost. Fuel problem rather difficult. Decided to reserve all coke for troops in trenches & in open. Remainder to get coal & wood. Coke & Wood obtained from MERVILLE. Coal from BETHUNE. An average of 5000 lbs coke a day is being sent out to trenches. Only 8 lbs hay per horse is being sent up on supply column. Ration is being supplemented by straw & a small quantity of bran. A consignment of warm fur waistcoats has arrived and a proportion was issued to all units.	Reinforcements 5 Officers & 574 O. R. for details see appendix. Casualties 2/Lt.Scott,5th Siege Batty and 2 men killed. 8 men wounded.
SAILLY November 24th	Weather less cold & decided thaw set in but still very raw and most trying for troops in trenches. A system of giving hot baths to the men (in a large building rigged up with tubs) was started and much appreciated by the men. It is hoped that every man in one Battalion a day will get a hot bath. 50 men get baths at a time. , this takes about ½ an hour.	Casualties 3 men killed. Lt.Burrowes 2/Queens and 5 men wounded. Casualties 3 men killed 4 men wounded.

Army Form C. 2118.

A. A. & Q. M. G's Branch, 7th Division.

WAR DIARY
or
INTELLIGENCE SUMMARY.
(Erase heading not required.)

Instructions regarding War Diaries and Intelligence Summaries are contained in F. S. Regs., Part II. and the Staff Manual respectively. Title pages will be prepared in manuscript.

Hour, Date, Place	Summary of Events and Information	Remarks and references to Appendices
November 25th	Weather much less cold. Question of provision of fuel getting rather serious. Estimate of requirements 20 tons a day if wood part of issue – 13 tons if no wood. Matter represented to Hd Qrs 4th Corps.	Reinforcements 18 Officers 140 Rank & File.
SAILLY November 26th	Weather much milder and as troops are now well provided with warm clothing they will be better equipped to meet any recurrence of frost & snowy weather. Horse shoes with Cogs & frost nails for horses also received.	Casualties (25/11) 2 men killed 4 men wounded. Casualties (26/11) 2 men killed 7 men wounded
November 27th	Weather very mild. Further consignment of warm clothing received.	Casualties (27/11) 1 man killed Major McInnes, D.S.O., R.E. & 8 men wounded.
November 28th	Mild weather continues. System of hot baths & Barbers Shop much appreciated by troops. Strength of Division now 14, 190, **Horses**	Casualties (28/11) 3 men killed 10 men wounded 2 men missing
SAILLY November 29th	No change in situation. Weather continues very mild. Under authority of G.H.Q. Officers (as can be spared) & 2 N.C.O's per unit are now being given short leave to England. G.O.C. Division has authority to grant up to 7 days. Larger periods referred to 4th Corps.	Casualties (29/11) Capt. Rose, R.E. and 4 men killed. 6 men wounded. 2 men missing.
November 30th	Situation unchanged. Fuel supply now assured for some weeks ahead.	Casualties 30/11 2 men wounded.

Appendix Q

Reinforcements received. 7th Division

Date	Unit	Officers	men
October 26th.	2nd Bn. Warwickshire Regt.	1	56
	1st Bn. Royal Welsh Fus.	1	90
	22nd F. A. Brigade		6
October 29th.	2nd Bn. Bedfordshire Regt.	1	20
	2nd Bn. R.S. Fusiliers	1	20
	2nd Bn. "Queens".	1	-
	1st Bn. Royal Welsh Fus.	7	-
October 30th.	2nd Bn. Bedfordshire Regt.	2	-
	22nd F. A. Brigade.	-	3
November 1st.	2nd Bn. Bedfordshire Regt.	2	96
	2nd Bn. R.S. Fusiliers	1	30
	22nd F. A. Brigade	-	2
November 3rd.	1st Bn. Grenadier Guards	1	96
	2nd Bn. Scots Guards	1	99
	2nd Bn. Border Regt.	1	96
	2nd Gordons.	1	93
	2nd Bn. Yorkshire Regt.	1	88
	2nd Bn. R.S. Fusiliers	1	50
	2nd Bn. Wiltshire Regt	1	96
	2nd Bn. "Queens".	1	112
	2nd Bn. Warwickshire Regt.	2	96
	1st Bn. S. Staffordshire Regt.	1	100
	Divisional Head Quarters	1	-
	3rd Heavy Brigade	-	3
November 6th	Divisional Head Quarters	1	-
	7th Signal Company	-	3
	2nd Bn. Bedfordshire Regt.	1	-
	1st Bn. Royal Welsh Fus.	1	109
November 7th	Divisional Head Quarters.	1	-
	2nd Bn. Bedfordshire Regt.	1	20
	2nd Bn. R.S. Fusiliers	-	30
	2nd Bn. Wiltshire Regt.	-	32
November 8th	Northumberland Hussars	4	-
	35th F.A. Brigade.	2	15
	1st Bn. Royal Welsh Fusiliers	2	99
November 9th	7th Signal Company	-	12
	2nd Bn. "Queens"	-	20
	1st Bn. S. Staffordshire Regt.	1	30

Appendix C

Reinforcements received 7th Division

Date	Unit	Officers	Men
10th November	35th F.A. Brigade	-	44
	21st Field Ambulance	2	--
November 11th	Div H.Q.	1	--
	35th F.A. Brigade	-	7
	3rd Heavy Brigade	-	10
	1st Bn Grenadier Guards	4	401
	2nd Bn. Scots Guards	7	250
	2nd Bn. Gordon Highlanders	1	91
	2nd Bn. Bedfordshire Regt	1	119
	2nd Bn. Wilts Regt	1	--
	2nd Bn. "Queens	2	207
	2nd Bn. Warwickshire Regt	-	160
	1st Bn. R. Welsh Fusiliers	2	303
	21st Field Ambulance	1	--
	23rd Field Ambulance	1	--
November 12th	Divisional Hd Qrs.	1	--
	35th F.A. Brigade	1	1
	1st Bn. Grenadier Guards	2	133
	2nd Bn. Scots Guards	5	285
	2nd Bn. Wiltshire Regt	1	60
	2nd Bn. "Queens	3	247
	2nd Bn. Warwickshire Regtz	-	250
	1st Bn. R. Welsh Fusiliers	-	151
	21st Field Ambulance	1	--
November 13th	35th F.A. Brigade	-	11
	2nd Bn. Gordon Highlanders	4	--
	22nd Infantry Brigade	1	--
	1st Bn. S. Staffordshire Regt	-	20
November 14th	35th F.A. Brigade	-	40
	7th Div. Ammn Column	1	4
	20th Infantry Brigade	1	--
	1st Bn. Grenadier Guards	4	--
	21st Infantry Brigade	1	--
November 15th	7th Signal Company	-	13
	2nd Bn. Bedfordshire Regt	-	100
	2nd Bn "Queens"	1	12
	22nd F.A. Brigade	-	12
November 16th	7th Signal Company	-	11
	7th Division Ammn Column	-	3
	2nd Bn. Yorkshire Regt	5	510
	22nd F.A. Brigade	-	45
November 17th	7th Signal Company	-	5
	14th Brigade R.H.A.	1	32
	35th F.A. Brigade	1	25
	7th Division Ammn Column	-	24
	1st Bn. Grenadier Guards	1	--
	1st Bn. R. Welsh Fusiliers	1	5
	22nd F.A. Brigade	-	7
November 18th	22nd F.A. Brigade	-	11
	35th F.A. Brigade	1	--
	7th Division Ammn Column	-	26
	1st Bn. Grenadier Guards	1	2
	2nd Bn. Bedfordshire Regt	1	--
	7th Division Train	-	34

Appendix C

Reinforcements received 7th Division.

Date	Unit	Officers	men
November 19th	1st Bn. Grenadier Guards	5	100
	2nd Bn. Border Regt	-	17
	2nd Bn. Gordon Highlanders	-	16
	2nd Bn. Bedfordshire Regt	3	100
	2nd Bn. R.S. Fusiliers	-	100
	2nd Bn. Wiltshire Regt	3	155
	2nd Bn. Warwickshire Regt	-	7
	R.A.M.C.	-	38
November 20th	54th Field Coy, R.E.	-	44
	55th Field Coy R.E.	1	32
	22nd Infantry Brigade H.Q.	1	1
	2nd Bn. Warwickshire Regt	2	98
	R.A.M.C.	-	16
	22nd F.A. Brigade	-	3
November 22nd	2nd Bn. Gordon Highlanders	1	89
	2nd Bn. Bedfordshire Regt	1	94
	2nd Bn. R.S. Fusiliers	-	65
	2nd Bn. Wiltshire Regt	1	9
	2nd Bn. R. Welsh Fusiliers	1	96
November 24th	R.A., H.Q.	-	1
	14th H.A. Brigade	-	35
	3rd Heavy Brigade	-	20
	22nd F.A. Brigade	-	6
	1st Bn. Grenadier Guards	1	-
November 26th	H.Q. R.A.	-	1
	22nd F.A. Brigade	-	2
	3rd Heavy Brigade	-	7
	2nd Bn. Border Regt	3	11
	2nd Bn. Gordon Highlanders	-	13
	2nd Bn. R.S. Fusiliers	4	5
	2nd Bn. Wiltshire Regt	4	1
	2nd Bn. "Queens"	2	120
	2nd Bn. R. Welsh Fusiliers	3	--
	R.A.M.C.	1	--
November 29th	7th Signal Company	1	2
	54th Field Coy, R.E.	1	-
	1st Bn. Grenadier Guards	1	-
	22nd Infantry Brigade H.Q.	-	1
November 30th	22nd F.A. Brigade	-	10
	54th Field Coy R.E.	1	1

APPENDIX:- D

Unit	Rank & Name	Date	Casualty
2nd Bn. Scots Guards	Maj.Lord E.C.Gordon-Lennox	22/10/14	Wounded
	Capt T.H.R.Bulkeley	22/10/14	Killed
	Capt.Hon D.A.Kinnaird	25/10/14	Killed
	Capt.C.F.P.Hamilton	27/10/14	Wounded
	Lieut W.H.Holbech	27/10/14	Wounded (Died)
	2/Lieut W.H.Wynne-Finch	27/10/14	Wounded
	Maj.Hon H.J.Fraser,M.V.O.	28/10/14	Killed
	Lieut A.R.Orr	28/10/14	Wounded
	Lt.Lord G.R.Grosvenor	28/10/14	Wounded
	Lt.Col.R.C.J.Bolton	28/10/14	Missing
	Major Visc.Dalrymple	28/10/14	Missing
	Capt C.V.Fox	28/10/14	Missing
	Capt Hon.J.S.Coke	28/10/14	Missing
	2/Lt.Lord Garlies	28/10/14	Missing
	Lieut.E.B.Trafford	28/10/14	Missing
	Lt.R&Steuart Menzies	28/10/14	Missing
	Lt.R.F.H.Gladwin	28/10/14	Missing
	Lt.Earl of Dalhousie	29/10/14	Wounded
	Capt H.L.Kemble,M.V.O.		Wounded
	2/Lt Gibbs		Killed
	Lt.D.R.Drumond	3/11/14	Killed
	Capt Hon.R.Coke	30/11/14	Wounded.
	2/Lieut C.Cottrell Dormer	28/10/14	Killed
2nd Bn.Border Regt.	Lt.P.J.E.~~Gorton~~ Egerton	17/10/14	Killed
	Major J.T.I.Bosanquet	27/10/14	Wounded
	Lieut T.H.Beves	27/10/14	Wounded
	Capt.E.H.Lees	28/10/14	Killed
	Capt C.A.J.Cholmondeley	28/10/14	Killed
	Captz R.N.Gordon	28/10/14	Killed
	Major W.L.Allen, D.S.O.	28/10/14	Killed
	Capt.C.G.W.Andrews	28/10/14	Killed
	Lieut J.B.B.Warren	28/10/14	Killed
	2/Lt.C.V.G.Surtees	28/10/14	~~Killed~~ W-M.
	2/Lieut T.J.Clancey	28/10/14	Killed
	Lt.H.P.O.Sleigh	28/10/14	Wounded & Mis
	2/Lieut C.H.Evans	28/10/14	Wounded & Mis
	Lt.Col.L.J.Wood	29/10/14	Wounded
	Capt.L.E.H.Molyneux-Seel	29/10/14	Wounded & Mis
	Lieut.H.V.Gerrard	27-1/11/14	Killed
	Capt G.E.Warren		Wounded
	Lieut W.Watson		Wounded
	Lieut C.W.H.Hodgson		Wounded Died 7/11/14
	Lieut. A.P.Johnson		Wounded.
	~~Lieut E.C.Clegg~~	28/10/14	S

Appendix:- B

Unit	Rank & Name	Date	Casualty
2nd Bn Gordon Highlanders			
	Capt. F.R.E.Sworder	28/10/14	Wounded
	Lieut T.H.C.Thistle	28/10/14	Wounded
	Lieut L.Carr	30/10/14	Wounded
	Capt.C.D.G.Huggins	30/10/14	Wounded
	2/Lt.W.Waring	30/10/14	Wounded
	Lt.Col.H.P.Uniacke	31/10/14	Wounded
	Lieut J.A.O.Brooke	29/10/14	Killed
	Lieut C.K.Latta	29/10/14	Killed
	2/Lt.G.McAuliffe (Camerons)	29/10/14	Killed
	2/Lt.Hon.S.Fraser	29/10/14	Killed
	Lt.P.M.Mackenzie	29/10/14	Wounded
	2/Lt A.Mc Bride (H.L.I.)	29/10/14	Wounded
	Lt.J.H.Fraser	30/10/14	Killed
	2/Lt.H.F.Webster (Black W)	30/10/14	Killed
	2/Lt.D.G.F.Macbean	30/10/14	Wounded
	2/Lt.J.P.Boyd	30/10/14	Wounded
	2/Lt.T.Pringle (Camerons)	30/10/14	Wounded
	2/Lt.T.F.Murdoch (Black W)	30/10/14	Wounded
	2/Lt.J.H.Duguid	30/10/14	Wounded
	Capt J.L.G.Burnett	31/10/14	Wounded
	Capt B.G.R.Gordon	31/10/14	Wounded
	Capt K.H.Bruce	31/10/14	Wounded
	Lt.Hon.W.Fraser	31/10/14	Wounded
	Lt.C.E.Anderson	31/10/14	Wounded
	2/Lt.Q.D.Bell	31/10/14	Wounded
	Lt.A.S.Graham	31/10/14	Wounded
	Capt C.N.McLean	31/10/14	Killed
	2/Lt.W.C.Robertson	31/10/14	Missing
	Major G.S.C.Crauford	1/11/14	Wounded
	Capt J.R.E.Stansfeld	2/11/14	Wounded.
21st Inf.Bde.Hd.Qrs			
	Capt A.L.Godman (Staff Capt)	1/11/14	Wounded
	Capt A.S.Bruce (M.G.Offr)	1/11/14	Wounded
2nd Bedford Regt.	2/Lt.C.O.Bell	18/10/14	Killed
	Capt F.H.Bassett	18/10/14	Wounded
	Capt C.H.Woolfe	18/10/14	Wounded
	Lt. Horsford	18/10/14	Wounded
	Lt.D.G.C.Wright	25/10/14	Killed
	Lt.A.E.Hopkins	25/10/14	Wounded
	Capt A.J.Patron	24/10/14	Wounded
	Capt A.G.Hall	26/10/14	Killed
	Lt.W.Bastard	26/10/14	Killed
	Lt.E.F.Punchard	29/10/14	Killed
	Capt W.E.H.Wetherell	29/10/14	Wounded
	Lt.R.E.Huntriss	29/10/14	Wounded
	2/Lt.Innes	29/10/14	Wounded
	2/Lt.Inskip	29/10/14	Wounded
	2/Lt.Small	29/10/14	Wounded
	2/Lt.Kuhn	29/10/14	Wounded
	2/Lt.R.R.L.Thom	29/10/14	Wounded
	2/Lt.Whittemore	29/10/14	Wounded
	Major J.H.Traill	29/10/14	Wounded
	Major R.P.Stares	30/10/14	Killed.
	Lt.J.A.Paterson	30/10/14	Killed.

APPENDIX:- B

Unit	Rank & Name	Date	Casualty
Bedford Regt (Continued)	Capt C.S.Garnett-Botfield	30/10/14	Wounded
	Capt.A.R.Lemon	30/10/14	Missing & Wounded.
	Lt,G.E.Gott	30/10/14	Wounded
	Lt.Dixon	30/10/14	Wounded
	Capt E.H.Lyddon	30/10/14	Wounded
	Lt.W.C.Anderson	30/10/14	Missing
	Lt.D.G.C.Thomson	31/10/14	Wounded & Missing.
	Lt.D.L.de T.Fernandes	23/10/14	Killed
2nd Bn.Yorks Regt	Lt.F.C.Ledgard	23/10/14	Killed
	Lt.R.Walmesley	23/10/14	Killed
	Capt C.G.Jeffery	23/10/14	Wounded
	Lt.C.G.Forsyth	23/10/14	Wounded
	Lt.W.F.I.Bell	23/10/14	Wounded
	Capt R.W.McCall	25/10/14	Wounded
	Capt.H.Levin	29/10/14	Wounded
	Major W.L.Alexander	29/10/14	Wounded
	Lt.A.T.Thorne	29/10/14	Wounded
	Capt.J.H.Stansfield	25/10/14	Wounded
	Major W.B.Walker	29/10/14	Killed
	2/Lt.M.T.Thwaites	29/10/14	Wounded
	2/Lt.L.Sykes	29/10/14	Wounded
	2/Lt.L.H.Marriage	29/10/14	Wounded
	Lt.Col.C.A.King	30/10/14	Killed
	Capt E.S.Broun	30/10/14	Killed
	2/Lt F.C.Hatton	30/10/14	Killed
	Lt W.H.Colley	30/10/14	Wounded
	2/Lt.D.C.Kidd	30/10/14	Wounded & Mis
	2/Lt.W.A.Worsley	30/10/14	Wounded & Mis
	2/Lt.R.H.Middleditch	30/10/14	Wounded & Mis
	Capt R.B.Corner	1/11/14	Wounded
	Lt.R.H.Phayre	26/10/14	Killed
	2/Lt.L.Studley	26/10/14	Killed
	2/Lt.H.G.Brooksbank	3/11/14	Wounded

APPENDIX:- B

Unit	Rank & Name	Date	Casualty
2nd Bn R.S.Fusiliers	Lt.J.E.Utterson-Kelso	22/10/14	Wounded
	Capt.F.Fairlie	23/10/14	Killed
	Capt A.C.Adair	23/10/14	Wounded
	2/Lt G.B.Bayley	25/10/14	Killed
	Lt.W.Tod	25/10/14	Wounded
	Lt.C.G.G.Mackenzie	25/10/14	Killed
	Lt.N.Kennedy	25/10/14	Wounded & Mis.
	2/Lt.C.Mc.C.Alston	25/10/14	Missing
	Capt.G.C.Fleetwood	26/10/14	Missing
	Lt.R.V.G.Horn	29/10/14	Wounded
	2/Lt.M.D.Buchanan	29/10/14	Wounded
	Maj.A.H.H.Forbes		Wounded
	Capt.J.G.Whigham		Wounded
	Lt.G.R.T.Kennedy		Wounded
	Lt.A.L.Thomson		Wounded
	2/Lt.Whitton		Wounded
	2/Lt.W.E.Clutterbuck		Wounded
	Major A.C.H.MacGregor		Missing
	Capt.A.G.L.E.Gallais		Missing
	Lt.H.W.V.Stewart		Missing
	2/Lt.E.P.O.Boyle		Missing
	2/Lt.J.L.Bowen		Missing
	2/Lt.Christie		Missing
	Lt.Col.Baird-Smith		Wounded & Mis.
	Capt.R.M.Burgoyne		Wounded & Mis.
	Lt.A.Ross Thomson		Wounded & Mis.
2ns Bn.Wilts Regt.	Capt A.C.Magor	17/10/14	Killed
	Capt C.G.M.Carter	23/10/14	Killed
	Lt.R.S.Grimston	23/10/14	Killed
	2/Lt.Burges (Ox.Uv.O.T.C.)	23/10/14	Killed
	Lt.E.Spencer	23/10/14	Killed
	2/Lt.F.L.D.Shelford	23/10/14	Wounded
	Lt.Col.J.F.Forbes	24/10/14	Missing
	Major J.R.Wyndham	24/10/14	Missing
	Major C.A.Law	24/10/14	Missing
	Capt E.L.W.Henslow	24/10/14	Missing
	Capt A.W.Timmis	24/10/14	Missing
	Capt.H.F.Coddington	24/10/14	Missing
	Capt C.H.E.Moore	24/10/14	Missing
	Capt G.LeHuquet	24/10/14	Missing
	Capt R.P.Culver	24/10/14	Missing
	Lt.R.Smith	24/10/14	Missing
	Lt A.S.Hooper	24/10/14	Missing
	Lt.A.H.Blockley	24/10/14	Missing.
	Lt.D.A.Anstod.	24/10/14	Missing
	2/Lt.R.P.Rogers	24/10/14	Missing
	2/Lt.C.H.R.Barnes	24/10/14	Missing
	2/Lt.E.L.Betts	24/10/14	Missing
	2/Lt.G.P.Oldfield	24/10/14	Missing
	2/Lt.F.Rylands	24/10/14	Missing
	2/Lt.W.P.Campbell	24/10/14	Missing
	2/Lt.M.R.Fowle	24/10/14	Wounded.

APPENDIX:- B

Unit.	Rank & Name	Date	Casualty.
Hd Qrs 22nd Inf.Bde.	Lt.F.V.Thicke (Int Corps)	31/10/14	Missing
	Capt G.H.James (Bde Major)	4/11/14	Killed
	Capt R.V.Barker (S.Capt)	3/10/14	Killed
	Lt C.B.Adams (Bde M.G.O)	30/10/14	Missing.
2nd Bn "Queens"	Capt H. Lewis	19/10/14	Wounded & Mis.
	2/Lt.C.S.Ingram	21/10/14	Killed
	Lt.R.I.G.Heath	21/10/14	Wounded
	Lt R.C.Williams	21/10/14	Wounded
	2/Lt G.M.Gabb	21/10/14	Wounded
	Capt H.C.Whinfield	21/10/14	Wounded
	2/Lt.D.Ive	21/10/14	Killed
	Lt.E.W.Bethell	25/10/14	Wounded
	Capt H.F.R.Master	20-22/10/14	Wounded & Mis
	Capt P.C.Esdaile	" "	Wounded
	2/Lt.J.G.R.Bird	25-27/10/14	Killed
	Lt.A.D.Brown	26/10/14	Wounded
	Lt.Col.M.C.Coles	29- 2/11/14	Wounded
	Maj.L.M.Crofts	" "	" "
	Maj.H.R.Bottomley	" "	" "
	Capt.T.Weeding	" "	" "
	Lt.D.R.Wilson	" "	" "
	2/Lt.R.H.Philpot	" "	" "
	Lt.A.C.Thomas	6/11/14	Wounded
	Lt.R.K.B.Furze	6/11/14	Wounded
	Capt W.H.Alleyne	7/11/14	Wounded & Mis.
	Lt.C.R.Haig	7/11/14	Killed
	Capt A.H.S.Roberts	7/11/14	~~Killed~~ Wounded
	Lt.J.A.L.Brown	7/11/14	Wounded
	2/Lt.J.G.Collis	7/11/14	Wounded
	Lt.G.A.White	5/11/14	Wounded
	2/Lt.Smith	5/11/14	Wounded
	2/Lt.C.Pascoe	7/11/14	Wounded
	2/Lt.J.D.Burrows	/11/14	Wounded
2nd Bn.R.Warwick Regt.	Lt.J.E.Ratcliff	19/10/14	Killed
	Lt.R.T.Stainforth	19/10/14	Killed
	Maj.G.N.B.Forster	19/10/14	Wounded
	Capt G.R.Taylour	19/10/14	Wounded
	Lt.J.H.G.McCormick	19/10/14	Missing
	Capt.C.O.B.H.Methuen	21/10/14	Killed
	Capt.T.Whaley	21/10/14	Wounded
	Lt.N.B.F.Collins	20-21/10/14	Missing
	Lt.G.H.R.B.Somerville	" " "	~~Wounded~~ & Mis.
	2/Lt.J.E.Medcalfe	" " "	Missing
	Lt.Col.W.L.Loring	25/10/14	Killed
	2/Lt.Deane	25/10/14	Killed
	Lt.J.P.Duke	25/10/14	Wounded
	Lt.J.S.Knyvett	25/10/14	Wounded
	2/Lt.N.H.L.Matear	29/10/14	Wounded
	Capt.F.B.Follett	31/10/14	Wounded
	Capt A.J.Peck	31/10/14	Missing
	Capt E.G.Sydenham	31/10/14	Missing
	Capt P.J.Foster	31/10/14	Missing
	Lt.E.H.Onslow	31/10/14	Missing
	Lt.H.W.Ozanne	31/10/14	Missing
	Lt.I.A.Brown	31/10/14	Missing

APPENDIX:- B

Unit	Rank & Name	Date	Casualty
2nd Bn.R.Warwick Regt (Continued)	Lt.J.Lucas	31/10/14	Missing
	2/Lt.Harrison (Sher.For.)	2/11/14	Killed
	2/Lt.P.J.Burn (Leicester R)	7/11/14	Wounded
	2/Lt.R.Hutton -do-	7/11/14	Missing
	Capt.E.C.Schooling	20-7/11/14	Wounded
	2/Lt.Vacher	29/11/14	Killed
1st Bn.R.Welsh Fusiliers			
	Capt.E.O.Skaife	20/10/14	Wounded & Mis.
	Capt.J.H.Brennan	20/10/14	Killed
	Lt.G.O.de P.Change	20/10/14	Killed
	Capt.W.Harris-St-John	20/10/14	Wounded
	Capt.S.Jones	20/10/14	Wounded
	Capt.W.G.Vyvyan	20/10/14	Wounded
	2/Lt.R.E.Naylor	20/10/14	Wounded
	Capt W.M.Kington,D.S.O.	21/10/14	Killed
	Capt.M.E.Lloyd	21/10/14	Killed
	Lt.E.C.L.Hoskyns	21/10/14	Killed
	2/Lt.G.P.J.Snead-Cox	21/10/14	Killed
	2/Lt.C.G.H.Peppe	21/10/14	Wounded & Mis.
	Lt.J.M.Courage	21/10/14	Wounded & mis. (believed Killed)
	Lt.L.A.A.Alston	21/10/14	Wounded
	2/Lt.J.M.J.Evans	21/10/14	Wounded
	Capt.J.G.Smyth-Osbourne	21/10/14	Missing
	Lt.D.M.Barchard	21/10/14	Missing
	2/Lt.Bingham	21/10/14	Missing
	2/Lt.A.Walmsley	21/10/14	Wounded
	2/Lt H.T.Ackland-Allen	23/10/14	Killed
	Lt.R.E.Hudson	23/10/14	Missing
	2/Lt.S.Williams	27/10/14	Wounded
	Capt D.J.Burk (D.C.L.I)	29/10/14	Wounded
	Lt.Col.H.D.S.Cadogan	30/10/14	Missing
	Lt.A.E.C.T.Dooner	30/10/14	Missing
	Lt.B.C.H.Poole	30/10/14	Missing
	2/Lt.E.Woodhouse	30/10/14	Missing
	2/Lt.R.L.B.Egerton	30/10/14	Missing
	2/Lt.A.M.G.Evans	30/10/14	Missing
	Capt T.H.Disney (3/Essex)	30/10/14	Missing
	Capt.E.E.Barrow (3.D.C.L.I.)	30/10/14	Missing
	Capt W.Vincent -do-	30/10/14n	Missing
	2/Lt.N.Pynn -do-	30/10/14	Missing
	Lt.C.V.de G Ryde(2.D.C.L.I)	30/10/14	Missing
	2/Lt.Proctor	27/10/14	Wounded
	2/Lt.F.R.Orme	7/11/14	Wounded & Mis.
	Maj.R.E.P.Gabbett	17/11/14	Wounded

APPENDIX:- B

Unit.	Rank & Name	Date.	Casualty.
1st Bn. S Staffs Regt.	Capt.C.G.Ransford	20-21/10/14	Wounded
	Lieut.C.W.Evans	20-21/10/14	Wounded
	Lieut.E.L.Holmes	23/10/14	Killed
	Capt.J.S.S.Dunlop	25/10/14	Killed
	Major H.J.Weichman	27/10/14	Wounded
	Capt.C.H.Green	27/10/14	Wounded
	2/Lieut.H.R.S.Bower	27/10/14	Wounded
	Capt.S.Bonner	29/10/14	Wounded
	Maj.J.B.Loder-Symons	31/10/14	Killed
	Lieut C.F.Crousaz	31/10/14	Killed
	Lt.Col.R.H.Ovens	31/10/14	Wounded
	Major A.G.Buckle	31/10/14	Wounded
	Lieut Archer Shee	31/10/14	Wounded & Mi
	Lieut R.Willoughby	31/10/14	Wounded & Mi
	Lieut W.A.P.Foster	31/10/14	Missing
	Lieut.C.Adams (Bde M.G. Offr)	31/10/14	Missing
	Capt.J.F.Vallentin	7/11/14	Killed
	Capt O de Trafford	20-7/11/14	Wounded & Mi
	Lieut R.W.McGeorge	" "	Wounded
	Lieut C.R.C.Bean	" "	Wounded
	Lieut C.E.C.Bartlett	" "	Wounded
	Lieut D.G.Twiss	" "	Wounded
	Lieut I.H.K.Shore	" "	Wounded
	Lieut C.G.Hume	" "	Killed
	2/Lieut.R.R.Riley	" "	Missing
	2/Lieut G.E.Parker	" "	Missing
	2/Lieut Burke	" "	Missing
	2/Lieut.Tomlinson	" "	Wounded.
7th Divisional Train	~~Capt.C.O.Hay~~	~~24/10/14~~	~~Wounded~~
~~21st Field Ambulance~~ R.A.M.C.	Lieut F.G.Thatcher	27/10/14	Wounded
	Capt.H.S.Dickson	28/10/14	Wounded
	Lieut.Butt	29/10/14	Missing
	Lieut.H.L.Shore	2/11/14	Wounded
	Capt.H.Robertson	30/10/14	Missing
	Lieut H.B.Winter	1/11/14	Missing
	Lieut S.W.Richardson	4/11/14	Killed
	Capt.T.Mc C.Phillips	4/11/14	Wounded
	Capt.K.Comyn	5/11/14	Wounded
23rd Field Ambulance	Lieut.S.R.Rayman	23/10/14	Missing
8th Bn. Royal Scots	Capt.J.A.Todd	20/11/14	Wounded & Mi
	~~2/Lieut.D.M.Stewart~~	~~1/12/14~~	~~Wounded~~
1st Medium Siege Battery	Capt C.L.Evans	5/11/14	Wounded
	2/Lieut E.C.Scott (5th Battery)	21/11/14	Killed

APPENDIX:- B

Unit	Rank & Name	Date	Casualty
68th Field Coy R.E.	Lieut J.M.Smeathman	26/10/14	Killed
	Captain L.St.V.Rose	28/11/14	Killed
Hd Qrs 20th Inf:Bde.	Brig.Genl.Ruggles Brise	2/11/14	Wounded.
1st Bn Grenadier Gds.	Major L.R.V.Colby	25/10/14	Killed
	Lieut.E.Antrobus	25/10/14	Killed
	2/Lieut.H.A.H.Somerset	25/10/14	Killed
	2/Lieut.S.Walters	25/10/14	Killed
	Capt.R.E.K.Leatham	25/10/14	Wounded
	Lieut.H.L.Aubrey-Fletcher	28/10/14	Wounded
	Major H.St.L.Stugley	29/10/14	Killed
	Capt.Lord R.Wellesley	29/10/14	Killed
	Capt.Hon.C.M.B.Ponsonby M.V.O.	29/10/14	Wounded
	2/Lieut R.S.Lambert	29/10/14	Wounded
	Major Hon.Weld Forester, M.V.O.	29/10/14	Wounded (Died)
	2/Lieut.R.O.R.Kenyon Slaney	29/10/14	Wounded
	Lt.Col.M.Earle,D.S.O.	31/10/14	Wounded & Missing.
	Captain G.Rennie	31/10/14	Wounded & Missing
	Lt.Hon.A.G.S.Douglas-Pennant	31/10/14	Wounded & Missing
	Lieut P.Van Neck	31/10/14	Wounded & Missing.
	Lieut.L.G.Ames	31/10/14	Wounded
	Lieut.Harcourt Powell	31/10/14	Wounded
	2/Lt.Sir C.H.J.Duckworth King	3/11/14	Wounded
	Lieut G.E.Hope	4/11/14	Wounded
	Lieut.E.S.Ward	15/11/14	Wounded

APPENDIX:- B

Unit	Rank & Name	Date	Casualty
22nd Bde R.F.A.	Major T.C.W.Malony, D.S.O.	21/10/14	Wounded
	Lieut. F.C. Hayter Chaylor	21/10/14	Wounded
	Major G.E.Bolster	23/10/14	Killed
	2/Lieut A.N.Coxe	2/11/14	Wounded
	2/Lieut F.R.P.Curry	8/11/14	Wounded
	Lieut. G.Sumpter	13/11/14	Wounded
35th Bde R.F.A.	Major H.R.Phipps	20/10/14	Wounded
	Lieut. J.C.C.Dennis	24/10/14	Killed
	Lieut. A.J.Woodhouse	30/10/14	Killed
	Lt.Col. E.P.Lambert	30/10/14	Wounded
	Major H.W.A.Christie	30/10/14	Wounded
	Lieut. E.Clayton	3/11/14	Wounded
	Lieut. H.N.H.Williamson	29/10/14	Wounded
	2/Lieut. R.W.Oldfield	20/11/14	Wounded
111th Heavy Batty R.G.A.	—		
112th Heavy Batty R.G.A.	—		
7th Div. Ammn Column.	—		
Hd Qrs Div:Engineers	—		
54th Field Coy R.E.	Capt. J.A.McEnery	26/10/14	Killed
	2/Lieut H.Wynne Jones (S.R.)	29/10/14	Killed
	Lieut. S.F.C.Sweeny	3/11/14	Wounded
	Lieut. C.A.West	20/11/14	Wounded
	Major D.S.McInnes	26/11/14	Wounded

APPENDIX:- B

7th Division
~~6th Division~~

List of Casualties - Officers from 18th October 1914

To November 30th 1914.

Unit	Rank & Name	Date	Casualty
Div: Hd Qrs.	Lt,Col.C.J.Perceval	22/10/14	Wounded.
	Captain J.V.Isacc	24/10/14	Wounded
	Captain W.S.Douglas	2/10/14	Wounded
	Captain P.R.Butler	2/11/14	Wounded.
7th Div: Signal Coy.	—		
Northumberland Hars.	Major L.Johnston	22/10/14	Wounded
	2/Lieut.C.H.Laing	22/10/14	Wounded
	Captain W.A.Kennard	24/10/14	Wounded
	Captain H.Sidney	25/10/14	Wounded
	2/Lieut.A.K.Pease	25/10/14	Wounded
	2/Lieut.S.Clayton	25/10/14	Wounded
7th Div: Cyclist Company	Captain L.Peel (Yorks)	24/10/14	Missing.
Hd Qrs & Pom-Pom Dett: R.A.	Major H.C.Cavendish.	13/11/14	Wounded.
14th Bde,R.H.A.	Lt.Col.H.D.White-Thomson, D.S.O.	22/10/14	Wounded.
	Lieut.H.L.Davies	24/10/14	Wounded. (Died 27/10/14

Appendix A.

CASUALTIES, 7th DIVISION. 18th OCTOBER 1914 to 13th NOVEMBER 1914.

Units &c.	Officers.			Other Ranks.		
	K	W	M	K	W	M
Divisional Headquarters.	-	4	-	5	6	-
7th Signal Company.	-	-	-	3	14	6
Northumberland Hussars.	-	6	-	3	17	1
Cyclist Company.	-	-	1	1	20	9
C.R.A.& Pom-Pom Detachment.	-	1	-	1	4	-
14th Bde R.H.A. ('F' Battery.)	-	2	-	7	20	1
22nd Bde R.F.A.	-	5	-	11	51	7
35th Bde R.F.A.	2	5	-	11	84	16
111th Heavy Btty R.G.A.	-	-	-	1	4	-
112th Heavy Btty R.G.A.	-	-	-	-	15	-
7th Divisional Amm. Column.	-	-	-	-	7	-
Divisional Engineers Headquarters.	-	-	-	-	-	-
54th Field Company, R.E.	2	1	-	5	32	1
55th Field Company, R.E.	1	-	-	5	16	2
20th Infantry Brigade, Headquarters.	-	1	-	1	6	-
1st Bn Grenadier Guards.	6	14	-	83	277	315
2nd Bn Scots Guards.	6	8	8	41	204	529
2nd Bn Border Regiment.	9	11	-	79	259	253
2nd Bn Gordon Highlanders.	7	21	2	88	289	161
21st Infantry Brigade, Headquarters.	-	2	-	5	6	1
2nd Bn Bedford Regiment.	9	18	2	75	324	151
2nd Bn Yorks Regiment.	8	17	-	104	374	153
2nd Bn Royal Scots Fusiliers.	3	15	8	91	268	488
2nd Bn Wilts Regiment.	5	2	19	55	116	574
22nd Infantry Brigade, Headquarters.	2	-	1	2	8	6
2nd Bn "Queens" Regiment.	3	25	-	75	441	283
2nd Bn R.Warwick Regiment.	7	9	12	88	357	342
1st Bn R.Welch Fusiliers.	7	15	15	72	228	724
1st Bn S.Stafford Regiment.	6	17	5	25	97	742
Divisional Train.	-	-	-	1	1	6
21st Field Ambulance.	1	3	3	1	2	5
22nd Field Ambulance.	-	-	-	-	-	3
23rd Field Ambulance.	-	-	1	-	-	22
TOTALS :-	85	202	77	935	3567	4801
		364			9303.	

Applicants
arabic num

Name (Block L
BREN
Date:
May

Reader's Ticket

| Group
| Letters
| W

(18
For Offi

244

SUBJECT.

adj
G.S.

7TH DIV

DEC 1914

WAR DIARY or INTELLIGENCE SUMMARY.

Army Form C. 2118.

Hour, Date, Place	Summary of Events and Information	Remarks and references to Appendices
SAILLY Dec. 1st 1914.	A most unexpected and highly appreciated surprise was furnished by a visit from H.M. The King — His Majesty arrived by motor from ESTAIRES at about 3 p.m. Orders in connection with H.M.'s visit were issued emphatically to Commanders concerned — the following troops lined the road from (in the following order) from RUE de LYS to the Corner a Set. Hd. 2/R. Scots Fusiliers Northumberland Hussars 2/Border Regt. RA (5co) detachments from RE (50 m) R.A.M.C. (100) A.S.C. (25) and 1/R. Welsh Fusiliers. His Majesty was received at CHATEAU MAISON BLANCHE by Major Gen. T. Capper C.B. DSO	Recommend Lts B. + Lt S. Kerr to be relieved on return.

Army Form C. 2118.

WAR DIARY
or
INTELLIGENCE SUMMARY.
(Erase heading not required.)

Hour, Date, Place	Summary of Events and Information	Remarks and references to Appendices
SAILLY Dec 1st /14	Comd. J.L. Stuart who presented the members of his Staff — The Majesty was graciously pleased to personally decorate the following Officers, N.C.O.s & men — D.S.O. Major A.B.S. Cator N Scots Guards 13th Major 20th Hussars Captain E.A. Osborne R.E. Con 37. Air Signal Co. Lieutenant H.S.M. KREYER 2nd Yorkshire Regt. C. Lamb 2nd Border Regt.	

Army Form C. 2118.

WAR DIARY or INTELLIGENCE SUMMARY.
(Erase heading not required.)

Instructions regarding War Diaries and Intelligence Summaries are contained in F.S. Regs., Part II. and the Staff Manual respectively. Title pages will be prepared in manuscript.

Hour, Date, Place	Summary of Events and Information	Remarks and references to Appendices
SAILLY Dec. 1st 1914.	Medal for Distinguished Conduct in the Field N° 29520 Sergt. G. Spain F. Battery R.H.A. " 53934 Bombardier R. Amey F. " " " 21652 Sergt. W.C. Warr 18b Battery R.F.A. " 4399 Corpl. J. Holmes " " " " " 4866 Coy Sergt Major R. Lovatt 2/Yorkshire Regt. " 6636 Sergt. W. Hitch " " " " 9495 Private F. Norfolk " " " " 19225 L/Corpl. F. Cole Royal Engineers " 19908 Sapper R. Blackie " " " 9939 Private Burns R.A.M.C. Other Officers & N.C.O's entitled up to 7 Dec. 14. (vide selected for Rewards) have been unfortunately to Appendix but this were indiscriminately for various causes not present to receive their medals from His Majesty. Major the Hon. J.R. Cole 2/Scots Guards Casualties. and one man wounded.	Not present <u>Awarded D.S.O.</u> Lieut. Lord C.N. Hamilton 1/Grenadier Gds Captain J.B. Paynter 2/Scots Guards Captain G.V. Fox 2/Scots Guards Lieut. H.W.V. Stewart 2/R. Scots Fusiliers Captain J.E.V. Isaac Rifle Bde (Reserve of Officers) <u>Awarded Medal for Distinguished Conduct in the Field</u> N° 8275 Sergt. A. Stuart 2/Yorkshire Regt. Regtl. Sergt. Major Batters 1/South Staffordshire Regt.

Army Form C. 2118.

WAR DIARY
or
INTELLIGENCE SUMMARY.
(Erase heading not required.)

Hour, Date, Place	Summary of Events and Information	Remarks and references to Appendices
SAILLY Dec 2nd 1914	No change in situation. Reinforcements 27 officers 1193 other ranks (all for infantry) arrived — 2/Lieut. Stewart 8th Royal Scots. Casualties 2/Lieut. Stewart 8th Royal Scots wounded. Other ranks 2 killed, 8 wounded —	Details of reinforcing drafts shown in Appendix — A
Dec. 3rd —	No change in situation. Casualties 3 men killed, 12 wounded, 2 missing.	Reinforcements (3rd) Major Hingston 1st Cmb. 2/Lt. Greenwood 5th Cmb. Battn. Capt B.G.R. Gordon Returned 2/Scottish Rifles Wounded. Capt S.C. Mitford Wounded.
Dec. 4th	No change — Casualties 8 men killed, 10 wounded, 2 missing. 10 Very pistols received — bringing up number so far issued to 7. S.A.A. up to 6.16. 2nd Bns is entitled to 4 & will be most up to reserve — the first "Balck Receipt" of clothing arrived in Railway vans issued	Reinforcements 1 Pers Off 4 men

Army Form C. 2118.

WAR DIARY
or
INTELLIGENCE SUMMARY.
(Erase heading not required.)

Instructions regarding War Diaries and Intelligence Summaries are contained in F.S. Regs., Part II. and the Staff Manual respectively. Title pages will be prepared in manuscript.

Hour, Date, Place	Summary of Events and Information	Remarks and references to Appendices
SAILLY Dec 5	No change. Casualties 1 man killed 2 wounded. Reinforcements Captain Fenton of Durham L.I. — Horse 3: Durham L.I. } attached 2/York & Lancs R. — Reserve 3: York & Lancs R. } 2/Welch R. — 2/Lieut. Selwyn R.F.A 2/Lieut Stig & Cruden (brought 25 & 29 officers & other ranks) arrived by march from General HQrs Quarters & were attached to 20. Bat. R.F. As a very large quantity of gifts & warm clothing has been received and the weather continuing to be very mild the warm clothing especially is not at present required except in trenches.	

(9 20 6) W 4141—463 100,000 9/14 H W V Forms/C. 2118/10

WAR DIARY
or
INTELLIGENCE SUMMARY.
(Erase heading not required.)

Army Form C. 2118.

Hour, Date, Place	Summary of Events and Information	Remarks and references to Appendices
SAILLY Dec. 5.	Arrangements have been made by each unit to establish in Store House a reserve of any load which from time when under required under 73 d. & 73 = arrangements. Large quantities barb. wire (entanglement) 500 wire cutters (small) and 22 miles Telephone wire D3 (for R.A.) received and issued.	
Dec. 6.	Slight u- arrangement of billeting area. 22nd F.A. Bde Amm. Col. & 35-7th Amm Col. moved to N.V. River & some of the Knots of Batteries in action moved back to billets previously occupied by Amm Columns S.2 River. Casualties 6 men wounded, 3 missing. R.A. 34 other ranks Reinforcements	

WAR DIARY
or
INTELLIGENCE SUMMARY.
(Erase heading not required.)

Army Form C. 2118.

Hour, Date, Place	Summary of Events and Information	Remarks and references to Appendices
SAILLY Dec. 7 - 9/14	No change <u>Casualties</u> 2 men killed. 9 men wounded. Endeavour to improve sanitary conditions in trenches. 300 iron pickets and lengths today for latrine buckets. 100 issued to each Bn. 10 more very photo W.ch & 10 more reported "available". Two fixing lamps — up to strength in this respect (2 each) Bn— trenching tool 20 = Inf. Bde. 100 Hand grenades demanded — Periscopes received and issued to P.A. R.E. & Infantry for observation in trenches. The outer cross wires found to be very primary and it was necessary to encase them in wood. This point was noted in the report in all a third while.	

Army Form C. 2118.

WAR DIARY
or
INTELLIGENCE SUMMARY.
(Erase heading not required.)

Hour, Date, Place	Summary of Events and Information	Remarks and references to Appendices
SAILLY Dec. 6-4/14	No change – Weather continues wet & raw but generally speaking mild for time of year. Casualties 2 men killed 3 wounded 1 missing Reinforcements Captain C.R. White Yorkshire Lr. "/Lieut. A.E. Robinson " Captain B. Cave–Browne–Cave Wiltshire R. Captain Cottingham 7th Dif. Amm. Column 2/Lt. Findlay ¼ Essex Highlanders 2/Lt. Castell } 2/1 Radnor Regt. Helm } A large consignment of warm clothing and fur waistcoats rec'd – also horse shoes with cogs – and 3000 lugs dyed boots. × We have been many complaints as to the different specialty of the boots supplied also as to the difficulty of getting the larger sizes. Two has died – a great deal of suffering some feet & frost bite – Ed while refused to boots was represented in a letter 6.4 Coys	

Army Form C. 2118.

WAR DIARY
or
INTELLIGENCE SUMMARY.
(Erase heading not required.)

Instructions regarding War Diaries and Intelligence Summaries are contained in F.S. Regs., Part II. and the Staff Manual respectively. Title pages will be prepared in manuscript.

Hour, Date, Place	Summary of Events and Information	Remarks and references to Appendices
SAILLY Dec 8th 1914	on 30th November and it was also recommended that boots sh'd be fitted with hob nails. Since then 100 caps & nail plates have been sent up. Boots of larger sizes, arrangements are being made to entrain &c	
Dec 9th	No change – Weather still mild but a lot of rain. Casualties 9 men wounded 1 missing Reinforcements 2/Lt Jeans & 2 men of Tills R/f Christy 4th A.&S. (Highlanders) attached 2/Gordon Highlanders 6th 73= Gordon Highlanders (why loaned the Division on 5 inst.) were found to be infected with mange – they are at once isolated & all precautions taken to prevent increase of outbreak – Report made to 4th Corps HQ	

Army Form C 2118.

WAR DIARY
or
INTELLIGENCE SUMMARY.
(Erase heading not required.)

Instructions regarding War Diaries and Intelligence Summaries are contained in F.S. Regs., Part II. and the Staff Manual respectively. Title pages will be prepared in manuscript.

Hour, Date, Place	Summary of Events and Information	Remarks and references to Appendices
SAILLY Dec 9th	The quality of the large drafts of men who joined on Dec 2nd was found to be very inferior - large numbers of elderly men (one of them owned to being a grandfather) were sent out. A great many men had either never fired a rifle at all or had at most fired a few rounds — a special report on this matter was made on 5th inst. and a separate report on the Gurkha rifle drafts (who were especially bad) was made on 6th inst. 120 HALES RIFLE Bombs were received (25 having been previously issued for experiment - report) - these were issued at the	

Army Form C. 2118.

WAR DIARY
or
INTELLIGENCE SUMMARY.
(Erase heading not required.)

Instructions regarding War Diaries and Intelligence Summaries are contained in F.S. Regs., Part II. and the Staff Manual respectively. Title pages will be prepared in manuscript.

Hour, Date, Place	Summary of Events and Information	Remarks and references to Appendices
SAILLY see 9th	Scale of 10 per Field Coy R.E. & 10 per Infantry Bn — Remainder kept in Reserve in Rwm — Column to be issued as applied for — hoop's loose eyed boots (85 g's < 10s) received & issued to Infantry also Drawers, socks, hose tops & shirts. Casualties 3 men killed, 6 wounded. Supply of 600 tons of coal for Civil population obtained.	
Dec. 10th	Arrangements made for large Central Store House at a factory at BAC S¹ MAUR & to be used in the event of a forward move. All units sent AB Indexes & Atp/Mt Sergts to meet A.A. & D.A.D.O.S. at the building at 2pm.	

Army Form C. 2118.

WAR DIARY
or
INTELLIGENCE SUMMARY.
(Erase heading not required.)

Instructions regarding War Diaries and Intelligence Summaries are contained in F.S. Regs., Part II. and the Staff Manual respectively. Title pages will be prepared in manuscript.

Hour, Date, Place	Summary of Events and Information	Remarks and references to Appendices
GAILLY Dec. 10th 1914	A separate room or part of a room was allotted to each unit and clearly marked in chalk to 20th ht — RE were trained to take Dy of a Guard of one NCO (full rank) & one a Corpl & 3 men to take over their duties at once in the event of a unit being ordered. 120 HALES BOMBS were issued 10 to each Fd Coy RE. < 10 to each Infantry Bn. Balance kept in Reserve in Div. Ammn Column to be issued as required	
Dec. 11—	Casualties. 1 man killed 7 wounded. Four 4.7 Guns issued — bringing Heavy Bde up to 6 complete guns — Damaged guns returned to Advanced Base — 1500 large size boots recd. < supply of water bottles, haversacks, mess tins & 2000 entrenching tools —	

WAR DIARY
or
INTELLIGENCE SUMMARY.
(Erase heading not required.)

Army Form C. 2118.

Hour, Date, Place	Summary of Events and Information	Remarks and references to Appendices
SAILLY Dec. 12=14/14	Casualties 2 men killed 7 wounded — Reinforcements Wounded 1 R.H.A. Battery (Territorial) R.A. 11 other ranks 200 French Territorial Troops attached to Bn. for clearing out ditches & fatigue work generally. (Welles unarmed but the Companies will — Casualties 4 men killed, 5 wounded Reinforcements 1 No Officer 200 219 other Ranks (for details see Appendix) B	
Dec. 13 =	Constant Infantry & large size clothing received. Two bags have been a difficulty getting for the 2 Battalions front owing to the division & Hospitals for Bns. knocked locally & not being issued.	

WAR DIARY
or
INTELLIGENCE SUMMARY.
(Erase heading not required.)

Army Form C. 2118.

Instructions regarding War Diaries and Intelligence Summaries are contained in F.S. Regs., Part II. and the Staff Manual respectively. Title pages will be prepared in manuscript.

Hour, Date, Place	Summary of Events and Information	Remarks and references to Appendices
SAILLY Dec. 13th (Continued)	The 1st Bn. S. Staffordshire Regt. relieved the 22nd Infantry Bde. having been in Corps Reserve since Nov. 11th. The 21st Inf. Bde. were withdrawn from the trenches at 5 p.m. and went in to Reserve. Trenches relieved by the 20th & 22nd Regts. Weather remains mild & wet.	
Dec. 14th 9/14	Casualties 1 man killed 3 wounded. Reinforcements 1 Officer & 97 men for 1/ South Staffordshire Regt. Worked Parties Captured 1 prisoner. Weather slightly improved — Bright morning — clouding over later.	21st Inf. Bde Offr. & Division temporarily placed under orders of G.O.C. 4th Div.
Dec. 15th 9/14	Casualties Captain Todrick 83 Royal Scots and 6 other ranks killed, 12 other ranks wounded, 3 missing	

(9 29 6) W 4141–463 100,000 9/14 H W V Forms/C. 2118/10

WAR DIARY
or
INTELLIGENCE SUMMARY.

Army Form C. 2118.

Hour, Date, Place	Summary of Events and Information	Remarks and references to Appendices
SAILLY Dec. 15th (continued)	Reinforcements R.A. - 10 other ranks 2. 4.7 guns issued to R.A. machine to 4.7 Batteries complete - A further consignment of 20 Periscopes received New Billets arranged for 7th Sus: Amm: Column at TROU BAYARD	
Dec. 16th	Casualties 2 men killed, 12 wounded. Captain Stansfield of Sudan Reinforcements rejoined from leave of 105 Highlanders being wounded Major Forbes – 1 Royal Scots Fusiliers 25 Binoculars for use of Infantry received	

Army Form C. 2118.

WAR DIARY
or
INTELLIGENCE SUMMARY.
(Erase heading not required.)

Instructions regarding War Diaries and Intelligence Summaries are contained in F.S. Regs, Part II. and the Staff Manual respectively. Title pages will be prepared in manuscript.

Hour, Date, Place	Summary of Events and Information	Remarks and references to Appendices
SAILLY Dec. 17th 1914	7th Sir Division Column moved from DOULIEU & their hors billets at TROU BAYARD. Arrangements made to hold all Cross Roads. Tactical at the same place (whilst the Div is stationary) with a permanent Piquet for the Regiment period. Casualties (on 16-5) 1 man killed 5 men wounded. 13 Reinforcements # officers 545 other ranks all for Infantry —	For details see Appendix C.
Dec. 18th 1914	Casualties (on 17th) Lieut. C.R. Cook 2/Border Regt killed Lieut. C.A.M. Eaton wounded, 5 other ranks killed & 5 wounded — At 3.30 p.m. Div. HQ. moved forward to	

(9 29 6) W 4141—463 100,000 9/14 H W V Forms/C. 2118/10

Army Form C. 2118.

WAR DIARY
or
INTELLIGENCE SUMMARY.
(Erase heading not required.)

Instructions regarding War Diaries and Intelligence Summaries are contained in F.S. Regs., Part II. and the Staff Manual respectively. Title pages will be prepared in manuscript.

Hour, Date, Place	Summary of Events and Information	Remarks and references to Appendices
SAILLY Dec. 18th	CROIX MARECHAL — An attack was delivered against enemy's trenches under Cover of darkness by the 20th & 22nd Inf. Bdes. This attack is detailed in 7th Div. General Staff War diary.	21st Inf Bde rejoined 7th Div during previous D. 18th —
Dec. 19th	Div. Hd. returned to SAILLY at 6am. No further fighting during the day (opposite 7th Div line) beyond the ordinary sniping & artillery bombardment. Casualties during night 18th/19th Dec. 13 Officers killed 19 wounded 5 missing = 37 215 Other ranks " 254 " 257 " = 750 723	For details see Appendix - D
Dec. 20th	Nothing of note occurred — 13 D² Telephones received — 3 returned by R.A. (an issue for use of Infantry — D3 instruments) extended by Ofc. Signal Coy	

Army Form C. 2118.

WAR DIARY
or
INTELLIGENCE SUMMARY.
(Erase heading not required.)

Instructions regarding War Diaries and Intelligence Summaries are contained in F.S. Regs., Part II. and the Staff Manual respectively. Title pages will be prepared in manuscript.

Hour, Date, Place	Summary of Events and Information	Remarks and references to Appendices
Dec. 26. 914	Infantry Brigades ordered to select places to install instruments which will be issued as follows 6 each to 21st & 22nd Inf. Bdes. 4 to 20th Inf. Bde (Gren[adiers] are in possession of a private apparatus). The issue of these telephones should greatly facilitate communication in the trenches. An issue of Dandy brushes has been made. A.D.V.S. considers that this will be a great assistance in keeping horses in condition as impossible to get all mud out of heavy winter coats with a body brush. A certain amount of range is prevalent but at present this is confined to 2/Scots Guards & 6th Bn Gordon Highlanders which have been isolated.	

Forms/C. 2118/10

Army Form C. 2118.

WAR DIARY
or
INTELLIGENCE SUMMARY.
(Erase heading not required.)

Hour, Date, Place	Summary of Events and Information	Remarks and references to Appendices
SAILLY Dec. 21st	Casualties during 20th - 5 other ranks killed 19 other ranks wounded 1 missing. Reinforcements T. Battery R.H.A. arrived and joined 14th R.H.A. Bde. Casualties during 21st - 3 men killed 10 wounded 2 missing.	
Dec 22nd	Amendment to Casualties reported for night 18th/19th Dec. 2nd Bedford Regt. 2 men previously reported missing now reported wounded - 2nd Queens 15 men previously reported missing now reported wounded - 1 man reported missing rejoined - 2nd Warwicks Captain Hadden previously reported wounded now reported wounded and a prisoner of war 2/Lieut. B. Bernard previously reported wounded now reported missing -	

WAR DIARY
or
INTELLIGENCE SUMMARY.
(Erase heading not required.)

Army Form C. 2118.

Hour, Date, Place	Summary of Events and Information	Remarks and references to Appendices
SAILLY Dec. 22nd 1914	Reinforcements 1/Grenadier Guards 2/Lt Stilwell, 2/Lieut. Barnard, 2/Lt Guthrie and 1 man - 2nd Grens Major L. M. Crofts (returned after being wounded) 2/Lt Greig and 19 other ranks - Nothing of note occurred during the day - The incessant rain is making the question of draining the trenches & keeping the trenches a very difficult problem - Casualties on 22nd 1 man killed, one officer (2nd Lieut. Johns 2/S.W. Borderers att 2 1/R. Welsh Fus.) and 11 other ranks wounded -	
SAILLY Dec. 23rd	Reinforcements 8 officers 755 other ranks - all for infantry (for details see Appendix)	E

Army Form C. 2118.

WAR DIARY
or
INTELLIGENCE SUMMARY.
(Erase heading not required.)

Instructions regarding War Diaries and Intelligence Summaries are contained in F. S. Regs., Part II. and the Staff Manual respectively. Title pages will be prepared in manuscript.

Hour, Date, Place	Summary of Events and Information	Remarks and references to Appendices
SAILLY Dec. 24.	Weather shows signs of a change. Wind in the North & decidedly colder and brighter — Casualties (23rd) 3 men killed, Lt Greenwood R.E. and 5 men wounded — Casualties not previously reported Lieut. & Q:M: Teece 1/Grenadier Gds wounded 21st inst. 1/S. Staffordshire Regt. 4 men wounded on 22nd. 6th Royal Scots 4 men wounded, 1 missing night 18th/19th Dec.	
Dec. 25th 1914 Xmas day	Sharp frost during previous night & cold winter weather returned — Her Majesty's Xmas Cards (also 1 from Lady Rawlinson) & Princess Mary's gift distributed to the troops.	

WAR DIARY
or
INTELLIGENCE SUMMARY.
(Erase heading not required.)

Army Form C. 2118.

Hour, Date, Place	Summary of Events and Information	Remarks and references to Appendices
SAILLY Dec. 25th 1914	Everything very quiet during the day and a sort of informal armistice held. Reinforcements. Drafts to infantry 11 officers 547 other ranks arrived also 66 other ranks R.E. (for details see Appendix) Canadians on 24th 5 men killed, Captain Jackson 3rd H.L.I. (attached 2/H.L.I.) Fasken, and 5 other ranks wounded. 2/Lt. B/F.B. Bernard 2/R. Warwickshire Regt. previously reported "wounded & missing" (16th/19th) is now reported killed. 2/Lt. C.V. Pearce previously reported missing (18th/19th) is now reported by a German officer to be a prisoner of war, wounded in the head & doing well.	

Army Form C. 2118.

WAR DIARY
or
INTELLIGENCE SUMMARY.
(Erase heading not required.)

Instructions regarding War Diaries and Intelligence Summaries are contained in F.S. Regs., Part II. and the Staff Manual respectively. Title pages will be prepared in manuscript.

Hour, Date, Place	Summary of Events and Information	Remarks and references to Appendices
SAILLY Dec. 26th	Sharp hostile during nights 25th/26th. Cold & weather much healthier than previous wet & damp — Casualties on 25th — 4 men killed, 4 wounded	
Dec. 27th	Thaw during previous night and a resumption of wet weather — An unpleasant change — Menace waived for 4 days that short leave may again be granted to Officers & N.C.O's Casualties (27th) 1 man killed, 4 wounded. 1 man R. West Fusrs. killed by W 18th/19th See not previously reported.	

WAR DIARY
or
INTELLIGENCE SUMMARY.
(Erase heading not required.)

Army Form C. 2118.

Hour, Date, Place	Summary of Events and Information	Remarks and references to Appendices
SAILLY Dec. 28th 1914	Weather very wet & "muggy". Casualties 1 killed, 1 wounded. 5 men of 1R. Rutter & 1 wounded man of 1R. Scots Gds. who were entered into the German trenches during a local armistice & made prisoners.	
Dec. 29th 1914	Lt. Col. Daly left today, having over temp command of 1R. 22nd Inf. bde. vice Brig. Gen. Lawford who proceeds on short leave tomorrow. A draft of 1 off. & 56 men arrived for 1R. tonight bringing it up to its original total. 1 R.E. officer & 9 N.C. officers also arrived T.o.r. F.H.A. Zouaves also ii) 2/Lt. W.F. Hayland C/K. P.R. attacked 1/T.W.F. Wounded. S.o.r. 1 killed, 6 o.r. wounded.	

WAR DIARY
or
INTELLIGENCE SUMMARY.

(Erase heading not required.)

Army Form C. 2118.

Hour, Date, Place	Summary of Events and Information	Remarks and references to Appendices
SAILLY 30.12.16	Officers & N.C.O's proceeding to England on leave. 2 N.C.O's per unit. Zaawalno went K.Z. Thomson 2/R Scots Fus. wounded or 5 killed. 15 wounded	
" 31.12.16	Weather still v. wet. River very high & low lying field flooded. Casualties 1 killed. 8 wounded	

(Appendix A).

Detail of Re-inforcements received by 7th Division on December 2nd 1914.

Units &c.	Officers.	Other Ranks.	Remarks.
1st Bn Grenadier Guards.	1	66	
2nd Bn Border Regiment.	4	570	
2nd Bn Gordon Highlanders... ...	2	-	
2nd Bn Bedford Regiment.	1	1	
2nd Bn Yorkshire Regiment... ...	4	76	
2nd Bn Royal Scots Fus:·	1	-	
2nd Bn "Queens"	4	150	
2nd Bn R.Warwick Regt:	7	140	
1st Bn R.Welch Fusiliers.... ...	3	190	
Total.	27	1193	

(Appendix B).

Detail of Re-inforcements received by 7th Division on December 15th 1914.

Units &c.	Offrs.	Other Ranks.	Remarks.
1st Bn Grenadier Guards.	1	45	
2nd Bn Border Regiment.	1	20	
2nd Bn Gordon Highlanders.	3	-	
2nd Bn Bedford Regiment.	2	30	
2nd Bn Yorkshire Regt.	-	34	
2nd Bn Wilts Regiment.	1	-	
2nd Bn R.Scots Fusiliers.	3	70	
2nd Bn The "Queens"	2	-	
2nd Bn R.Warwick Regt	3	20	
Total	16	219	

(Appendix *C*).

Detail of Re-inforcements received by 7th Division on December 17th 1914.

Units &c.	Offrs.	Other ranks.	Remarks.
1st Bn Grenadier Guards.	1	60	
2nd Bn Gordon Highlanders... ...	2	39	
2nd Bn Bedford Regiment.	2	60	
2nd Bn Wilts Regiment...	2	300	
2nd Bn R.Scots Fusiliers	1	-	
2nd Bn The "Queens".	2	45	
1st R.Welsh Fusiliers...	3	40	
8th Bn Royal Scots.	-	1	
Total.	13	545	

7th Division. (APPENDIX D.)

CASUALTIES. Operations 18th/19th December 1914.

Units &c.	Officers K	Officers W	Officers M	Other ranks K	Other ranks W	Other ranks M	Remarks.
54th Field Coy, R.E.	-	2	-	-	4	-	
55th Field Coy, R.E.	-	1	-	4	2	-	
1st Grenadier Gds.	-	-	-	1	5	-	
2nd Scots Guards.	2	3	1*	81	62	30	* Also wounded.
2nd Border Regt.	1	3	-	6	22	88	
2nd Yorks Regt.	-	1	-	1	7	1	
2nd Bn "Queens".	1	5	2	26	39	23	
2nd Bn R.Warwick R.	7	3	2	96	97	102	
1st Bn R.Welch Fus.	-	1	-	-	17	3	
1st S.Staffs Regt.	1	-	-	-	-	-	
8th Bn R.Scots.	1	-	-	2	4	-	
Totals.	13	19	5	217	259	247	
Grand Total.		37			723		

Names of Officers:-

54th Field Coy, R.E.	Lieut: E.L.Morris, R.E.	Wounded.
	2/Lieut: J.B.H.Doyle, R.E.	Wounded.
55th Field Coy, R.E.	Captain J.O.H.Moore, R.E.	Wounded. (died).
2nd Scots Guards.	Captain H.Taylor.	Killed.
	Lieut:Hon:F.Hanbury-Tracey	Killed.
	Captain Sir F.L.P.Fitz-Wygram	Wounded.
	Lieut:Hon:J.St V.B.Saumarez	Wounded.
	Lieut: G.C.L.Ottley	Wounded. (died)
	2/Lieut:R.F.R.Nugent.	Wounded & Missing. (Prisoner of war).
2nd Border Regt.	Captain H.A.Askew	Killed.
	Captain C.Lamb. D.S.O.	Wounded. (died).
	Lieut: N.Castle.	Wounded.
	Lieut: M.S.N.Kennedy.	Wounded.
2nd Yorks Regt.	2/Lieut:A.J.Pickup (late Artists Rifles)	Wounded.
2nd Bn "Queens"	2/Lieut: D.P.Ramsay	Killed.
	Captain P.J.Fearon	Wounded.
	Captain R.T.Lee.	Wounded.
	Lieut: A.M.Allan.	Wounded.
	2/Lieut: F.T.Burkitt.	Wounded.
	2/Lieut: B.Butterworth	Wounded.
	2/Lieut: C.G.Rought(late Artists Rifles)	Missing. (prisoner.)
	2/Lieut: A.E.Walmisley	Missing. (- do -)
2nd R.Warwick Regt.	Major R.H.W.Brewis	Killed.
	Captain R.J.Brownfield	Killed.
	Captain C.A.R.Hodgson	Killed.
	2/Lieut: B.Campbell	Killed.
	2/Lieut: G.B.Monk (late Artists Rifles)	Killed.
	2/Lieut: A.R.L.Tucker	Killed.
	2/Lieut: B.Bernard.	Killed.
	2/Lieut: B.A.Standring(late Artists Rifles)	Wounded. (died)
	Captain E.C.Mulgrue	Wounded.
	2/Lieut:R.F.Richardson	Wounded.
	Captain J.B.Haddon	Missing.(prisoner).
	2/Lieut:G.V.Pearce	Wounded & Missing. (died).
1st R.Welch Fus:	2/Lieut:G.R.Gore	Wounded. (died).
1st S.Staffs.Regt.	2/Lieut: H.R.S.Bower	Killed.
8th Royal Scots.	Lieut: A.Burt.	Killed.

1st Bn. S.Staffordshire Regiment

STRENGTH RETURN --- 15/12/14

Captain	F.S.N.	Savage Armstrong	1st Bn.	C.O.
Captain	H.J.de.	Trafford	3rd Bn.	
Captain	W.F.	Helmore	4th Bn.	
Lieutenant	H.R.S.	Bower	1st Bn.	
Lieutenant	F.M.	Soly (attached from 3rd E.Surreys)		
2/Lieut.	N.R.	Freeman (attached from 1st D.C.L.I.)		
2/Lieut.	K.	Frost (attached Prob.Artists' Corps)		
2/Lieut	F.	West --do--		
2/Lieut.	A.	Silcock --do--		
2/Lieut.	H.L.	Mackintosh --do--		
2/Lieut	J.S.D.M.	Armour (attached from 3rd Scottish R.)		
2/Lieut.	D.E.C.	Bacon --do--		
2/Lieut.	P.W.Le.	Gros (attached from 3rd Warwicks)		
Lieutenant	O.W.	Evans	1st Bn.	ADJUTANT
Captain	F.H.	White	1st Bn.	QUARTERMASTER

15 officers

Strength of OTHER RANKS:- 4 6 5

Appendix V(a)

7th DIVISIONAL ROUTINE ORDERS No. 75

15th December 1914

GENERAL STAFF

1. HAND GRENADES

A limited number of W.D. Pattern hand grenades and of Hale's pattern hand grenades (which are somewhat similar to Hale's rifle bombs) are on charge of Brigade Ammunition Columns for issue to the Infantry Brigades to which they are affiliated.

Infantry Brigadiers will arrange with Officers Commanding affiliated Field Companies R.E. for 4 Sappers in each section of R.E. and for 8 men in each Infantry battalion to be thoroughly instructed in the use of these grenades.

It is suggested that the Infantry should be selected from the men who have shown most aptitude in throwing improvised hand grenades, and that these men should be earmarked to form a Brigade grenade detachment.

The instruction should, if possible, be given at or near the billets of the Field Company concerned, who have been supplied with grenades for the purpose.

It is important that the instruction should be expedited so that these grenades may be used practically with as little delay as possible.

2. MAPS

In future only the following maps should be used in writing orders, reports, etc.
(a) For details of trenches the $\frac{1}{10,000}$ maps of Right, Left Centre and Left sections of the defence.
(b) For local tactics the $\frac{1}{40,000}$ " Country S.W. of ARMENTIERES" map.
(c) For general use the $\frac{1}{80,000}$ Sheets.

                        A. R. Hoskins   Colonel
                        General Staff.

ADMINISTRATIVE STAFF.

3. SICK.

The following are the percentages of Sick and Wounded in the 7th Division for 14th instant:-

20th Infantry Brigade
Admitted to Hospital Sick, 1 Officer, 13 men, Wounded 3 men.
Percentage of admissions to Brigade strength = .39%

21st Infantry Brigade
Admitted to Hospital, sick 11 men, Wounded 1 man.
Percentage of admissions to Brigade strength = .39%

22nd Infantry Brigade
Admitted to Hospital, sick, 11 men, Wounded Nil.
Percentage of admissions to Brigade strength = .26%

Northumberland Hussars.
Admitted to Hospital, sick, 2 men, Wounded Nil.
Percentage of admissions to Regtl strength = .45%

Royal Artillery
Admitted to Hospital, sick, 5 men, Wounded 2 men.
Percentage of admissions to R.A. strength = .15%

Royal Engineers.
Admitted to Hospital, sick 1 man, Wounded Nil.
Percentage of admissions to R.E. strength = .16%

Army Service Corps
Admitted to Hospital, sick 2 men, Wounded Nil.
Percentage of admissions to A.S.C. strength = .5

R. A. M. C.
Admitted to Hospital, sick, 1 man, Wounded Nil.
percentage of admissions to R.A.M.C. strength = .15%

Total admissions from 7th Division = Sick 1 Offr, 46 men, Wounded 6 men.
Percentage of admissions to Division strength = .3%

P. T. O.

4. CLAIMS - COMPENSATION AND REQUISITIONS.
All claims for compensation and all requisition claims that cannot be traced are to be forwarded to this office. It should be stated on compensation claims that the damage was inspected by an officer, and the name of the officer should be given for future reference if further information should be required.

5. BATH HOUSE
The 20th Infantry Brigade will have the use of the Bath House tomorrow.
17th & 18th December:- 22nd Infantry Brigade.

19th December:- 20th Infantry Brigade.

20th December:- 22nd Infantry Brigade.
O. C. Divisional Troops or detached units desiring use of the Bath House will notify hours at which most convenient and dates will be allotted.

A.C.Daly   Major
A. A. & Q. M. G., 7th Division.

Nominal Roll Officers departing to front 24
16/12/1914

Rank	Name	Unit	Unit to which posted	Remarks
Lieut	Greville G.C.S.	1st Grenadier Gds	1st Grn Gds	
2"	Rowley L.N.G.	"	"	
2 "	Ramsay	3rd Gordons	2nd Gordon Hdrs	
Lieut	Campbell, adjt	attd 2nd army	2nd Gordon Hdrs	
"	Williams W.H.	East Surrey	2nd Bedfords	
2 Lt	Duchesne S.J.	"	"	
"	W.P. Spencer	3rd Wilts	2nd Wilts	
"	S.J. Belsham	"	"	
"	R.S. Stenckey	3 Queens	2nd Queens	
"	T.J. Burkett	"	"	
Lieut	A.K. Richardson	Royal Welsh Fus	1st R Welch Regt	
2 "	Foote J.	"	"	
"	Blount B.C.L.	3 R Welch Fus.	"	
"	Wilson W.H.	6 Rifle Brigade	2 R Scots Fus	

Rouen.
16.12.1914.

Henr W Lucy 2/Lt for Captain
adjt 7th Infy Base Depot

Appendix VIII

7th DIVISIONAL ROUTINE ORDERS. No.80
22nd December 1914.

GENERAL STAFF.

1. GRENADE COMPANIES - FORMATION OF.

It has become necessary for us to use Hand Grenades in the phase of operations with which we are confronted. That they may be used effectively, a proper understanding of their capabilities and a thorough training in their use is necessary.

It has therefore been decided to make a special organization in each Brigade to this end. In each Brigade a separate Company will be formed from specially selected men drawn from each battalion. The composition of the Company will be as follows:-

- 1 Officer, Commanding the Company.
- 1 Specially selected Non-commissioned officer as acting Sergeant Major and Q.M.Sergeant with 3 sections from each Battalion each consisting of 1 N.C.O. and 9 men.

These Companies are to be formed immediately and their instruction by the R.E.Company affiliated to their Brigade is to be taken in hand without delay. They are to understand each pattern of bomb or grenade and the throwing of them.

When they have passed a satisfactory standard they will be entitled to wear a red cloth grenade on the sleeve of the great-coat and tunic.

During the period of instruction, and while the Brigades are stationary, they will be billeted and live with the R.E. affiliated to the Brigade. When on the march they will move as a Company, and a 2 wheeled cart will be allotted to the Company by the Brigade.

Adequate arrangements are to be made for the storage of the bombs in the trenches and the replenishment of the supply from the ammunition supply system.

It must be understood that if necessary all or any of these Brigade Companies are at the disposal of the Divisional Command for any special emergency.

It must be understood that the instruction under the R.E. which must commence immediately, must be thorough as far as our knowledge goes at present. One section from each battalion will undergo the first course of instruction under the R.E.Company affiliated, and this section will be followed by another from each unit until all three sections per Battalion are thoroughly instructed.

2. TELEPHONE LINES - CARE OF.

During the recent strong gales, telephone posts have been continually blown down. As the wire lying in the mud deteriorates rapidly, it is the duty of all ranks to assist in maintaining communications in good order by re-erecting any fallen posts that they may notice.

3- DOCUMENTS - CARE OF.

The greatest care must be taken by all officers and men when in the trenches or when going into action, that they have no papers maps or documents on their persons which could be of use to the enemy.

This must be impressed on all officers and men who join units from time to time.

A. R. Hoskins   Colonel

General Staff.

P. T. O.

7th D.O. No.80 dated 22/12/14.

ADMINISTRATIVE STAFF

4. **INSTRUCTIONS RE COLLECTION OF MATERIAL THAT CANNOT BE CARRIED ON THE MARCH.**

All fur undercoats when not actually required in the trenches should be collected and dried under Battalion arrangements and stored in the Divisional Store. When Commanding Officers consider the weather sufficiently severe they will be reissued and must be collected again and dried as soon as the weather becomes milder. It is most important that they should not be permitted to lie about in wet trenches.

(2) In the event of a sudden move Units will send a demand to the O.C.Train for sufficient transport to carry such articles as cannot be taken on the march, to Battalion Stores. Here they will be sorted, cleaned and dried, before being stored in the Divisional Store.

(3) Arrangements will be made for the removal of such stores to the Divisional Store either by wagons left behind for the purpose or by transport hired locally.

(4) No more should be kept in the Battalion Stores than is required for the immediate requirements of Units.

(5) The Factory near the Divisional Store is available as a drying room by arrangement with the Quartermaster, Scots Guards.

(6) O.C. Units are responsible that their Transport is not overloaded through the carriage of unauthorized loads.

(7) All spare tools surplus to establishment, loopholes, etc, not in use, should be collected and taken to Battalion Stores.

(8) Instructions as regards storemen have already been issued, until Battalion Stores are closed 1 man per Battalion must be left behind as storeman.

5. **SENTRIES**

Routine Order No.76 (2) of 18th December is cancelled and the following substituted.

Sentries will halt all persons, motors and mounted men approaching their posts between 4-30 p.m. and 7 a.m.

South of the railway line all civilians must be in possession of a white residential pass signed by the A.P.M. 7th Division.

North of the railway line civilians may pass up to 8 p.m. without a pass.

Both North and South of line, no civilian is allowed out between 8 p.m. and 6 a.m. without a <u>special</u> pass signed by an A.P.M. stating reasons for being out.

All Foreign Officers and British Officers travelling in Motor Cars should be in possession of a green pass signed by an A.P.M.

Whenever there is any doubt as to the bona-fides of any individual Civil or Military of whatever rank, the Sentry will detain the person concerned and refer the case to an officer who if not satisfied will send the suspect under escort to the office of the A.P.M. at SAILLY BRIDGE.

6. **PRINCESS MARY'S XMAS PRESENT TO THE TROOPS AT THE FRONT.**

Extracts from 4th Army Corps Order No.422 dated 10/12/14.

x x x x x x x x

(3) Every Commanding Officer will give a receipt for the Boxes received for his units, and render a certificate to the Senior Supply Officer on the 27th that every Officer and man present with his Unit on the 25th or 26th received one box only. Any balance left over will be handed to the Senior Supply Officer with the Commanding Officer's Certificate.

x x x x x x x

(continued)

Sheet (2)

(5) Every man who entrains for the Front on the 23rd or 24th will receive his box from his unit. A supplementary demand being made on the Senior Supply Officer if necessary.

(6) Every man who leaves his Unit or Hospital for the Base on the 23rd or 24th will receive his box on arrival at the Base.

(7) Any man who entrains for the Base on the 25th will receive his box from his unit before starting. Similarly, any man who entrains for the front on the 25th will receive his box before entrainment.

(9) It must be distinctly understood that, while every effort will be made to ensure that each Officer and Man receives one Box, should by accident anyone not receive it, the non-receipt is not to form the subject of subsequent official correspondence.

7. CHRISTMAS PUDDINGS.
The plum puddings which have been kindly provided for the 4th Corps by a Committee presided over by Lady Rawlinson will be issued with rations at the refilling point on the 24th instant, the allowance will be about 3/8 lb per man.

8. FORAGE.
There have been a number of complaints from Units that they are not receiving their full allowance of forage. On investigation it almost invariably transpires that the shortage is due to their representative not indenting for the full amount.

The following is the scale of forage ordered vide 7th Div. Routine Order No.50 dated 22/11/14 and is available:-

HORSES	Oats	Hay	Bran
Riding or Draught	12	8	2
Heavy Draught	15	8	2
Clydesdale and Shire	19	8	2

When bran is not available 2 lbs Oats will be issued in lieu.
The balance of the hay ration will be made up in straw procured locally, or, if no local supply is available, arrangements will be made by the Senior Supply Officer.

In future the responsibility of asking for the correct amount will rest with the Unit, and the Indent (B.55) will show clearly, in the Column "Remarks" the strength of Animals under the following heads, viz:- Riding and Draught, Heavy Draught, Clydesdale or Shire.

9. SANITATION.
It has been noticed that many of the billets are in an insanitary condition, empty tins and vegetable refuse being thrown about outside the houses.
O. C. Units must see that all refuse is buried in proper refuse pits.

10 HORSES - MANGE
The restrictions contained in D.Os 66 (5) and 74 (6) are cancelled.

P. T. O.

11. SICK.
The following are the percentages of Sick and Wounded in the 7th Division for the 21st inst:-

20th Infantry Brigade.
Admitted to Hospital, sick, 1 Officer, 38 men, Wounded 1 Officer, 6 men.
Percentage of admissions to Brigade Strength = 1.05%

21st Infantry Brigade
Admitted to Hospital, sick 16 men, Wounded 3 men.
Percentage of admissions to Brigade Strength = .56%

22nd Infantry Brigade.
Admitted to Hospital, sick, 1 Officer, 10 men, Wounded 6 men.
Percentage of admissions to Brigade Strength = .39%

Royal Artillery.
Admitted to Hospital, sick 1 man, Wounded Nil.
Percentage of admissions to R.A. strength = .03%

Royal Engineers
Admitted to Hospital, sick, 1 man, Wounded Nil.
Percentage of admissions to R.E. Strength = .17%

R. A. M. C.
Admitted to Hospital, sick, 4 men, Wounded Nil.
Percentage of admissions to R.A.M.C. strength = .59%

Total admissions from 7th Division = Sick 2 Officers, 71 men (includes 1 man of Details)

Wounded 1 Officer, 15 men.

Percentage of admissions to Division Strength = .5.

A. C. Daly   Major
A. A. & Q. M. G., 7th Division.

38

Nominal Roll officers to front 22.12.1914
7th I Base Depot

Rank	Name	Unit	Unit to which posted	Remarks
Lt	Ashmead Bartlett	4 Bedford Rgt	2 Bedford Rgt	
2/Lt	Powell. F	4 " "	" "	
2/Lt	G Westmacott	1st G. Gds	1st Gren Gds	✓
2/Lt	A Stretton	2 R Warwicks	2 R Warwick Rgt	
Lt	L A Allston	3 R Welch Fus	1st R Welch Fus	
Capt.	L.W. Jones Bateman		1st Norfolk Rgt	
2/Lt	Wilson Rae	3rd Surrey Rgt	1st E Surrey	Absent.

Rouen
22.12.14

Kaplan
A.A.G 7th I.B. Depot.

(Appendix *E*).

Detail of Re-inforcements received by 7th Division on December 23rd 1914.

Units &c.	Offrs.	Other Ranks.	Remarks.
1st Bn Grenadier Guards.	1	41	
2nd Bn Bedford Regt.	2	-	
2nd Bn Yorks Regiment	1	120	
2nd Bn R.Warwick Regt	1	70	
1st Bn R.Welsh Fusiliers	1	25	
1st Bn South Staffords.	2	500	
Total	8	756	

(Appendix F)

ORDER TO PROCEED

You will proceed, in accordance with instructions received.

From ..D.A.G. III a Echelon......

By { Letter
     Telegram No XIII dated 22 12/14
     Telephone }

with the detachment under your command by the

Train {
(Hour) I — 17.25 hrs 24 12/14
(Place) II — Rouen
(Station) III — Martinville
(Platform) IV —
}

To ......Railhead IV th Corps..... where you will report and show this authority.

RANK	NAME		REGT OR CORPS	
	7th Division			
2nd Lt	A.V.H. WOOD	other ranks	1st Grenadier Gds.	20
2nd Lt	R.G. DONE	other ranks	2d. Border Regt.	130
	E. MOLSON	other ranks	2d. Royal West Surrey Regt.	45
2nd Lt	A.S. MAUNSELL	other ranks	2d. Royal Warwicks	240
2nd Lt	H.D.O. LYLE	other ranks	1st Royal Welch Fusiliers	30
2nd Lt	A. BLAIR	other ranks	8th Royal Scots	82
				6 547

{ 20th Bde. — WOOD
  22nd Bde. — DONE, MOLSON, MAUNSELL, LYLE, BLAIR }

December 24th 1914

A. Nicholson
Col.
Com.ndt Base Depots.

ORDER TO PROCEED

RANK	NAME	7th Division Contd.	REGT OR CORPS
Captain	R. DUCKWORTH.		1st Son li Staffords
"	H.F. BIDDER.		"
2nd Lt	T.G.W. PHILLIPS		"
"	G.D. RAMSBOTTOM		"
"	H.N. HUME		

You will proceed, in accordance with instructions received.

From _J. a. g. Tues. Ech 2gu_

By: { Letter
Telegram No. R.O. XII dated 20/12/14
Telephone }

with the detachment under your command by the

Train { (Hour) I – 17hrs 24/12/14
(Place) II – Rouen }

From { (Station) III – Martinville
(Platform) IV – }

To _Rai Elzad IV ci Corps._

where you will report and show this authority.

G. Nicholson Col.

Com^ndt Base Depots.

December 24th 1914

Os 22nd Bde Hd Qrs

Casualty Return

Officers

Killed
Wounded
Missing
Sick
} Nil

Other Ranks

Killed
Wounded
Missing
Sick
} Nil

Reinforcements Nil 5 Officers

(Capt R Duckworth, S. Staffs
" H F Bedder, 3/R Sussex
2/Lt G B Ramsbotham - " -
" T G Vaughan-Phillips
    3/S Staffs Bde
2/Lt H N Hume, 1/Hampshire

R. M. Savoy [signature]   Capt
                    OC 1/South Stafford Regt

Hour
Date 26-12-14

(4711) Wt. W 3391-411. 10/12. 15,000 Pads. WY. & S., LTD. Sch. 18.
"B" Form.   Army Form C 2122.

MESSAGES AND SIGNALS.   No. of Message_____

Prefix………..Code……………m	Received	Sent	Office Stamp.
Office of Origin and Service Instructions. Words.	At………………m. From…………… By……………	At………………m. To…………… By……………	ZU 29-12-16

TO | 21st Bde | | | |

Sender's Number.	Day of Month	In reply to Number	AAA
*Y06	29th		

2nd Lt G F Hadow has reported himself here for duty with 2nd Btn Yorkshire Regt

From YORKS
Place
Time 6.35 pm

* This line should be erased if not required.

2nd Battn Border Regiment

Nominal Roll of Officers of Above

Rank & Name			Remarks
Capt	Askew	H.A.	Capt. R.F. Hanbury L Eads
"	Lamb	C	Lt. G.P. Nunneley "
"	Jenkins	N.G	2.12.14
Lieut	Watson	W	Machine Gun Officer
"	Kennedy	W.S.N.	Lt. W. Hatch Barnwell. 12/12/14
2nd Lt	Hutton	B	
"	Kerr	W	Lt. G P L Drake Brockman
"	Owen	W	" C.R. Cooch.
"	Horsley	A	" N Castle
Hon Lt & O.M.	Mitchell	J.W.	" H.F.D Aclm
			Transport Officer
Attached from Artists Rifles on Probation			
2nd Lt	Klose	M.A	
"	Cuthbertson	F.J	
"	Sampson	H.J	
"	Wornum	G.H	
Medical Officer			
Lieut	Ormsby	W	RAMC

Sailly sur la Lys
29th Nov 1914

Jack Mitchell Lt & Q.M
for OC 2nd Border Regt

6th Battalion Gordon Highlanders

Nominal Roll of Officers.

Rank	Name	Duties
Lieut Colonel	C. McLean	
Major	W.A. McDonald	
Major	G.A. Wilson	
Captain & Hon Major	C.J. Reynolds	
Captain	J. Dawson	
Captain	J.M. Cook	
Captain	J.G. Cowie	
Captain	G. Smith	
Captain	G.A. Stephen	
Captain	W.B. Welch	
Captain	J. Kellas	
Captain	J.G. Fleming	
Lieutenant	A. Grant	
Lieutenant	G. McCombie	
Lieutenant	G.E. Gordon Duff	
Lieutenant	D.G. Clark	
Lieutenant	L.S.P. Davidson	
Lieutenant	Sir J. Seton Bart	
Lieutenant	H.C. Closter	
2nd Lieutenant	M. McK. Wood	
2nd Lieutenant	F.W. Peter Hay	
2nd Lieutenant	P. Kynoch Shand	
2nd Lieutenant	F.C. Mitchell	
2nd Lieutenant	A.S.C. Burn	
2nd Lieutenant	W.H. Newson	
2nd Lieutenant	F.C. Farquharson	

Rank.	Name.	Duties.
Captain.	J.A.L. Campbell.	Adjutant.
Hon: Major.	H.W. Cooper.	Quarter Master.
Major.	J. Bair Stevens.	Medical Offr.
Rev. Captain	J.E. Adams.	Chaplain.

Sd/ E.J. Reynolds, Major. for
Lieut: Colonel.
8/12/1914. Commanding, 6th Gordon Highd

2nd Battn Scots Guards

Roll of Officers

~~Captain Hon. R. Cote~~ v. Commanding Officer
" ~~H. Taylor~~
Lieutenant G. H. Loder   Adjutant
" ~~Sir F. Fitzwygram~~
" E. C. F. Warner
" Sir E. Hulse
" ~~C. A. Cator~~
" ~~Hon. F. Hanbury-Tracey~~
" Lord Lisburne
" ~~St. J. Saumarez~~
" ~~R. H. Nugent~~
" C. Massey
2nd Lieut. Lord Clive-Swinton
"   "   ~~G. C. L. Otley~~
"   "   H. H. Liddell-Grainger
Lieut and Qmr F. Ross

(At present Sick) Capt. G. Paynter.
                   2nd Lieut H. Atkinson-Clark

Daily Report Jan 12 - 1914   95

1st Bn Grenadier Gds	Killed	Wounded	Missing
Officers	nil	nil	nil
Other Ranks	nil	nil	nil

	Reinforcements Received	Enemy's casualties
Officers	2/Lieut C. T. Goschen	nil
Other Ranks	nil	nil

Sick Admitted to hospital: 6.

Mitchell
Lieut. for Lieut Col
Commdg 1st Bn Grenadier Gds.

— 1/R War R —

Return of Killed, Wounded, Missing, Sick &c.

Officers
Killed
Wounded } Nil
Missing
Sick

Other Ranks
Killed
Wounded } nil
Missing
Sick   3

— Reinforcements —

Officers Capt. A. D Vaughan.
Other Ranks. Nil.

ADVaughan   Capt.
30-12-14   Comdg 1/R War R.

Daily Return

2nd Border Regt	Killed	Wounded	Missing
Officers	Nil	Nil	Nil
Other Ranks	Nil	Nil	Nil
	Reinforcements	Every 5 casualties	
Officers	Lieut C.W. Wilson, Lieut H.R. Wright Sanguine, 2 Lieut S. Horsley - from York	Nil	
Other Ranks	Nil	Nil	

30/12/1914

2nd Bn The Queens Rgt.   30.12.14
Return of killed, wounded, missing, sick &c

Officers:
   Killed.   nil
   Wounded. nil
   Missing.   nil
   Sick.   nil

Other ranks
   Killed.   nil
   Wounded.   nil
   Missing.   NIL   { Absent from 12.30
   Sick.   nil   29.12.14 2 men.

From Hospital: nil

Reinforcements:—
   Lt. C. Carlile
   2nd Lt. P. Rossiter

30.12.14

[signature]
Capt & Adjt. for O.C.
2/Queens Rgt.

1st Bn. R. W. Inf.

Report of Killed, Wounded, Missing, Sick etc.

Officers.
   Killed. —
   Wounded. 2/Lt Acyland W.F.
   Missing. —
   Sick. —

Other Ranks.

   Killed   3
   Wounded.   4
   Missing. —
   Sick. —

Re-inforcements
Officers. 2nd Lieut C.F. Woodward.
Other Ranks. One O.R.

                      J.C. Wood Captain
                      for O.Commdg
30/12/14.   1st R.W. Inf.

be rendered to Officers i/c Records for transmission to the War Office.   Army Form B. 158.

CAVALRY, ARTILLERY and INFANTRY only.

Regiment, etc., or Depôt 1st Bn Grenadier Guards.

Station Rue du Quesnes.

Date 29/11/14

LIST OF OFFICERS.

* Married or Single	Officers doing duty with the Unit NAME	Date of being taken on the strength of the Unit †	Stations (if on Detachment)
	Lieut.-Colonel— Lieut Col. G. P. Fisher Rowe	20/11/14	
	Majors— Major G. Corkran	19/11/14	Sick 25/12/14
	" G. Trotter, D.S.O	27/11/14	
	" G. W. Duberly	18/11/14	
	Captains— Hon. R. Legge, M.V.O.	17/11/14	
	Earl Stanhope	20/11/14	
	J. A. Morrison	20/11/14	
●	Capt. E O Stewart	2.12.14	Sick 16/12
	Lieutenants— G. H. Douglas Pennant	12.12.14	
	C. Mitchell	30/10/14	
	C. Sykes	18/11/14	Sick 21/12/14
	C. H. Greville	17.12.14	
	C. L. B. H. Blundell	16.12.14	Sick 22/12/14
	C. T. R. S. Guthrie	21.12.14	
	C. F. Burnand	"	
	F. O. S. Sitwell	"	
	G. R. Westmacott	23.12.14	
	2nd Lieutenants— M. A. A. Darby		
	C. Fisher Rowe	18/11/14	
	C. L. Blundell	18/11/14	
	R. Williams	20/11/14	
●	Lord Brabourne	20/11/14	
	Lord W. Percy	20/11/14	
	T. Parker-Jervis	16.12.14	
	E. H. J. Duberly	16.12.14	
	Adjutant— 2 Lieut C Fisher Rowe		
	Quartermaster— Lieut & QmR J. Leece		
	Riding-Master—		

WARRANT OFFICERS.

Master Gunner—
Serjeant-Major— Sgt. Major J. E. Parkin.
Bandmaster—

OFFICERS ATTACHED.
(Including Special Reserve and Territorial Force Officers. Authority to be quoted.)

Rank	Name	Corps	Authority	Date of joining
Lieut	A. M. McCutcheon	R.A.M.C., S.R.		8/11/14
2nd Lieut	A. A. Moller	Artists Rifles. O.T.C.		13/11/14
"	R. Drake	- do -		13/11/14
"	E. J. S. Edlmann	- do -		13/11/14
"	F. E. J. Crisp	- do -		13/11/14

* The letter "M" or "S" in red ink is to be placed before the names of Officers.
† For Units of Royal Artillery, Depôts of all Arms and Special Reserve Units.
NOTE.—The word "Sick" to be inserted against the names of all Officers who are on the Sick List, and the words "Assistant Adjutant," "Instructor of Gunnery," &c., against the name of an Officer holding such appointment.

Officers absent on duty.
(Exclusive of seconded Officers, but including Officers posted and not joined.)

Married or Single.	Rank and Name	On what duty, at what station, from what time

Officers and Warrant Officers absent with Leave.

Rank and Name	By whose permission, and date of order	On what account	From what time	To what time
2/Lieut M.A.A Darby	G.O.C 4th Army Corps	On leave to England	29/11/14	8/12/14
Lieut C Mitchell	~do~	~do~	29/11/14	8/12/14

Officers and Warrant Officers who have *joined* during the preceding month, showing whether from leave of absence, on appointment, &c.

Rank and Name	Date and cause	Rank and Name	Date and cause	Officers Attached Rank & Name	Date & cause
Lieut Col J B Lister Rowe	To Command Battalion 29-11-14	2/Lieut C Eicher Rowe, For duty.	12-11-14	Lieut A McCutcheon, R.A.M.C	To complete establisht 8/11/14
Major G Cochran	For duty with Battalion 19-11-14	" C Blundell -do-	12-11-14	2/ A.B.Mollo, Artists Rifles	ditto
" C W Duberly	-do-	12-11-14	" Rhys Williams -do-	20-11-14	" R Drake -do-	Temporary transferred officers
Capt Earl Stanhope	-do-	20-11-14	" Lord Brabourne -do-	20-11-14	" T.G Tillmann -do-	for duty
" J A Morrison	-do-	20-11-14	" Lord W. Percy -do-	20-11-14	" 2/Lt Crisp -do-	13-11-14
Hon P. Lyon MOO	-do-	12-11-14				
Lieut E Sykes	-do-	12-11-14				

Officers and Warrant Officers who have *quitted* during the preceding month, showing whether on leave of absence, removal, death, &c.

Rank and Name	Date and cause
Capt & Adjt G E O Rasch	Sick. Admitted to hospital 8/11/14.
Lieut E Ward	Wounded. 15/11/14
" Lord C Hamilton	Sick. Admitted to hospital 16/11/14
" H.W.R. Mackenzie	Wounded (accidentally) 17-11-14.
" C.S. Rowley	Sick. Admitted to hospital.

Officers absent without leave.

Rank and Name	Since what time

Lieut Col.
Commanding.
Commdg 1st Bn Grenadier Guards

To be rendered to Officers i/c Records for transmission to the War Office.　　　Army Form B. 158.

CAVALRY, ARTILLERY and INFANTRY only.

Regiment, etc., or Depôt 2nd Gr Bedfordshire
Station Thurbain
Date 30th November 1914

LIST OF OFFICERS.

* Married or Single	Officers doing duty with the Unit NAME	Date of being taken on the strength of the Unit †	Stations (if on Detachment)
	Lieut.-Colonel—		
	Majors—		
M	**Captains**— W. H. Deane		Commmg Officer from 24/11
M	C. B. Cumberlege		
S	C. C. Foss		Adjt.
	H C Jackson	2.12.14	
	A E Samer	12.12.14	
S	**Lieutenants**— C. E. G. Shearman		
S	S. D. Mills		
S	E. G. Fanning		Sick
	R. S. St C. Mayne 3/E. Surrey	12.12.14	
	W. H. Williams	17.12.14	
	H. Duchesne		
	2nd Lieutenants— Attached Officers Continued		
S	2nd Lieut J. W. F. Wyld 1/Hampshire R.	20-11-14	
S	2nd Lieut R. Dabell Artists Rifles	13-11-14	Temporary 2nd Lieut
S	2nd Lieut C. H. Brewer	13-11-14	" "
S	2nd Lieut H. Williams	13-11-14	" "
S	2nd Lieut H. de Burratti	13-11-14	" "
S	2nd Lieut B. Whitehouse Loyal N. Lancs R	20-11-14	" "
S	2nd Lieut A. C. Talbot Essex R	20.11.14	" "
C	**Adjutant**— Captain C. C. Foss		
M	**Quartermaster**— Captain & Qr Mr H. Crossingham		
	Riding Master—		

WARRANT OFFICERS.

	Master Gunner—		
S	**Serjeant-Major**— J. W. Thurley		Promoted 16.10.14
M	**Bandmaster**—		

OFFICERS ATTACHED.
(Including Special Reserve and Territorial Force Officers. Authority to be quoted.)

	Rank	Name	Corps	Authority	Date of joining	
S	Lieut	W. D. Goudie	R.A.M.C.	War Est		
S	Captain	J. S. Collinge Wells	4th Bedf R	Reinforcement	16-11-14	
M	2nd Lieut	G. William Wilson	5th Middlesex R	"	1-11-14	Sick 23-11-14
S	2nd Lieut	G. H. Waddy	Gloucester R	"	29-10-14	
S	2nd Lieut	W. B. Carstake	R W Surrey R	"	1-11-14	
M	Captain	C. Davenport Hanley	3rd Bedf R	"	2-11-14	Sick 16 12/1

* The letter "M" or "S" is to be placed before the names of Officers.
† For Units of Royal Artillery, Depôts of all Arms and Special Reserve Units.
NOTE.—The word "Sick" to be inserted against the names of all Officers who are on the Sick List, and the words "Assistant Adjutant," "Instructor of Gunnery," &c., against the name of an Officer holding such appointment.

GALE & POLDEN, LTD. PRINTERS, ALDERSHOT.　Forms
(73,692). Wt. 8585—526. 30,000. 8/14. W 26.　B. 158

Officers absent on duty.

(Exclusive of seconded Officers, but including Officers posted and not joined.)

Married or Single.	Rank and Name	On what duty, at what station, from what time
		Nil

Officers and Warrant Officers absent with Leave.

Rank and Name	By whose permission, and date of order	On what account	From what time	To what time
		Nil		

Officers and Warrant Officers who have *joined* during the preceding month, showing whether from leave of absence, on appointment, &c.

Rank and Name	Date and cause

Officers and Warrant Officers who have *quitted* during the preceding month, showing whether on leave of absence, removal, death, &c.

Rank and Name	Date and cause
2nd Lieut. G. William Wilson (5th Middlesex R.)	Invalided 28-11-14. Sickness

Officers absent without leave.

Rank and Name	Since what time
	Nil

W. H. Dennis Captain Commanding.
2nd Bn. Bedfordshire Regiment

To be rendered to Officers i/c Records for transmission to the War Office.   Army Form B. 158.

CAVALRY, ARTILLERY and INFANTRY only.

Regiment, etc., or Depôt 2nd Battalion Yorkshire Regiment
Station In the Field
Date 30 November 1914

LIST OF OFFICERS.

* Married or Single	Officers doing duty with the Unit NAME	Date of being taken on the strength of the Unit †	Stations (if on Detachment)
	Lieut.-Colonel—		
M	**Majors—** E. S. Moon-Blundell (local Lieut.) Commanding		
	C. Lindley 3rd S. Wales Borderers	16-11-14	
	Captains— E. S. Moon-Blundell (local Major)		wounded 1-11-14
	G. E. Green		
	H. E. Milner	16-11-14	Sick 12/13/14
	B. H. Leatham	2.12.14	
S	**Lieutenants—** H. S. Grayson (acting Adjutant)		
S	W. A. Colley		wounded 2-11-14
S	B. W. Marde		Hospl (Sick) 9-11-14
S	G. F. Gladstone		Hospl (Sick) 9-11-14
	C. G. Briggs (3 W Yorks)	12.12.14	
S	D. A. Laird R.A.M.C. Medical Officer	1-11-14	
S	**2nd Lieutenants—** W. A. A. Chaunce Transport officer		
S	H. C. Brocklehurst		wounded 3-11-14
S	A. J. Pickup 28 London Rgt	13-11-14	
S	M. S. B. Cross "	13-11-14	
S	W. L. Hollis "	13-11-14	
S	G. Cutler "	13-11-14	
S	D. Parker 3rd W. Riding Rgt	16-11-14	
S	J. B. Sperling 1st RW Kent Rgt	16-11-14	
S	L. S. Monteagle 3rd E Sussex Rgt	16-11-14	
M	Boseley	2.12.14	
	Adjutant—		
	Quartermaster— Lieutenant C. Pickard		
M	**Riding Master—** W. Wyatt	2.12.14	

WARRANT OFFICERS.

	Master Gunner—		
M	**Serjeant-Major—** H. Wilcox		
	Bandmaster—		

OFFICERS ATTACHED.
(Including Special Reserve and Territorial Force Officers. Authority to be quoted.)

Rank	Name	Corps	Authority	Date of joining

* The letter "M" or "S" in red ink is to be placed before the names of Officers.
† For Units of Royal Artillery, Depôts of all Arms and Special Reserve Units.
NOTE.—The word "Sick" to be inserted against the names of all Officers who are on the Sick List, and the words "Assistant Adjutant," "Instructor of Gunnery," &c., against the name of an Officer holding such appointment.

Officers absent on duty.
(Exclusive of seconded Officers, but including Officers posted and not joined.)

Married or Single.	Rank and Name	On what duty, at what station, from what time

Officers and Warrant Officers absent with Leave.

Rank and Name	By whose permission, and date of order	On what account	From what time	To what time
M Lt. Maj Wilcox	Headquarters 3rd Infantry Bde	Seven days furlo'	30-11-1914	6-12-14

Officers and Warrant Officers who have *joined* during the preceding month, showing whether from leave of absence, on appointment, &c.

Rank and Name	Date and cause
Major E. Lowthe 3 S Wales Borderers Capt H. L. Boulton 3 Lincoln Rgt Lieut D. Paton 3 W. Riding Rgt " J. F. Burbury 1st W. Kent Rgt " J. B. Gladstone 3 R. Sussex Rgt " A. J. Pickup " M.S.F. Brewis 28 London Rgt " H.J. Hollis (Artists Rifles) " G. Cuttle	Joined Battalion on the 16th November 1914 as Reinforcements from Havre. Joined Battalion on the 13th November 1914 as temporary Second Lieutenants on probation

Officers and Warrant Officers who have *quitted* during the preceding month, showing whether on leave of absence, removal, death, &c.

Rank and Name	Date and cause
Major E. Lowthe 3 S Wales Borderers	To Hospital 10-10-14
Capt E. J. Colson 2nd Yorkshire Rgt	wounded 1-11-14
Lieut H. F. Cubby " "	wounded 2-11-14
Lieut J. B. Gladstone " "	To Hospital 9-11-14
Lieut M. W. Meade " "	To Hospital 9-11-14
Lieut J. F. Burbury 1st W. Kent Rgt	To 13 Bde 20-11-14
" H.G. Zwonbrunck 2nd Yorks Rgt	wounded 3-11-14

Officers absent without leave.

Rank and Name	Since what time
—	—

N.S. Ratchitt for Major Commanding.
2nd Battalion Yorkshire Rgt

be rendered to Officers i/c Records for transmission to the War Office.   Army Form B. 158.

CAVALRY, ARTILLERY and INFANTRY only.

Regiment, etc., or Depôt _1 Bn. Royal Scots Fusiliers_

Station _La Gorgue (France)_

Date _30th November 1914_

LIST OF OFFICERS.

* Married or Single	Officers doing duty with the Unit NAME		Date of being taken on the strength of the Unit †	Stations (if on Detachment)
	Lieut.-Colonel—			
	Majors— A. H. Forbes.		15.12.14.	
S	Captains— R. B. Crawford	1 Bn RSF	2.12.14	Sick.
	J. B. Traill	B SR	19.11.14	
M	J. Parker		22.11.14	
	Lieutenants—			
S	N. C. Thomas	R.S.Fus		
S	J. B. Peace	a. S. Fus	1-11-14	
	J. E. Utterson Kelso.		12.12.14	
	2nd Lieutenants—			
	2/Lt. W. A. Wilson	6/R.B.	15.12.14	
	C. W. Brown	3/R.S.F	12.12.14	
	R. S. Crawford		12.12.14	
S	H. E. Glittrick	3 S.Fus		
S	W. J. Kennedy	2 S.Fus	4.11.14	
S	W. M. Beckenham	2 S.F.	25-11-14	
S	M. W. Parr	S.F.	25/11/14	
S	N. C. S. Teasdale	4 KRR Corps	25/11/14	
S	R. M. Graham	Essex Regt	25/11/14	
S	G. B. Sibary		10.12.14	
S	Adjutant— Lieut. N.C. Thomson	R. Scots Fus		
M	Quartermaster— Lieut & Qmr A Spence	R. S. Fus		
	Riding Master—			

WARRANT OFFICERS.

	Master Gunner—			
M	Serjeant-Major— W. S. Wilson			
M	Bandmaster— N. Robertson Away at Depot Ayr.			

OFFICERS ATTACHED.
(Including Special Reserve and Territorial Force Officers. Authority to be quoted.)

	Rank	Name	Corps	Authority	Date of joining	
S	Lieut	Ingram W. H.	R.A.M.C.	S. of C.	28.11.14	Duty of med of
S	Lieut	White J. A.	Artists Rifles		Sick	
S	—	Stuart J.	—	21 Inf Bde	13.11.14	Temporary Leave (amputation)
S	—	Raynor Parker S.C.	—			
S	—	White L.	—			

* The letter "M" or "S" is to be placed before the names of Officers.
† For Units of Royal Artillery, Depôts of all Arms and Special Reserve Units.
NOTE.—The word "Sick" to be inserted against the names of all Officers who are on the Sick List, and the words "Assistant Adjutant," "Instructor of Gunnery," &c., against the name of an Officer holding such appointment.

Officers absent on duty.

(Exclusive of seconded Officers, but including Officers posted and not joined.)

Married or Single.	Rank and Name	On what duty, at what station, from what time
		Nil

Officers and Warrant Officers absent with Leave.

	Rank and Name	By whose permission, and date of order	On what account	From what time	To what time
S	Lieut.		Private affairs	1-11-14	5-11-14
S	Lieut.		Private affairs	21-11-14	
M				30-	5-12-14

Officers and Warrant Officers who have *joined* during the preceding month, showing whether from leave of absence, on appointment, &c.

	Rank and Name	Date and cause
M	4312 Sgt. Major E.J. Titmas	16-10-14 On Promotion, posted 1 R. Sqn.

See on reverse as stated against each officer

Officers and Warrant Officers who have *quitted* during the preceding month, showing whether on leave of absence, removal, death, &c.

	Rank and Name	Date and cause
M	Sergeant Major H.J. Page	16-10-14 On Promotion to Lieutenant 1 R. Sqn.

Officers absent without leave.

Rank and Name	Since what time
	Nil

for T. Jackson Captain Commanding.

Nominal Roll
of
OFFICERS

HQ 20th Bde.

Brigadier General F.J. Heyworth Cmdg 20th Bde.
Lt Col A.B. Cator Brigade Major
                   Scots Guards
Lieut A.H. Palmer Yorkshire Regt
                   Cmdg No 2 Section
                   7th Sig Coy R.E.
~~Capt H. Taylor 2/Scots Guards~~
                   ~~B.M.G. Officer~~

Major Viscount ~~Lord~~ Bury
                   Scots Guards

Lieut J. Fox A.V.C.

Rue du Quesnes   A.H. Palmer Lieut
30/11/14   for B.M. 20th Bde

2nd Bn. The Gordon Highlanders

Roll of Officers.

Captain W. B. J. Mitford. 2.12.14

Lieut. J. M. Hamilton (Commanding Officer).

Lieut. H. M. Sprot

2nd Lieut. W. J. Graham (Acting Adjutant)

2nd Lieut. J. A. Letters.

Hon. Capt. J. Mackie. (Quartermaster)

Captain W. B. J. Reid. 3/Seaforth 2/12/14

"Attached" B. G. R. Gordon. 3/12/14

2nd Lieut. W. A. Tabb. Royal Highlanders

2nd Lieut. E. R. Mulloch ⎫
2nd Lieut. A. D. Chater ⎬ On probation
2nd Lieut. S. Horsley ⎬ from
2nd Lieut. O. Horsley ⎭ Artists Rifles.

2nd Lt. T. P. Finlay 7/12/14   A + S H[rs]

Lieut. J. G. Priestley. R. A. M. C.

In the Field⎫   M Hamilton. Lieut.
30/11/14 ⎭ Comdg. 2nd Bn. The Gordon Highlanders

2nd Lt. T. C. Christie. A + S. H[rs] 8/12/14
Capt W. Alexander. ⎫
2nd Lt. R. E. Gillespie ⎬ 3/Gordons. 13/12/14
"   D. M. Bain. ⎭
Captain J. R. E. Stansfeld. 15/12/14
" Lt. A. D. P. Campbell (I.A) 17/12/14
"   L. N. G. Ramsay. 3/GH

M	¨	¨ Col A.F. Band Smith	Missing 31/10	2 RSF
M		Major O.C.S. MacGregor	Wounded 31/10	"
M		¨ J.A.F. Forbes	Wounded 28/10	2 RSF
M		Captain C.M. Burgoyne	Missing 30/10	"
S		¨ J.C. Whigham	Wounded 30/10	"
M		¨ A.G. A. Lattai	Missing 31/10	"
M		¨ C.L. Rowe	Wounded (date not known)	
M		¨ J. Hardie	Killed in action 22/10	
M		¨ R.C. Adair	Wounded 22/10	"
M		¨ G.E. Rylwood	Missing 30/10	"
S	Lieut	H.W.V. Stewart	Missing 31/10	"
S		Q & Adj R.V.C. Kerr	Wounded 20/10	"
S		¨ N. Kennedy	Wounded 24/10	"
S		¨ A. Ross Thomson	Missing 30/10	"
S		¨ C.G.G. Mackenzie	Killed in action 2/11	"
S		¨ L.R.F. Kennedy	Wounded 30/10	"
S		¨ A.C. Fox	Wounded 22/10	"
S		¨ ¨ ¨ ¨ ¨	¨ ¨ 3/11	"
S	Lieut	J.E. Atkinson Kerr	Wounded 22/10	"
S		¨ C. McB. Alston	Missing 24/10	"
S		¨ J.L. Bower	Missing 2/11	"
S		¨ A.S.M. MacGregor Mills	Wounded 30/10	"
S		¨ M.B. Buchanan	Wounded 3/11	"
S		¨ E.P.O. Boyle	Missing 3/11	"
S		¨ J.A. Chapple	3 RSF	
S		¨ R. Blathwyte	3 RSF	
M	Serg Major W.J. Pugh	Commissioned 16/10	2 RSF	To 1 RSF
M	Bandmaster W. Roberton	Posted to Depot	"	
S	Lieut G.B. Bayley	KOSB Killed in Action 25/10		

(2U/64)

A.F.W.B158

2Bn. Wiltshire Regt.

Nominal Roll of Officers.

Rank	Name	Remarks
Capt.	Beaver. P.S.L.	Officer Commanding.
Major	Wilson. H.C.B.	Attached from K.O.Y.L.I.
2/Lieut.	Legg. P.P.	
-do-	Hunter. H.M.	
-do-	Ransom. H.B.	Acting Adjutant.
-do-	~~Jeans. D.M.~~	Sick in Hospital.
-do-	Sargeaunt. W.S.	
-do-	Brooks. D.	
-do-	Francis. E.L.	
-do-	Waylen. B.C.	
-do-	Strawson. W.J.	
-do-	Shepherd. J.S.	} Attached on probation from
-do-	Kitcat. A.J.	} Artists Rifles
-do-	Carden. R.A.	}
Lt.&Q.M.	Hewit. S.	Quartermaster
Lieut.	Beaumont. B.B.	R.A.M.C. Medical Officer.
Capt	B Cave-Brown-Cave	8 12/14
"Lt"	D.M. Jeans.	

Killed Capt. E.L. Makin. 12 12/14

30th Novr. 1914

P.L. Beaver. Capt
Comdg. 2Bn. Wilts. Regt.

To be rendered to Officers i/c Records for transmission to the War Office.   Army Form B. 158.

CAVALRY, ARTILLERY and INFANTRY only.

Regiment, etc., or Depot _Headquarters 22nd Infantry Brigade_
Station _Fleurbaix France_
Date _20th November 1914_

LIST OF OFFICERS.

Married or Single	Officers doing duty with the Unit — NAME	Date of being taken on the strength of the Unit	Stations (if on Detachment)
	Lieut.-Colonel		
M	~~Lieut.-Colonel~~ Brig-General J.T.B. Lawford, Commanding 22nd Infty Brigade	8.9.14	
	Majors—		
	Captains—		
M	E.C.L. Thurlow, Somerset Light Infantry, Brigade Major	20.11.14	
S	A.J. Fellowes, Rifle Brigade, Staff Captain	13.11.14	
	Lieutenants—		
S	J.M. Dawson, A.V. Corps, Veterinary Officer	17.9.14	
	R.N. O'Connor	13.12.14	
	2nd Lieutenants		
S	J.J. Liggett, Corps of Interpreters, Interpreter	12.11.14	
S	C.H.B. Blount, 2nd Bn. The Queens (R.W.S.R.)	5.11.14	

Adjutant—
Quartermaster—
Riding Master—

WARRANT OFFICERS.

Master Gunner—
Serjeant-Major—
Bandmaster—

OFFICERS ATTACHED.
(Including Special Reserve and Territorial Force Officers. Authority to be quoted.)

Rank	Name	Corps	Authority	Date of joining

* The letter "M" or "S" is to be placed before the names of Officers.
† For Units of Royal Artillery, Depots of all Arms and Special Reserve Units.
NOTE.—The word "Sick" to be inserted against the names of all Officers who are on the Sick List, and the words "Assistant Adjutant," "Instructor of Gunnery," &c., against the name of an Officer holding such appointment.

Officers absent on duty.
(Exclusive of seconded Officers, but including Officers posted and not joined.)

Married or Single	Rank and Name	On what duty, at what station, from what time

Officers and Warrant Officers absent with Leave.

Rank and Name	By whose permission, and date of order	On what account	From what time	To what time

Officers and Warrant Officers who have *joined* during the preceding month, showing whether from leave of absence, on appointment, &c.

	Rank and Name	Date and cause
M.	Captain E.C.L. Hartles S.R.I. Bde Major	2.11.14 On appointment
S.	Captain R.T. Fellowes R.B. Staff Captain	13.11.14 On appointment
S.	Lieut J.I. Biggott Interpreter	12.11.14 On appointment
S.	Lieut C.H.B. Blount 2nd Queens	5.11.14 On Acting Appointment

Officers and Warrant Officers who have *quitted* during the preceding month, showing whether on leave of absence, removal, death, &c.

	Rank and Name	Date and cause
M	Captain G.D. James The Buffs Brigade Major	Killed in action 12.11.14
M	Lieut R.N. O'Connor Scottish Rifles Brigade Signalling Officer	To hospital (Sprained ankle) 2/11/14
S	Lieut R.C. Thomas 2nd Queens (R.W.S.) Lieut P.R.B. Zuggs 2nd Queens (R.W.S.)	Wounded 5/11/14 (Temporarily attached on Body Captain)

Officers absent without leave.

Rank and Name	Since what time

R.T. Fellowes Captain
Commanding.

be rendered to Officers i/c Records for transmission to the War Office.　　　Army Form B. 158.

CAVALRY, ARTILLERY and INFANTRY only.

Regiment, etc., or Depôt __2nd Battn The Buffs Regt__

Station __RUE DE BIACHE__

Date __1st December, 1914__

LIST OF OFFICERS.

* Married or Single	Officers doing duty with the Unit NAME		Date of being taken on the strength of the Unit †	Stations (if on Detachment)
	Lieut.-Colonel—			
	Majors—			
M	Captains—	Montague Bates F E	11-11-14	
M		Hewitt A S	12-11-14	
		Kirkpatrick H.F. Buffs	2-12-14	
		Slacke P.C. "	"	
S	Lieutenants—	~~For Pat~~ Gruffer B V J	25-11-14	
		11 Lt P.G. Hendry	17.12.14	
		~~Lt F.F. Burkett~~	"	
		11 Lt R.S. O'Bryon	12.12.14	
		~~Lt F A Walmesley~~ B/Queen	12.12.14	
S	2nd Lieutenants—	~~Butterworth~~ H	25-11-14
S		West P C	9-10-14	
S		Burrows J D	11-11-14	
S		Allan A M	12-11-14	
S		~~Ramsay~~ D P	12-11-14	
S		Austin C F	13-11-14	
S		Mascom H	13-11-14	
S		~~Rought~~ C G	13-11-14	
S		Humphreys D F	13-11-14	
		Cooke J B	2-12-14	
S	Adjutant—	Lieutenant Ross R H		
M	Quartermaster—	Captain West C H J		
S	~~Riding Master~~ ~~Medical Officer~~	Lieutenant Buchanan J S		

WARRANT OFFICERS.

	Master Gunner—		
M	Serjeant-Major—	Q. M. Sgt Routley H	
	Bandmaster—		

OFFICERS ATTACHED.
(Including Special Reserve and Territorial Force Officers. Authority to be quoted.)

	Rank	Name		Corps	Authority	Date of joining
M	Captain	Montague Bates	F E	East Surrey Regt		11-11-14
M	"	Hewitt	A S	R West Kent Regt		12-11-14
S	Lieut	Gruffer	B V J	E Surrey Regt	Sick 16?/12	25-11-14
S	2/Lieut	West	P C	E Kent Regt		9-10-14
S		~~—~~				
S		Ramsay	D P	R Sussex Regt		12-11-14

* The letter "M" or "S" is to be placed before the names of Officers.
† For Units of Royal Artillery, Depôts of all Arms and Special Reserve Units.
NOTE.—The word "Sick" to be inserted against the names of all Officers who are on the Sick List, and the words "Assistant Adjutant," "Instructor of Gunnery," &c., against the name of an Officer holding such appointment.

Officers absent on duty.

(Exclusive of seconded Officers, but including Officers posted and not joined.)

Married or Single.	Rank and Name	On what duty, at what station, from what time

Officers and Warrant Officers absent with Leave.

Rank and Name	By whose permission, and date of order	On what account	From what time	To what time

Officers and Warrant Officers who have *joined* during the preceding month, showing whether from leave of absence, on appointment, &c.

	Rank and Name		Date and cause
M	Major	Monteagle Browne	E	11-11-14	From Royal North Lancs Regt.
M	Captain	Montague Bates	F S	11-11-14	From East Surrey Regt
M	"	Hewett	O S	12-11-14	From Royal West Kent Regt
S	Lieut	Griffies	B V I	25-11-14	From East Surrey Regt
S	2/Lieut	Butterworth	H	25-11-14	From Base
S	"	Oliver	O M	12-11-14	From Base
S	"	Ramsay	D P	12-11-14	From Royal Sussex Regt
S	"	Nott	P C	9-10-14	On appointment (London Gazette 9-10-14)
S	"	Burrows	J D	16-11-14	From Royal West Kent Regt
S	"	Austin	C F		
S	"	Musson	H	13-11-14	On appointment (from 28th Bn County of London Regt)
S	"	Ronget	C G		
S	"	Humphreys	D F S		

Officers and Warrant Officers who have *quitted* during the preceding month, showing whether on leave of absence, removal, death, &c.

	Rank and Name		Date and cause
M	Major	Monteagle Browne	E	13-11-14	To Royal Warwickshire Regt
S	Captain	Allegra	W H	7-11-14	Wounded & missing
M	"	Roberts	A H S	7-11-14	Wounded
S?	Lieut	White	G A	3-11-14	Wounded
S	"	Thomas	O C	6-11-14	Wounded
S	"	Furze	E K B	6-11-14	Wounded
S	"	Longbourne	J A	7-11-14	Wounded
S H	Adjt	Haigh	C R	7-11-14	Killed
S	2/Lieut	Collis	J G	7-11-14	Wounded
S	"	Blount	C H B	6-11-14	(To 22nd Inf Bde Staff)
M	2/"	Smith	W	4-11-14	Wounded
M	"	Pascoe	C	7-11-14	Wounded
S	"	Burrows	J D	22-11-14	Wounded
M	Sgt Major	Lucas	C	7-11-14	Killed

Officers absent without leave.

Rank and Name		Since what time

H Montague Bates Captain Commanding.
2nd Bn The Queen's Regt.

be rendered to Officers i/c Records for transmission to the War Office.   Army Form B. 158.

CAVALRY, ARTILLERY and INFANTRY only.

Regiment, etc., or Depôt __2/R War R__
Station __In the Field__
Date __30-11-14__

LIST OF OFFICERS.

* Married or Single	Officers doing duty with the Unit NAME	Date of being taken on the strength of the Unit †	Stations (if on Detachment)
	Lieut.-Colonel—		
	Majors— R. H. K. Brewis	11-11-14	
	Captains— J. P. Hadden	2.12.14	
	R. L. Bromfield		
	C. F. Hodgson		
	I. H. G. White		
	F. C. Mulgrew	2.12.14	
	Lieutenants— H. J. Walmsley Dresser	5.12.14	
	2nd Lieutenants— R. F. Richardson		
	H. Stevens	17-10-14	Such 28 13/12
	B. Bernard		
	B. Campbell	2.12.14	
	J. Pennington		
	C. F. H. Chavasse		
	2/Lt. W. G. O. Booker	12.12.14	Such 27 13/12
	N. H. A. R. Tusker		
	Adjutant—		
	Quartermaster— Lieut. & Qr. Mr. M. Hyde		
	Riding Master—		

WARRANT OFFICERS.

Master Gunner—
Serjeant-Major—
Bandmaster—

OFFICERS ATTACHED.
(Including Special Reserve and Territorial Force Officers. Authority to be quoted.)

Rank	Name	Corps	Authority	Date of joining
2/Lieut	Jerbage R.F.W.	28th County of London (Artists) Rifles.	S. 10/12/14	1/2
"	Pearcy J.B.			1/1
"	Stirling A.A.			14

* The letter "M" or "S" is to be placed before the names of Officers.
† For Units of Royal Artillery, Depôts of all Arms and Special Reserve Units.
NOTE.—The word "Sick" to be inserted against the names of all Officers who are on the Sick List, and the words "Assistant Adjutant," "Instructor of Gunnery," &c., against the name of an Officer holding such appointment.

Officers absent on duty.

(Exclusive of seconded Officers, but including Officers posted and not joined.)

Married or Single.	Rank and Name	On what duty, at what station, from what time

Officers and Warrant Officers absent with Leave.

Rank and Name	By whose permission, and date of order	On what account	From what time	To what time
2Lieut H Stevens	2nd J B orders of 28-11-14.	Private affairs.	29-11-14.	6-12-14.

Officers and Warrant Officers who have *joined* during the preceding month, showing whether from leave of absence, on appointment, &c.

Rank and Name	Date and cause
2Lieut B Bernard	On Appointment.

Officers and Warrant Officers who have *quitted* during the preceding month, showing whether on leave of absence, removal, death, &c.

Rank and Name	Date and cause

Officers absent without leave.

Rank and Name	Since what time
Nil	

R.W. Brown Major
2nd R War R
Commanding.

To be rendered to Officers i/c Records for transmission to the War Office.   Army Form B. 158.

CAVALRY, ARTILLERY and INFANTRY only.

Regiment, etc., or Depot 8th Bn. The Royal Scots

Station Bac-St-Maur

Date 30th November 1914

LIST OF OFFICERS.

Married or Single	Officers doing duty with the Unit		Date of being taken on the strength of the Unit	Stations (if on Detachment)
S	Lieut.-Colonel—	Brook A.		
S	Majors—	Gemmill E.		
M		Tait J.		
M		~~Todrick~~		Killed 14/11/14
M		McEwen B.		
M	Captains—	McRae W.A.R.M.	5-9-14	
M		Rowbottom	2-11-14	
S		Mitchell J.B.		
S		Watson J.W.		
S		Richardson J.		
M	Lieutenants—	~~Bent~~ A.		
S		Kerr R.B.		
S		Plew J.J.		
M		Turner J.T.		
		Greenshield J.B.	2-11-14	
S		Inch W.H.	12-12-14	
M	2nd Lieutenants	Stewart D.M.		
		Young		
S		Dingle J.S.		
M		Kemp J.C.		
S		Thorburn R.M.		
M		Nicol J.L.		
		Elder J.H.		
		Wallace W.E.		
S		Martin J.	2-11-14	
M	Adjutant—	Blair / Grant Suttie G.J.	Sick 16/11	
	Quartermaster—	Clark J.	26-12-14	
	Riding Master—			

WARRANT OFFICERS.

Master Gunner—
Serjeant-Major—
Bandmaster—

OFFICERS ATTACHED.
(Including Special Reserve and Territorial Force Officers. Authority to be quoted.)

	Rank	Name	Corps	Authority	Date of joining
Widower	Major	Crombie J.C.	R.A.M.C.(T)	War Establishment	5-8-14

* The letter "M" or "S" is to be placed before the names of Officers.
† For Units of Royal Artillery, Depots of all Arms and Special Reserve Units.
NOTE.—The word "Sick" to be inserted against the names of all Officers who are on the Sick List, and the words "Assistant Adjutant," "Instructor of Gunnery," &c., against the name of an Officer holding such appointment.

Officers absent on duty.
(Exclusive of seconded Officers, but including Officers posted and not joined.)

Married or Single	Rank and Name	On what duty, at what station, from what time

Nil

Officers and Warrant Officers absent with Leave.

Rank and Name	By whose permission, and date of order	On what account	From what time	To what time

Nil

Officers and Warrant Officers who have *joined* during the preceding month, showing whether from leave of absence, on appointment, &c.

Rank and Name	Date and cause

Nil

Officers and Warrant Officers who have *quitted* during the preceding month, showing whether on leave of absence, removal, death, &c.

Rank and Name		Date and cause
Captain	Todd J.A.	To Hospital. Wounded. 20:11:14
"	Ballantyne G.H.	To Hospital. Sick. 26:11:14
2nd Lieut	Maxwell R.	To Hospital. Sick. 28:11:14

Officers absent without leave.

Rank and Name	Since what time

Nil

E. Wallace 2nd Lieut & Lt.Col. Commanding.
8th Bn. The Royal Scots.

1st Bn. R.W. Fus.rs

Return of Officers of above Bn.

Rank	Name	Remarks
Major	Gabbett R.B.	
Capt.	Holroyd C.P.	2.12.14
"	Minshull-Ford J.	
"	Wood G.C.	
	Blackall C.W.	2.12.14
Lieut	Sore S.G.	
"	Walmsley A.	
"	Cottrill J.	
"	Johns S.B.	S.W.B.
Capt & Q.M.	Parker E.A.	ordered to 1st Corps 18/12/14
Lieut	Rees J.J.	
"	Parkes A.F.	Artists
"	Winters J.W.	Kiffles
"	Jones L.	
"	Jerman R.N.	from 11 E.
"	Aulin P.H.	2/ Devons
"	Ledger R.K.	6/ Rifle Bde.
"	Heyland W.F.	6/ R.R.R.
Lieut	Fry W.K.	Ramc
" Lt	Lane H.	Rif. Bde. 2.11.14
" Lt	J.C. Poole	A Sussex 17/12/14
" "	R.C.L. Blosse	
30/11/14	A.K. Richardson	

Seventh Division

1st R.W. Fus.rs has been supplied with A.F.B. 158 to complete and return tonight. These will be forwarded when received.

E. Wood Col.
O.C. Major
Comdg 1/ R.W. Fus

Nominal roll of Officers R.A.M. Corps serving in the Field Ambulances of the 7th Division

Unit	Rank and Name of Officer		Date of joining unit
21st Field Ambulance	Major	Hayes E.G.	14th Sept 1914
	"	Kelly W.D.G.	21st " "
	Lieut	Button P.N.	15 " "
	"	Marr D.M.	15 " "
	"	Jardine E.D.	15 " "
	"	Argo G.E.	10th Nov 1914
	"	O'Reilly C.J.	—
	"	Stafford S.B.	12th Nov 1914
	"	Quinlan W.J.	4th " "
	Lieut & QMr	Wickersham J.	19th Sept 1914
	Maj.	B.H.E. Dunbar	26.12.14
22nd Field Ambulance	Major	Archer L.A.	15 Sept 1914
	Captn	Wells A.G.	—
	Lieut	Nelson J.B.	—
	"	Higgins J.	—
	"	Charles F.P.	—
	"	Greenlees J.R.C.	16th Sept 1914
	"	Maltby H.W.	2nd Nov 1914
	"	McCusker J.	16 " "
	"	Pope H.M.	26 " "
	Lieut & QMr	Senior E.SG	20 Sept 1914
23rd Field Ambulance	Major	Crawford W.J.	14th Sept 1914
	"	Brown G.H.J.	15 " "
	Captn	Wright W.G.	4th " "
	Lieut	Buckley G.D.M.	11 Nov 1914
	"	Hart E.SG	14th Sept 1914
	"	Linnell J.W.	7th Nov 1914

Unit	Rank and Name of Officer		Date of joining unit
23rd Field Ambce (contd)	Lieut	Mackie D	15 Sept 1914
	"	Moynan R.N.O	14 Nov 1914
	"	Wedd B H	11 Sept 1914
	Lieut M	Jackson J	21 Sept 1914

Major
D.A.D.M.S. 7th Division

7th Divisional Train

Nominal Roll of Officers of the above formation

11 December 1914

Rank & Name		Date of Joining Division	Remarks
Major	H. G. Burrard	4-9-14	
Capt	A. W. Alexander	4-9-14	
"	N. Wintle	15-9-14	
"	E. T. Wright	22-9-14	
"	T. A. Prendergast	24-9-14	
"	R. S. Harger	22-9-14	
Lieut	G. W. Lunn	25-9-14	
2/Lieut	G. W. Grassett	11-11-14	
"	A. J. C. E. Phillippo	11-11-14	
"	D. Chandler	11-11-14	
"	W. H. Lewis	11-11-14	
"	B. C. Frederick	28-10-14	
Tempy 2/Lt	A. A. Morphy	23-9-14	
"	E. C. Sherman	23-9-14	
"	W. H. Waller	24-9-14	
"	C. N. Lowe	23-9-14	
"	W. N. Brown	23-9-14	
"	H. S. Collins	23-9-14	
"	L. H. Featherstonhaugh	23-9-14	
"	A. G. Birch	23-9-14	
"	T. Whittington	23-9-14	
"	A. R. Whittington	23-9-14	
Tempy Lt	A. L. Christie R.A.M.C.	11-11-14	Attached
---	G. T. F. Budge A.V.C.	18-9-14	
Tpy 2/Lt	H. Appleyard (Interpreter)	26-9-14	

The A.A. & Q.M.G.
7th Divn

H. G. Burrard Major
A.S.C.
Commdg 7 Divl Train

3. Infantry Brigade.
_____

        The General Officer Commanding wishes to know what routine system is adopted by you in your Section of the defence, or what you propose to adopt.

        He considers that now that we have been, and possibly may still be, some time in the trenches, a regular and precise routine, such as on a Man-of-War, would be advantageous and tend to efficiency in the defence. Regular hours for standing to arms, breakfast, digging, dinners, etc., should be adopted and the exact order and punctuality be maintained.

        (Sgd) A.R.Hoskins
        Colonel,

1-12-14.   General Staff, 7th Division.

22nd Infantry Brigade.

The General Officer Commanding wishes to know what routine system is adopted by you in your Section of the defence, or what you propose to adopt.

He considers that now that we have been, and possibly may still be, some time in the trenches, a regular and precise routine, such as on a Man-of-War, would be advantageous and tend to efficiency in the defence. Regular hours for standing to arms, breakfast, digging, dinners, etc., should be adopted and exact order and punctuality be maintained.

Colonel,
1-12-14.   General Staff, 7th Division.

Headquarters
7th Division.

I beg to report that the following is the routine system that is being adopted in my Section of the defence at present.

1. Stand to arms for one hour before dawn.
2. General clean up of rifles etc.   7. — 8. am.
3. Breakfasts.   8. — 8.30 am
4. Working parties.   9. — 12 noon.
5. Dinners.   12.30 — 1.30 pm
6. Working parties   1.30 — 4 pm
7. Night sentries mount.   4 p.m.
8. Teas.   5 p.m.

During darkness working parties of garrison will improve and work on fire trenches and no one will leave the fire trenches except water & ration parties.

P.T.O.

Work on support and Communication
trenches by night will be carried out
by working parties from the Local Reserve.

Stanfield
Brigadier General
Commdg. 22nd Inf Bde.

Dec. 2nd 1914.

7th Division

With reference to your Q45.3 dated 1/12/14 I propose to adopt the following routine system in my Section of the defence.

Stand to Arms	6.0 am
Inspection of Rifles	7.30 am
Day relief	7.45 am
Breakfast	8.0 am
Working	9.0 am to 12.0 noon
Dinners	12.30 pm
Working	1.30 pm to 3.30 pm
Rifle Inspection	3.45 pm
Teas	4.0 pm
Night relief	4.30 pm
Rations	5.30 pm
Night work	according to circumstances and light.

Hendaix
7.10 pm.

Watt? Brig Genl.
Comdg 21st Inf Bde

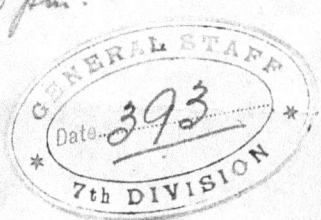

Daily Routine in Trenches for a Company
2nd Battn Border Regiment

Stand to arms from 5-30am to 6-30am and from 4pm to 5pm.

Breakfasts and cleaning rifles between 6-30am and 8-30am

Rifle Inspection 8-30am.

Two digging parties of 20 strong work in shifts of 2 hours from 9am to 4pm. Dinners between 12 noon and 2pm.

Two men per section go for water and 2 for rations at 5.pm.

From 5pm to 5-30am 2 men per section dig and 4 men are on "sentry go" and six men resting. All these work in two-hour shifts

Sailly sur la Lys
9/12/1914

Henry A. Askew. Captain
Commanding 2nd Border Regt

20th D⁻

The J.O.C. is quite satisfied so long as there is a sound and definite system in the Brigade with which we are satisfied.

The Border Regt. may have such a system but it is not clear from their paper attached to your message.

Can you please elucidate this?

6.12.14
A J Hoskins Colonel
[signature] G.S. Capt

4th Division

Attached is an amended Trench Routine of 2nd Border Regiment.

[signature] Capt
Staff Captain
8/12/1914
20th Inf. Bde. 4th Division

"A" Form.   Army Form C. 2121.

MESSAGES AND SIGNALS.

Prefix___ Code___ m. Office of Origin and Service Instructions.	Words.	Charge.	This message is on a/c of: ___Service.	Recd. at___ m. Date ZT 3-12-14 From___ By___
	Sent At 9a m. To YG By OrCy		(Signature of "Franking Officer.")	

TO — 7th Div

Sender's Number	Day of Month	In reply to Number	AAA
BM34	2d		

Herewith attached a detail of routine carried out by the units in my brigade as requested in your O 45 B of the 1st inst.

[Stamp: GENERAL STAFF 7th DIVISION 397]

From   20TH BDE
Place
Time   8am

The above may be forwarded as now corrected.   (Z)

Censor.   Signature of Addressor or person authorised to telegraph in his name
* This line should be erased if not required.

Daily Routine in the Trenches
1st Battn. Gren. Gds.

1. Standing to Arms

The battn stands to arms every morning from 5.30 AM to 6.30 AM, and also for an hour at dusk.

2. 6.30 AM to 8 AM — Breakfast (according to companies)

7.15 AM — Memorandum, inspections of rifles, feet etc.

3. Digging — 2 men per section digging all day in three hour shifts.

Night digging two shifts of 20 men from 9 pm onwards, in shifts of 3 hours each.

4. Dinners — By sections or platoons at any time convenient. There are also many intermediate meals.

5. Sentries — Sentries by day, one double sentry per section for one or two hours at a time. Some coys. prefer the two hours sentries by night, one double sentry to each six men. Night sentries mount at 6 pm and day sentries when company is dismissed from standing to arms.

6. Fatigues — Fatigues for collecting water, timber, bricks & vegetables are found by two men per section at night so as not to weaken the line too much in one place.

Report.   20th Inf Bde.

Routine in the Trenches.

With Reference to your B.M. 84 of 2nd inst.
the following routine is carried on in the trenches.

Stand to Arms.   Half an hour before daylight till
half an hour after.
This was 6 am till 7 am when we
were last in the trenches.

Breakfast.   7.45 - 9 am.
The men will have this in relays.

Dinners   12.30 - 2 pm.
The men have this by relays.

Digging.   By 2 hour reliefs - at night.
This is not possible by day owing to
the proximity of the enemy.
By day the men are employed
revetting and improving the Fire trench.

Fatigues.   All men undergoing Field Imprisonments
work at the saps by reliefs night and
day continuously.

continued

an N.C.O. is told off to keep a roster and personally supervise this work in each sap.

Sentries   By Day
            1 Sentry to each section by
            hourly reliefs.

            By Night.
            2 Sentries to each section of the
            trenches about 15 to 20 yards.
            Posted in Pairs.
            Hourly Reliefs.
            An N.C.O. in each platoon is
            constantly on watch patrolling to
            see that the sentries are on the alert.

Herewith attached is copy of Battalion orders.
Nov 27th 1914. re sentries.

G. H. Loder Capt.
Cmdg
2nd Battn Scots Gds

Battalion Orders.   Copy.

Nov. 27th 1914.

(1) Sentries by night.

The order as to double Sentries was not always attended to

The Company officers must select in the trenches the most suitable places to post their Sentries:-

These should not be more than 15 to 20 yards apart.

Whilst on this duty the Sentry must stand so as to observe the ground line of the barbed wire entanglement:

Care should be taken to avoid those portions of the parapet on which the fixed German rifles are trained:-

An N.C.O. will be detailed to patrol allotted sections of the Company Fire trench all night. (1 N.C.O per Platoon in 2 hour reliefs).

His duties will consist in:

(1) Seeing that these orders are adhered to
(2) No waterproof sheets are put up in the Fire trench.
(3) The Passage to be kept clear of all obstacles.
(4) On the Alarm being given to warn the men in the dug outs to occupy their fire position.

1 Officer or Platoon Sergt. (If a Sergt is in command of a Platoon) will patrol and visit all the Sentries in his Company once in every 2 hours during the night between 6 pm and 6 am.

G.H. Coder Capt.
Cmdg. 2nd Battn Scots Gds

Daily Routine in the Trenches

2nd Battn Gordon Highlanders

Morning

	5.30 AM to 6.30 AM	Stand to arms and latrines cleaned out.
	6.30 AM to 7.30 AM	Working Parties.
	7.30 AM to 9 AM	Breakfast, clean up, and rifle inspection
	9 AM to 12.30 pm	Working Parties

Afternoon

	12.30 pm to 1.30 pm	Dinner
	1.30 pm to 4.30 pm	Working Parties and Tea
	4.30 pm to 7 pm	Water and Ration parties, latrines cleaned out, remainder in fire trench.
	7 pm to 5.30 AM	2 men out of 6 on look-out.

Continuous digging is carried on day and night at the support trench, except between 4.30 pm and 7 pm, and 5.30 AM to 6.30 AM when men cannot be spared from the fire trench. By day one section per platoon is on duty in the fire trench.

7th Division
Routine Orders
1914.

7th Division Routine Orders No. 1.

Southampton
3rd September 1914

Camps

1. **Composition of 7th Division and allotment to Camps.**

Subject to such alterations as may be found necessary, the Division will be encamped at Lyndhurst (L) and Baddesley Common (B), as shown below:—

Headquarters	L
Divisional Signal Co.	L
20th Infantry Brigade H.Q.	L
2nd Bn York R.	L
2nd " Bord R.	L
2nd " Wilts R.	L
2nd " Gord Highrs	L
21st Infantry Brigade H.Q.	L
2nd Bn R War R.	L
2nd " W Yorks R.	L
1st " R W Fus.	L
2nd " Devon R.	L
22nd Infantry Brigade H.Q.	L
2nd Bn The Queens (R W Surr R)	L
2nd Bn Beds R.	L
1st " S Staffs R.	L
2nd " Northn R.	L
Northumberland Yeomanry	L
H.Q. Div. Art.	L
XIV Bde R.H.A.	B
XXII Bde R.F.A.	L
XXXV Bde R.F.A.	B
109th (Hvy) Batty R.G.A. & Am: Col.	L
7th Div Am Col	B

H.Q. Div Eng:	L
54th Fd. Co. RE	L
55th Fd Co RE	L
Div. Train	L + B
21st Fd Amb	L
22nd " "	L
23rd " "	B

An Ordnance Depot will be established at Lyndhurst Road Station, and a Supply Depot at Lyndhurst and Baddesley Common Camps.

The 54th Field Company moved to Lyndhurst Camp yesterday. The Hd Qrs 20 Inf Bde, the 2nd Bn York R. and the 2nd Bn Border R will move on the 4th Septr; the 2nd Bn Wilts R. and the 7th Div Signal Co on the 5th Septr.

The remaining units of the Division will proceed direct to the camps shown against their names on arrival.

Div Hd Qrs will remain for the present at the Polygon Hotel, Southampton.

R. F. A. Hobbs
Captain
D.A.A. & Q.M.G.
7th Division

g.so. 1.

7th Division Routine Orders No 2.
Southampton
5th September 1914.

1. Personnel for Water Duties &c
   As there is no RAMC personnel available to provide the men detailed in W.E. for attachment to units, NCOs & men from each unit will be specially selected and trained in water duties and sanitation. The number of NCOs & men so trained will be in accordance with the numbers laid down in W.E. of the 7th Division for RAMC (attached to units). The vacancies in the unit caused by the selection of these NCOs & men should be made good.

2. Mobilization
   Units will report deficiencies as laid down in para 5 of "Instructions for the mobilization of units of the 7th Division returning from abroad". Equipment will be drawn in the ordinary way from the Ordnance. Any deficiencies which cannot be complied with after application as laid down above, will be reported direct by units to DIRMOBIZE, LONDON. All units will report at once to this office through the usual channel when they are mobilized.

J.J. Clarke
Lieut Colonel
AA & QMG
7th Division

G.80.1

7th Division Routine Orders No 3

Southampton
7th September 1914

1. Messages from Aeroplanes

The following information and instructions regarding messages dropped from Aeroplanes are published for information

"Notes on Messages Dropped from Aeroplanes.

The message is enclosed in a canvas bag which is fastened with two spring clips and contains a weight.

Two streamers of blue, yellow and red cloth each 4½ feet long are attached.

The written message will be found inside the bag.

Only one seeing one of these dropped from an aeroplane should at once open the bag and take steps to forward the message inside to the person for whom it is intended"

All ranks will be acquainted with this order which will be read on three successive parades.

J.J. Clarke
Lieut Colonel
A.A. & Q.M.G.

980

7th Division Routine Orders No 1.

Southampton
7th September 1914

1. **HeadQuarters**

HeadQuarters 7th Division will be established at LYNDHURST Camp from 4 pm the 10th September 1914. The Office will be at the Grand Hotel, Lyndhurst.

Postal address - LYNDHURST.
Railway station - LYNDHURST ROAD
Telephone No. - No 23 LYNDHURST (for the present pending establishment of a military exchange).

2. **Bounds**

All Public Houses in the neighbourhood of LYNDHURST are placed out of bounds to the troops of the 7th Division.

H.J. Clarke
Lieut Colonel
A.A. & Q.M.G.

7th Division Routine Orders No 5

Lyndhurst
11th Sept 1914

1. Bounds
SOUTHAMPTON is placed out of Bounds to all troops of the Division.

2. Bugle and Trumpet Calls
Until further notice:-
Reveille will sound at 5-30 am
Retreat   "   "   " 6-30 pm
First post "   "   " 8-45 pm
Last post "   "   " 9-15 pm
Lights out "   "   " 9-30 pm
All troops will be in Camp by 9 pm

3. Strangles
A case of strangles having occurred, any horse showing sign of discharge from the nose or general symptoms of cold should not be watered at the general watering troughs. Any cases noticed should be at once reported to the D.A.D.V.S.

4. Water Supply.
(a)   The greatest care must be exercised in husbanding the water supply in all Camps and waste must be reduced to a minimum.
(b)   High stand pipes for filling water carts must not be used for filling Buckets, mess tins &c. These must be filled at the low taps
(c) Horses of all units, except Divisional HeadQrs, Yeomanry and Artillery, will be watered only at the general watering troughs on the main road, just east of the Supply Depôt.

(d). When

(d). When the surroundings of water taps or troughs become wet, the ground should be covered with bundles of heather under regimental arrangements.

(e). Troops are warned that the water in streams, pools and ditches in the New Forest is unsafe for drinking purposes.

(f) Water troughs must be emptied and cleaned out once a day.

(g) Units will detail water piquets to ensure that troughs are filled before watering is commenced, and that taps are turned off &c. The 54th Field Co. R.E. will be responsible for the general watering troughs.

4. <u>Routine Orders</u>.

Routine Orders will be issued at 12 noon daily. At that hour orderlies from Head Quarters of Divisional Mounted Troops, Cyclists, Artillery, Engineers, Signal Co;, A.S.C., R.A.M.C. and Infantry Brigades will attend at Divisional Head Qrs (Grand Hotel, Lyndhurst) to receive copies of orders for distribution.

J.R.J. Clarke
Lieut. Col.
A.A. & Q.M.G. 4th Divn.

<u>NOTICE</u>.
The Committee of the New Forest Golf Club have very kindly made all Officers of the 4th Division Honorary Members of the Club during their stay at Lyndhurst.

4th Divisional Routine Orders. No. 6

Lyndhurst
12th Sept 1914.

General Staff

1. Training Areas

Training Areas round LYNDHURST are lettered as follows:-

A. Between the LYNDHURST – TOTTON and the LYNDHURST – LYMINGTON Roads.

B. Between the LYNDHURST – LYMINGTON and the LYNDHURST – BURLEY – RINGWOOD Roads.

C. North of the TOTTON – LYNDHURST – BURLEY – RINGWOOD Roads.

The attached table gives the allotment of areas to Infantry, Yeomanry and Artillery units. Cyclists, R.E., A.S.C. and R.A.M.C. may use any suitable area, but must be careful not to interfere with the training of the units to which the area is allotted.

Infantry and Artillery units allotted to the same area will, whenever possible, arrange to carry out combined training. For this purpose Infantry Brigadiers should communicate direct with the Officers Commanding Artillery Brigades.

	M	T	W	T	F	S
20th Infantry Brigade	A	B	C	A	B	C
21st –do– –do–	B	C	A	B	C	A
22nd –do– –do–	C	A	B	C	A	B
14th Field Artillery Brigade	A	B	C	A	B	C
35th Field –do– –do–	B	C	A	B	C	A
22nd Field –do– –do–	C	A	B	C	A	B
3rd Heavy Brigade	A	C	B	A	C	B
Northumberland Yeomanry	B	A	C	B	A	C

Montgomery
Lieut Col
General Staff

Administrative Staff

2. **States**
A state showing by units the strength in officers, other ranks, horses and amount of transport in possession, will be furnished to Divisional Headquarters by 12 noon tomorrow 13th instant.

These states will be collected by Head Qrs of Divisional Artillery, Engineers, Signal Company, A.S.C., R.A.M.C. and 20th Infantry Brigade for transmission.

Similar states, except as to amount of transport in possession, will be submitted daily at 12 noon from the 14th instant inclusive and should be sent by the orderlies detailed to fetch Divisional Routine Orders.

F.L.J. Clarke
Lieut Col
A.A. & Q.M.G.
7th Division

7th. Divisional Routine Orders. No. 7.

Lyndhurst.
14th. September. 14.

1. Composition of 7th. Division and allotment of Camps.
(a.) With reference to Routine Order No. 1. of 3rd. Sept: the composition of the Infantry Brigades of the Division will be as follows: with effect from tomorrow 15th. instant.

20th. Infantry Brigade - Commander Brig: Genl. H. G. Ruggles-Brise.
    1st. Bn. Grenadier Guards.
    2nd. Bn. Scots. Guards.
    2nd. Bn. Border Regiment.
    2nd. Bn. Gordon Highlanders.

21st. Infantry Brigade - Commander. Brig: Genl. H. E. Watts. C.B.
    2nd. Bn. Bedfordshire Regiment.
    2nd. Bn. Yorkshire. Regiment.
    2nd. Bn. Rl. Scots. Fusiliers.
    2nd. Bn. Wiltshire Regiment.

22nd. Infantry Brigade - Commander Brig: Genl. S. T. B. Lawford.
    2nd. Bn. Rl. West Surrey Regiment.
    2nd. Bn. Rl. Warwickshire Regiment.
    1st. Bn. South Staffordshire Regiment.
    1st. Bn. Rl. Welsh Fusiliers.

(b) Consequent on above the following changes will be made in the allotment of Camps-

The (new) 20th Brigade will be encamped on the Golf Course. Orders will be issued from this Office for the 2nd. Bn. Border Regiment to move from their present Camp as soon as Camp Equipment is available.

The

The (new) 21st. Brigade will be encamped in their present Camp of the (old) 20th. Brigade. The 2nd. Rl. Scots" Fusiliers on arrival will take over the vacant Camp originally intended for the 2nd. Bn. Gordon Highlanders. The 2nd Bn. Bedfordshire Regiment on arrival will take over the Camp vacated by the 2nd. Bn. Border Regiment. The 22nd. Infantry Brigade will be encamped to the East of the Old Gravel Pit and North East of the 7th. Division Headquarter Camp.

J.R.J. Clarke
Lieutenant Colonel.
A. A. & Q. M. G. 7th. Division.

7th Division Routine Orders. No. 8.

Lyndhurst,
15th. September. 1914.

1. Bicycles.

Units will arrange to draw bicycles as authorised by War Establishments 7th. Division from Ordnance Officer, Gun Wharf Portsmouth at once.

Men should proceed to Portsmouth by rail and return by road.

2. Brigade Areas.

The Camps at Lyndhurst and Ashurst will be formed into the following Brigade Areas for the purpose of sanitation, cleanliness etc.

No.1. - Artillery Brigade Area. - To include Camps of the 14th. R.H.A. Brigade and Heavy Batteries R.G.A.

No.2. - 20th. Brigade Area. - To include 20th. Infantry Bde, Supply Depôt, Divisional R.E., Signal Company and Cyclists Company.

No.3. - 21st. Bde. Area. - To include 21st. Infantry Bde, 3. Field Ambulances, and Reception Hospital.

No.4. - 22nd. Brigade Area. - To include 22nd. Infantry Bde, Divisional Headquarters, Divisional R.A. Headquarters and Northumberland Hussars.

No.5. - Ashurst Area. - To include 35th. & 22nd Brigades R.F.A. and Ordnance Depôt at Lyndhurst Road Station.

A Field Officer or Captain of the day will be appointed to each Brigade Area, who will be responsible for reporting to O.C. Units any want of proper sanitation or cleanliness in the Camps.

3. Drying Tents.

2. Drying Tents.
(a.) Marquees for drying wet clothing will be supplied as under:-

 Each Artillery Brigade _____ 1.
 Each Infantry Brigade _____ 4.
 Divisional R.E. _____ 1.
 — do — A.S.C. _____ 1.
 — do — R.A.M.C. _____ 1.
 — do — Headquarters _____ 1.
 Northumberland Hussars. ___ 1.

(b.) 2. Braziers with a supply of coke and coal will be provided for each Marquee — also framework for hanging clothes on.

(c.) Headquarters of Artillery and Infantry Brigades, Divisional R.E., A.S.C., R.A.M.C., and O.C. Northumberland Hussars will each arrange to draw the number of Marquees and Braziers allotted to their Units from the Ordnance Depôt Lyndhurst Road Station and will indent on the Supply Depôt for an initial supply of coke and coal.

(d.) The C.R.E. will arrange to erect the necessary framework in each Marquee.

          J.L.J. Clarke

          Lieutenant Colonel.
        A.A. & Q.M.G. 7th. Division.

G.06.

7th Division.

Evening Conferences.

Conferences will be held at Division Headquarters at 9. p.m. every evening except Sundays.

The following is the provisional programme of subjects for discussion:-

Septr.	15th.	Security.
"	16th.	Replenishment of Ammunition.
"	17th.	March discipline.
"	18th.	Medical arrangements and Replacement of Casualties.
"	19th.	Billets and Brigade Areas.
"	21st.	Attack:- Cooperation of all Arms; Fire and movement.
"	22nd.	Defence and Counter attack.
"	23rd.	Retreats. Morale.
"	24th.	Supply and requisitions.
"	25th.	Village & Wood Fighting

A.A. Montgomery
Lieut. Colonel.
General Staff.

15th. Septr. 14.

G.S.O.1

<u>7th. Division Routine Orders. No. 9.</u>

Lyndhurst.
16th. Sepr. 1914.

<u>General Staff.</u>

1. <u>Training Areas.</u>

With reference to the allotment of Troops to Training Areas in Routine Order No. 1. of 12th. September the following amendments will be made to the table at the bottom of the page:-

For "14th. Horse Artillery Brigade", read "36th. Field Artillery Brigade."

For "35th. Field Artillery Brigade", read "14th. Horse Artillery Brigade."

H.M. de F. Montgomery
Lieutenant—Colonel.
General Staff.

<u>Administrative Staff.</u>

2. <u>Civilian Cooks.</u>

Intimation has been received that Mr. C. H. Senn, 329. Vauxhall Bridge Road, London. S.W. has available for immediate despatch 400. male cooks.

3. <u>Travelling (Troop Trains.)</u>

All Troops travelling by rail are warned against throwing bottles from the train.

4. <u>Camps.</u>

The 2nd Border Regiment will move out of their present Camp, in the 21st. Infantry Brigade Area tomorrow. 17th. inst. and encamp in the 20th. Infantry Brigade Area under arrangements to be made by the respective Brigade Headquarters.

J.J. Asserie
Lieut: Colonel.
A.A. & Q.M.G.

7th Division

Evening Conferences

The following will be substituted for the programme issued on the 15th September:—

16th Septr.	Replenishment of Ammunition
17th "	Retreats & Rear Guards
18th "	Medical & Sanitary Organization
19th "	Attack; fire & movement; co-operation of all arms.
21st "	Billets & Brigade Areas
22nd "	Defence and Counter attack
23rd "	March discipline & replacement of casualties
24th "	Wood & village fighting
25th "	Supply Organization
26th "	Intercommunication.

16th Septr 1914.

RhdMontgomery
Lieut. Colonel
General Staff

7th. Division Routine Orders. No. 10.

Lyndhurst.
17th. September 1914.

1. **Blankets:-**
The issue of a second Blanket is approved. - Units not in possession of ground sheets will be equipped first. Indents to be forwarded to Ordnance Officer, Lyndhurst Road, Depot at once.

2. **Picquets:-** Infantry Brigades in rotation commencing with the 20th. Infantry Brigade this day will find a Picquet of 1. Sergt., 1. Corporal & 10 men daily, mounting at 5. p.m. The N. C. O. in command of this Picquet will report at 5. p.m. daily to the Assistant Provost Marshal at the Grand Hotel Lyndhurst, from whom they will receive their orders. Regimental Picquets will be withdrawn and will only be detailed in exceptional circumstances.

3. **Inoculation:-** O. C. Northumberland Hussars, Headquarters of Divisional Artillery, Engineers, Signal Coy, A.S.C., R.A.M.C., and Infantry Brigades will forward a return at once to the A.D.M.S. 7th. Division showing the percentage of Officers and men that have been inoculated against Enteric fever in each Unit.

4. **Forage:-** Following scale of forage is authorised for Heavy Draught Horses — 17 lbs Oats, 16 lbs. Hay per diem.

5. **Entire Horses:-** Units in possession of entire horses are not permitted to keep them in their lines, and must make arrangements either to billet them or tether them at Lyndhurst Road Station, until instructions are received from the War Office as to their disposal.

Clarke Lieut: Colonel.
A.A.& Q.M.G. 7th. Division.

G501

7th Division Routine Orders. No. 11.

Lyndhurst.
18th September 1914.

1/ Dress:-
N. C. O's and men when walking out beyond the limits of their Brigade Areas will wear Bandoliers or Belts, and Puttees.

2/ Baggage:-
Units must be prepared to despatch to depots or agents, under regimental arrangements, all baggage surplus to the amount authorised to be taken oversea.

3/ Horses:-
Any Units of R.E. and Infantry including Headquarters of Infantry Brigades that have not yet sent in Requisitions for Horses other than "Train" should at once do so to Headquarters Southern Command, Salisbury.

J.J. Clarke
Lieut. Col.
A.A. & Q.M.G. 7th. Division.

7th Division Routine Orders. No. 12.

G.S.O.4

Lyndhurst.
19th September 1914

1. Baggage:-
With reference to para 2 of Routine Order No. 9 dated 15.9.14. Surplus baggage must be packed ready for despatch by the evening of the 20th inst.

2. War Establishments:-
A few copies of War Establishments 7th Division still being available for issue, a small supply of same can be obtained on application to the 7th Division Staff Supply Officer.

3. Mobilization:-
All Units will report at once to this Office through the usual channel when their mobilization is complete.

4. Delivery of Telegrams:-
In future the post office messengers will deliver telegrams to the nearest camp telephone office, the Headquarters of the Brigade or other unit controlling the telephone will be responsible for the delivery of the telegram to the addressee and will arrange for an operator to sleep in the telephone office at night. Sufficient orderlies for the distribution of telegrams will be detailed daily. Telegrams intended for the R.E. and R.A.M.C. will be delivered at the Telephone in the Supply Depot, and the R.E., A.S.C., and R.A.M.C. will detail orderlies by mutual arrangement.

5. Inspection of Equipment:-
Officers Commanding Units will please cause all equipment and stores including vehicles to be thoroughly examined and overhauled where necessary.

6. Indents:-
Indents should be submitted at once to C.A.O. Portsmouth Fortress for all items required to complete equipment; also for items required to replace others unserviceable. It is most essential that the whole of the items should

should be included in one indent.

7. **Vehicles:-**

All transport vehicles will have a distinguishing mark painted on both sides in a conspicuous place, under regimental arrangements. The mark will consist of a patch about 9 inches square of the colours given below on which the official abbreviated name or number of the unit will be marked in black.

The colours for the patches will be:-

Division Headquarters	Red & White.
R.A.	Red & Blue.
Other Divisional Troops	Blue.
20th. Infantry Brigade	Red.
21st. " "	Green.
22nd. " "	Yellow.

8. **Chaplains:-**

The following C. of E. Chaplains having joined, will be posted and attached as under:-

The Rev. E. H. Kennedy posted to the 20th. Infantry Brigade, and attached to the 21st Field Ambulance.

The Rev. J.P. George posted to the 21st Infantry Brigade, and attached to the 22nd. Field Ambulance.

Church parades will be held tomorrow under arrangements to be made by Brigade Area Commanders.

The Rev. C. H. Compton, Rector of Lyndhurst will conduct the C. of E. service in the 22-nd. Brigade Area at 10. a.m.

J.K.J. Clarke
Lieut. Colonel.
A.A. & Q.M.G. 7th. Division.

Notice.

Found:-

Five (5) Cartridges S.A. Ball .303 inch, in charger. Can be obtained upon application to the Ordnance Officer.

7th Divisional Station Orders No 13.

Lyndhurst
20th September 1914.

1. District Court Martial.

A District Court Martial as under will assemble at Headquarters Camp Divisional R.E. at 10 a.m on 21st September for the trial of —

[redacted]

and such other person or persons as may be brought before it.

President.
Major J.I.S. Boringuel, 2/Border Regiment.

Members.
A Captain to be detailed by Headquarters Divisional R.A.
A Subaltern to be detailed by Headquarters 22nd Inf. Bde.

The accused will be warned and all witnesses directed to attend. Proceedings to be forwarded to Headquarters 7th Division.

2. Bicycles:-

Government Bicycles are not to be used for any but purely military purposes.

3. Train Transport Drivers:-

All Train transport drivers will be furnished by the Company of the 7th Divisional Train concerned, and steps are being taken so that these Companies can be brought up to War Establishment at short notice.

It will be necessary to provide many of the train vehicles for the 7th division from civilian sources, and it is not proposed to bring the train up to War Establishment until it is known how many complete turns out (i.e. wagons, horses, harness and drivers) will have to be provided by each of of the Companies

4. Forage:

With reference to routine order No 4 of 17th instant forage may be issued on the following scale to heavy draught horses of the Shire and Clydesdale stamp, employed on heavy draught work.—

Oats 19 lbs.   Hay 15 lbs.

5. Horseshoes:

In cases where horseshoes cannot be provided from local resources, mobilization sets can be used provided indents to have them replaced are at once sent to the Ordnance Officer 7th Division, Gun Wharf, Portsmouth.

6. Canteens:

Troops are only allowed to use the canteens of their own units, and must not make use of any others.

J. J. Leahe
Lieut: Colonel.
A.A.Q.M.G. 7th Division.

7th. Division Routine Order No. 14.

Lyndhurst.
21st. September 1914.

1. **Chaplains:-**
With reference to Routine Order No 8. dated 19/9/14, the Rev. E.J. Kennedy will be attached to the 23rd. Field Ambulance, and the Rev. J.P. George, to the 21st. Field Ambulance and not as therein stated.

2. **Brigade Areas:-**
The following alterations are made in the Brigade Areas:-

No.2. 20th Brigade Area:- To include 20th. Infantry Brigade and Supply Depot.

No.3. 21st Brigade Area:- To include 21st Infantry Brigade only.

No.4 22nd Brigade Area:- To include 22nd. Infantry Brigade, Divisional R.E., Signal Co., Cyclists Co., A.S.C., Field Ambulances, Northumberland Hussars, and Divisional Head-quarters.

The main road from Lyndhurst Road Station to Lyndhurst is to be considered as outside Brigade Areas, and all men using it are to be properly dressed as laid down in Routine Order No 11 para 1. of 18th. September 1914.

3. **Drying Tents:-**
With reference to Routine Order No 3. dated 15/9/14 the marquees are now ready for issue at the Ordnance Depot, Lyndhurst Road Station, and may be drawn on application.

4. **Forage:-**
All Riding Horses over 16 hands high, can be issued with the revised scale of forage, as under:-
Oats. — 15 lbs.   Hay. — 15 lbs.

J.J. Clarke
Lieut: Colonel.
A.A. & Q.M.G. 7th. Division.

7th Division Routine Orders No. 15.

                                                          Lyndhurst.
                                            22nd Sept: 1914.

GENERAL STAFF.

1. DIVISIONAL ROUTE MARCH.

       The Division will carry out a route march tomorrow 23rd September, the leading troops leaving LYNDHURST at about 3 a.m.

       Operation Orders will be issued to all concerned this afternoon.

       The object of the march is to test march discipline, Staff arrangements for watering en-route and the employment of an advanced guard covering the Division on the march.

       As far as the watering place, the march will be carried out under peace conditions; from there onwards it will be covered by an advanced guard to which orders will be issued in due course.

       On return to LYNDHURST troops will proceed independently to their Camps and dismiss.

       The length of the march will be about 15 miles.

       The O.C., 22nd Brigade R.F.A. will command the skeleton force consisting of :-

    22nd F.A.Bde (as available).

    4 Officers and 100 men from each Infantry Brigade. (as far as possible base details and unfit men).

       He will report to Div.H.Q. for instructions at 5 p.m. today.

       The Infantry of the skeleton force will assemble at on the TOTTON-LYNDHURST road, in order of seniority of Bdes, facing S.W., head at LYNDHURST ROAD STATION, under Bde arrangements; O.C.Bde detachments will report there to

                                                          the

Sheet 2. (22/9/14.)

the O.C.22nd F.A.Bde at 8-30 a.m.

All Units of the Devision except the Div.Ammn.Col. will turn out at War Establishment including Train and spare horses as far as their strength permits.

Haversack rations will be carried.

Rifles are not to be loaded.

The equipment of the men of Battalions, which are not yet fit, may be lightened at the discretion of Infantry Brigadiers.

A memorandum will be issued with Operation Orders this evening drawing attention to points of march discipline to which the Major General Commanding wishes special attention to be paid.

       H. M. de F. Montgomery, Lieut:Colonel,
         General Staff.

ADMINISTRATIVE STAFF.

2. VETERINARY SERVICES.

When in Brigade Areas, units which are not provided with a Veterinary Officer in War Establishments will be in charge of the Vetsrinary Officer appointed to the Headquarters of the Infantry Brigade quartered in the Brigade Area.

On the line of march, such units will apply to the nearest Veterinary Officer.

       J. L. J. Clarke, Lieutenant Colonel,
        A. A. & Q. M. G.

7th. Division Routine Order No 15.

Lyndhurst.
22nd. September 1914.

After Order.

3. Damage to Trees.

On no account are trees to be cut down for any purpose whatever. Wood for fires should be obtained from Supply Depot on requisition, wood for other purposes from the Engineers.

J.F. Clarke
Lieut: Colonel.
A.A. & Q.M.G. 7th. Division

Notice.

Found at the Railway Station, Lyndhurst Road, a Rifle Short M.L.E. mark 1*. numbered $\frac{A.O.C.}{406}$, and can be obtained by the owner, upon application to the Ordnance Officer Lyndhurst.

7th. Division Routine Order No. 13.

Lyndhurst.
23rd. Septr. 1914.

1. **BOARD.** A Board of Officers will assemble at the Grand Hotel stables on Friday the 25th instant at 9.a.m. for the purpose of assessing the value of any private chargers the property of Officers for purchase by the State. The Board will be composed as under:-

    President:-

    Brigadier General H.K. Jackson, D.S.O., Commdg Divnl R.A.

    Members:-

    A Field Officer to be detailed by Head Qrs 20th Infty Bde.
    A Field Officer to be detailed by Head Qrs 21st Infty Bde.
    The D.AD of Veterinary Services, 7th Division.

    All Officers concerned must arrange to have their horses sent to be inspected as above with a declaration of value, countersigned by their Commanding Officers.

2. **UNITS returning from ABROAD, Mobilization of:-**

    The following alteration is to be made to paragraph 5 of "Instructions for the Mobilization of Units of the 7th Division returning from Abroad":-

    "In the case of other other ranks" For "To Officer i/c Records" substitute "To the War Office".

3. **DEFICIENCIES:-** In future, a "Return" is to be rendered daily to Head Quarters 7th Division, not later than 3.p.m. showing deficiencies in horses and Wagons 1st and 2nd Line Transport, Equipment, and other essential articles. Minor details are not to be reported.

4. **MOBILIZATION:-** Attention is directed to Order No.3. of Routine Order No.12 dated 19th instant. The rendering of the report required is to be made immediately Mobilization has been effected.

5. **REQUISITIONS for CASH:-** The following "Extract" from Southern Command Orders dated 2nd September 1914, is published for the information of, and compliance by all concerned:-
    " It having been observed that Os.C. Units and others are in the habit of telegraphing for money to pay their men and to meet other expenses, this procedure is only to be adopted in very exceptional cases, normally, the following instructions will be adhered to:-

1. Cash

Sheet 2 of Routine Order No. 16:-

1. Cash will be obtained from the Cashier of the Command in which the sub-accountant is serving.

2. Requisitions for cash (Army Form .:N: 1487) for the pay of Units will be despatched so as to reach the Cashier's Office not later than the first post on the Wednesday preceding the actual pay-day (i.e., Friday).

3. Requisitions (A.F."N"1487) from other sub-accountants will reach the Cashier's Office not later than two clear days before the money is required.

4. If, under very exceptional circumstances, it becomes necessary to telegraph for an Imprest, the telegram will give the name of the Officer operating on the account, and will state that "Requisition follows".
The confirmation of the telegram and a covering A.F.N.1487 explaining the urgency will be sent by the first post or the draft will be stopped as a precautionary measure.

5. The name of the Bank in which it is desired that sums are to be lodged to credit of sub-accountants will invariably be shown on the Army Form N, 1487.

6. If an open draft is desired, this will be clearly stated on the requisition and the entry initialled by the Officer preferring it.

(C.R., S.C., No. 3/12507 (P).

(sd) J.L.J. Clarke, Lieut: Colonel,
A.A. & Q.M.G., 7th Division.

NOTICES:-

LOST:-

1. A black box marked "Quartermaster's Stores, 2/Queens Regiment" and labelled "For use on Voyage". Finder to communicate at once with O.C. 2/Queens.

2. Pannier- labelled " 1/South Stafford Regt, containing 2 Lamps, Signalling "B" and 50 Flags, 2 Foot." Finder to communicate at once with O.C. 1/South Stafford Regt.

3. Horse, from Lines of 35th Brigade R.F.A., night of 22nd instant, Description of animal not known. Might bear a label addressed "35th Brigade R.F.A." Finder of a stray horse to communicate at once with O.C. 35th Brigade R.F.A.

7th Division Routine Orders No: 17.

Grand Hotel,
LYNDHURST. Hants.
24th September 1914.

1. REQUISITIONS FOR CASH.

      Order No: 5 of Routine Order No: 16 dated 23rd instant, is to be repeated in Brigade Orders.

2. RETURNS.

      All Infantry Units will forward a return to Headquarters after every divisional day showing the number of men who fell out during the march.

3. ARMLETS.

      Armlets will be worn in future by Officers of Headquarters Units at all Field Operations.

4. CHAPLAINS.

      The Reverend the Hon: H.Pool, Church of England Chaplain is posted to the 22nd Infantry Brigade and will be attached to the 22nd Field Ambulance.

5. FIELD IMPREST ACCOUNTS.

      Officers Commanding Units &c. will render to the Field Cashier, Headquarters, 7th Division as soon as possible lists showing the Rank and Name of Officers who will require Imprest Accounts for the pay &c. of Troops in the Field.
      Where Imprests are required for other purposes, the service should be stated.

6. FORAGE & ANIMAL ACCOUNTS.

      The attention of Officers Commanding Units is drawn to the necessity for closing and rendering their Forage and Animal Accounts to the Local Auditor concerned prior to embarkation, and to give the fullest possible information in their accounts in regard to the source of receipt of fresh horses and explanations of any subsequent casualties.
      Attention is also drawn to the necessity for closing and rendering Equipment and Clothing Accounts to the Local Auditor in accordance with paragarphs 20-25, Appendix 1, Equipment Regulations, Part 1, and paragraphs 55-63 Clothing Regulations, Part 111. (C.R.S.C. 2/15063 (A.2).)

7. UNITS FROM ABROAD. DRAFTS REQUIRED TO COMPLETE WAR ESTABLISHMENT

      Reference Order No: 2 of Routine Order No: 16 dated 23rd instant, it is to be noted that applications for Officers and other ranks required to complete War Establishment are to be submitted to Headquarters, Southern Command, Salisbury and NOT direct to War Office.

      J. L. J. CLARKE, Lieutenant Colonel,
    A. A. & Q. M. G., 7th Division.

MARCH DISCIPLINE.

Special attention should be paid to the following points and paragraphs in Field Service Regulations Part 1.

HALTS. Every Unit will halt at ten minutes to the hour and resume the march at the hour. Watches will be set at Divisional Head Quarters.

These halts do not apply to the advanced guard which will halt as tactical conditions admit. Units will not close up at the halts unless orders are received from Divisional Head Quarters that they are to do so. During halts each Brigade is responsible for it's own local security. The fairway must be left clear and all riding horses should be backed well into the side of the road, with their heads towards the fairway. Equipment will be taken off during halts.

MAINTAINING TOUCH. Every Unit is responsible that touch is maintained with the Unit following it. This is especially important at night or when a Unit is detached from the column to a flank thus causing a gap in the main column.

INTERVALS. The intervals mentioned in F.S.R.1. 25 (3) are a luxury and will only be maintained when tactical conditions admit. They will normally be reduced and must in no case be exceeded.

FALLING OUT. Men should only be allowed to fall out for purposes of nature during the halts. They will use their entrenching tool when necessary. Men who fall out sick will stay on the side of the road and report to the Officer i/c of the first ambulance wagon which passes. No one will be left in charge unless the man is dangerously ill. Men who fall out for any reason will not attempt to catch up their Unit on the march but only at the halt. They will march in the first available space.

LED HORSES -

LED HORSES.   F.S.R.1, 27 (2).

WATERING at FORDS.   F.S.R.1. 35 (1).

VEHICLES.   No vehicles which are not authorised by War Establishments or Divisional Head quarters will be allowed. F.S.R.1. 33.(5).

F.S.R.1. 28 (1).   Men with vehicles may put their packs on the vehicle but will in all cases carry their rifles slung. Wagons temporarily broken down will be pulled off well clear of the road and after repair will rejoin the column in the nearest available space. They will not attempt to rejoin their proper place in the column.

SMOKING.   No cigarette smoking is allowed on the line of march.

PASSING TROOPS.   In open country mounted officers and orderlies passing along the column will keep well clear of the road. Motors will go slowly unless on urgent military business and will not pass the column more often than necessary.

Officers Commanding Companies &c may pull out of the column to see the march discipline of their Unit and then trot up to rejoin their position.

CLOSING UP.   A regular pace will be maintained and an Officer will march in rear of each company, squadron, battery, &c., to to see the Units keep well closed up.

COMPLIMENTS.   The Commander-in-Chief, Southern Command will see the Division tomorrow at Beaulieu about 11.0.a.m. Troops in the main column of march (advanced guard excepted) will salute the Commander-in-Chief on passing him unless they are carrying out some tactical operation. As the Commander-in-Chief will be present, troops will not salute the Divisional General.

With reference to the "List of Conferences" published on 16th instant, the following alterations will be made:-

For "22nd instant" substitute " 23rd instant".
For "23rd instant" substitute " 22nd instant".

7th Division Routine Orders No: 18.
****

LYNDHURST.
25th Sept 1914

1. TRAFFIC.

The Cemetery Road is not to be used for wheeled traffic except under very exceptional circumstances.

2. CAMP EQUIPMENT.

A limited supply of the undermentioned stores has been received by the Ordnance Officer, Lyndhurst and Units that have not already been supplied with such can obtain them on indent, viz:-
  Lanterns, tent, folding.
  Hammers, miners, sledge.
  Buckets, water, canvas.
  Mallets, heel peg.
  Ropes, head.
  Braziers (vide Order No: 3 of Routine Order No: 8 of 15/9/1914).
  Mauls, G.S.

Units that have not drawn the drying tents referred to in Routine Order No: 8 of 15th instant should do so as soon as possible.

3. PRIVATE HORSES FOR PURCHASE BY THE STATE.

With reference to Order No: 1 of Routine Order No: 16 dated 23rd instant, Officers whose horses were accepted by the Board, are AT ONCE, to forward to 7th Division Headquarters Office, a statement (in duplicate) showing name and address of Bankers or other person to whom it is desired that payment be made by the War Office for the horse or horses purchased.

A certificate (in duplicate) is, at the same time, to be forwarded by the Commanding Officer of the Unit concerned, stating that the horses (number of same to be shown) accepted by the Board have been taken on the strength of such Unit for Military service.

4. RETURNS.

Officers Commanding Units will forward to Divisional Head Quarters, through the usual channels, by 9 a.m. on Sunday the 27th instant, a return of officers by name who have passed through the Staff College.

J. L. J. CLARKE, Lieutenant Colonel,
A. A. & Q. M. G., 7th Division.

N O T I C E S.
....

LOST.
(a). During night of 24th-25th, an Officer's charger, No: 105, wearing horse rug, Dark Bay, about 16 hands, rope gall near hind. Finder to communicate at once with Hdqrs, 22nd Infantry Brigade.
(b). 1 Case marked "Machine Gun, 1st S. Stafford Regt" containing 2 spare part boxes, 1 Belt filling machine, 4 panels pairs, 4 large leather girth straps, 10 small girth straps, 2 shovel caps, 4 shovels G.S., 2 Picks, 2 Pick handles, 2 bridoons, 4 pairs of Prism Glasses. No: 2 Box with tripod and Lamp Box with 2 Lamps. 1 Bale containing 200 towels. Finder to communicate at once with O.C. 1st S. Stafford Regiment.
(c). Horse, description unknown, coming from Lyndhurst Road Station to join the 22nd Bde R.F.A. as a remount. Finder of a stray horse is at once to communicate with O.C., 22nd Bde R.F.A.

7th Division Routine Orders No: 19.

************ ********

Grand Hotel,
LYNDHURST.
26th September 1914.

1. COMPULSORY ALLOTMENT OF PAY.

The compulsory allotment by men at Home under Army Order 21 and 542 of 1914 will be suspended with effect from Monday last in any case in which the man is unwilling to make it.

Men should be warned that allotment may be imposed if wife appeals and separation allowance is proved insufficient.

Paymasters will issue &c. to families as already instructed pending further orders which will be issued from the War Office.

2. CHURCH PARADES.

Church parades will be held to-morrow under arrangements to be made by Brigade Area Commanders.

The Reverend C.H.Compton, Rector of Lyndhurst will conduct the Church of England service in No: 1 Brigade Area at 10 a.m.

Roman Catholic services will be held as under:-
(i). By Father Bernard Vaughan near the Scots Guards Camp for Nos: 1 & 2 Brigade Areas at 9-30 a.m.
(ii).By the Reverend J.Holley near the Wilts' Camp for Nos: 3 & 4 Brigade Areas at 9-30 a.m.

3. MAP CASES.

Officers are warned against wearing talc map cases; they have been found to reflect the sun and draw the enemy's fire.

4. UNITS FROM ABROAD. DRAFTS REQUIRED TO COMPLETE WAR ESTABLISH-
MENTS.

Reference Order No: 7 of Routine Order No: 17 dated 24th instant, applications for Officers and other ranks required to complete War Establishment are NOW to be made DIRECT to War Office. When it is desired to also inform Headquarters, Southern Command, telegram should end with "Addressed War Office repeated Southern Command."

5. RETURNS.

Officers Commanding units will render through the usual channels to Divisional Headquarters by 9 a.m., Monday 29th inst. a return of all Officers qualified as Interpreters in FRENCH and GERMAN.

J. L. J. CLARKE, Lieutenant Colonel,
A. A. & Q. M. G., 7th Division.

NOTICE.
****

LOST:- On 23rd instant between Brockenhurst Station and Race Course Green Camp a black kit bag, marked "16495 Gr.Harvey H.J." Finder please communicate with O.C., 111th (Heavy) Battery Royal Garrison Artillery.

7th Division Routine Orders No: 19 (continued).
****

Grand Hotel,
LYNDHURST.
26th September 1914.

AFTER ORDERS.

6. TRANSPORT - REQUIREMENTS OF.

All Units in the Division whose first line wheeled transport is not complete will send a representative to meet the D.A.Q.M.G. at the Grand Hotel, Lyndhurst at 8 a.m. to-morrow Sunday. Each representative must be prepared to give information as to transport already in possession and also as to transport required, both first and second line. Transport will then be issued.

7. MACHINE GUNS.

An examination and adjustment of machine guns on charge of Units of the 7th Division has been ordered by the Chief Inspector of Small Arms, and two examiners have arrived at Lyndhurst Camp for the purpose.
The order in which the examination will be carried out is as follows:-

20th Infantry Brigade............1st Grenadier Guards.
2nd Scots Guards.
2nd Border Regiment.
2nd Gordon Highlanders.

21st Infantry Brigade............2nd Bedford Regiment.
2nd Yorkshire Regiment.
2nd Royal Scots Fusiliers.
2nd Wiltshire Regiment.

22nd Infantry Brigade............2nd R.W.Surrey Regiment.
2nd Royal Warwickshire Regiment.
1st Royal Welsh Fusiliers.
1st S.Stafford Regiment.

The guns will be left suitable for firing Mark VII ammunition and Officers Commanding Units will be good enough to afford every facility to the examiners.

8. RETURNS.

Reference Order No: 5 of today's date for "29th" read "28th."

9. INTERPRETERS.

A revised copy of the 7th Division War Establishments has been received giving the following detail of interpreters with the Division. The Officers are being detailed by the War Office. Os C.Units will arrange for batmen, horses, saddlery and bicycles :-

	Offrs.	Batmen.	Horses.	Bicycles.
Divl Headquarters	3	3	6	-
Northumberland Hussars	4	4	8	-
Cyclist Company	1	1	-	2
14th R.H.A.Brigade	1	1	2	-
22nd R.F.A.Brigade	1	1	2	-
35th R.F.A.Brigade	1	1	2	-
7th Divl Ammn. Column	1	1	2	-
7th Divl Train Headquarters	1	1	2	-

Deficiencies -

Sheet 2.

Routine Order No. 19. "Orders, After" Contd:-

10. DEFICIENCIES.

With reference to Order 3 of Routine Order No. 16 dated 23rd instant, the "Return" issued with "After Orders" this day is to be completed and forwarded to Divisional Head Quarters by 8.0.p.m. this evening, the 26th instant.

A similar Return is to be rendered by 8.0.p.m. daily commencing 27th instant.

J.L.J. Clarke, Lieut: Colonel,
A.A. & Q.M.G., 7th Division.

7th Division Routine Orders No 20.
****

a

Grand Hotel,
LYNDHURST. Hants.
27th September 1914.

GENERAL STAFF.

1. DIVISIONAL OPERATIONS.

The Division will carry out field operations tomorrow the 28th September. The leading troops will start about 6 a.m. Operations Orders will be issued early this afternoon. Each Infantry Brigade will detail one Officer and 40 men to act as a skeleton force. The Officers Commanding these Brigade detachments will report to Major C.A.Law, 2nd Wilts Regiment at 5 p.m. at the Wilts Regiment Camp for Orders. Each Brigade detachment will take out 12 Signalling flags: the 21st Brigade detachment will, in addition, take out 6 red flags. The skeleton force will not carry packs or ammunition.

All Units of the Division will turn out as far as possible at War Establishment. The equipment of Units which are not yet fit may be lightened at the discretion of Brigadiers.

Haversack rations and feeds will be carried.

Rifles are not to be loaded.

At the conclusion of operations units will close and await orders for the return march.

H.MONTGOMERY, Colonel,
General Staff.

ADMINISTRATIVE STAFF.

2. NUMBERING HORSES:

Units are responsible that all Horses in the Division are marked on the hoofs as follows. On the near hind initials of unit and on the off hind a regimental number. The forefoot are to be left for Army Numbers where allotted. Lettering irons can be obtained on loan from the Mobile Veterinary Section. Infantry Brigades should obtain them in rotation commencing with the 20th and arrange to carry out the numbering in conjunction with their affiliated Artillery Brigades.

3. BLANKETS AND GROUND SHEETS.

Units will forward to the Ordnance Officer, Lyndhurst as early as possible a statement showing their ACTUAL strength (on date of rendering statement) and the number of Blankets and Ground Sheets in possession respectively.

4. WARRANT OFFICERS: RETENTION OF.

In future an application for the retention of a Warrant Officer under para: 270 King's Regns, and Article 770 Royal Warrant for Pay &c. will be made in letter form, accompanied by a Medical Certificate as to fitness, and not on Army Form B.221 as has been the custom heretofore.

This letter,after approval has been given by the G.O.C. will be filed with the Warrant Officers' Duplicate Attestation, a copy being sent to the Officer i/c Records.
(Authority:- Southern Cmd Order No: 1168 of 1914.)

J. L. J. CLARKE, Lieutenant Colonel,
A. A. & Q. M. G., 7th Division.

NOTICE.
*****

LOST from Lines of 1st Bn S.Staffordshire Regiment one Light Draught Horse. Please return to Transport Officer, 1st S.Stafford Regiment.

7th Division Routine Orders No: 20 (Continued).

Grand Hotel,
LYNDHURST. Hants.
27th September 1914.

AFTER ORDERS.

GENERAL STAFF.

5. DIVISIONAL OPERATIONS.
Reference Order No: 1 of to-day's date, for "Major C.A.Law, 2nd Wilts Regiment" read "Major W.L.Alexander, 2nd Bn Yorkshire Regiment".

ADMINISTRATIVE STAFF.

6. PRIVATE HORSES FOR PURCHASE BY THE STATE.
Officers who have not yet complied with Order No: 3 of Routine Order No: 18 dated 25th instant, must forward the required certificates without further delay.

7. CYCLIST COMPANY: N.C.Os and MEN TRANSFERRED TO.
N.C.Os and men who have joined the Cyclist Company will be paid by the Officer Commanding Cyclist Company from Monday 29th instant inclusive. This refers to all Infantry Battalions except 2/Yorks Regiment and 2/Border Regiment whose N.C.Os and Men are already on pay from Cyclist Company.

8. ROUTINE ORDERS: DRAFTS FOR.
Drafts for insertion in Routine Orders must reach Divisional Headquarters not later than 10-30 a.m.
Drafts received after that hour will not be published until following day except under exceptional circumstances.

J. L. J. CLARKE, Lieutenant Colonel,
A. A. & Q. M. G., 7th Division.

NOTICE.

L O S T during the night of 24th-25th, an Officer's charger, No: 105, wearing horse rug, Dark Bay, about 13 hands, rope gall near hind. Finder to communicate at once with Headqrs, 22nd Infantry Brigade.

7th DIVISION ROUTINE ORDERS No: 21.

Grand Hotel,
LYNDHURST. Hants.
28th September 1914.

1. BOUNDS.

No N.C.Os or Men are allowed to proceed East of the Bridge over the River Test at TOTTON unless in possession of a pass signed by an Officer.

Lyndhurst Road Station and Yard are placed out of bounds except for men on duty or in possession of a pass signed by an Officer.

2. PASSES.

A limited number of passes for six hours or under may be granted to N.C.Os and Men of good character, at the discretion of Commanding Officers.

3. FATIGUES.

Fatigue parties are not to be allowed on the platforms of Lyndhurst Road Railway Station except when necessary to carry out their work. Officers and N.C.Os in charge of fatigue parties are to see that this order is carried out.

4. DUTIES.

A Brigade on duty will be detailed daily.

The Brigade on duty will find all Guards, Picquets and Fatigues, except the permanent working party at the Supply Depot.

The following Guards will be mounted daily at 9 a.m.:-
(i). TOTTON ROAD BRIDGE.
    1 Sergt., 1 Corporal and 6 men.
(ii). TOTTON RAILWAY STATION.
    1 Sergt. and 3 Men.
(iii). LYNDHURST ROAD STATION.
    1 Officer, 1 Sergt., 2 Corporals and 15 men.
(iv). ORDNANCE DEPOT, LYNDHURST ROAD STATION.
    1 N.C.O. and 6 men.

The following working parties will be furnished daily, reporting at 8-15 a.m.:-
(i). To Ordnance Officer, Ordnance Depot.
    1 N.C.O. and 20 men.
(ii). To A.S.C.Offr on duty at LYNDHURST Road Station.
    1 N.C.O. and 25 men.
(iii). To Supply Officer, Supply Depot.
    1 N.C.O. and 25 men.

5. PICQUETS.

Three picquets each consisting of 1 Sergt, 1 Corporal and 12 men will mount daily at 6-30 p.m. for duty under the Assistant Provost Marshal, reporting to that Officer at the Grand Hotel.

Brigade on duty tomorrow 29th instant:- 22nd Infty Bde.

6. SUPPLIES.

In the absence of further instructions, Regimental Supplies will NOT be drawn prior to embarkation.

J. L. J. CLARKE, Lieut: Colonel,
A. A. & Q. M. G., 7th Division.

NOTICES :-

7th Divl Routine Orders No: 21. (Sheet 2.)

NOTICES.

L O S T .   A Sergeants small deck box containing documents and marked No: 6510 P.Inskip (on brass plate) and Bedford Regt in white stencil. Would finder please communicate with O.C., Bedfordshire Regiment.

F O U N D . Horse, Bay Gelding, Blaze, White Stockings, with sore withers, found in lines of 54th Field Company, R.E. on night of 27th instant.
Applications to O.C., 54th Field Company, Royal Engineers.

7th Division Routine Orders No: 21. (continued).
****

                                      Grand Hotel,
                                          LYNDHURST. Hants.

                                      28th September 1914.

                AFTER ORDER.
                ****

7. FIELD DRESSINGS.

     Units not complete with Field Dressings are to AT ONCE inform Ordnance Officer, Lyndhurst of numbers required.

                         J. L. J. Clarke, Lieutenant Colonel,
                            A. A. & Q. M. G., 7th Division.

7th DIVISION ROUTINE ORDERS No: 22.

Grand Hotel,
LYNDHURST. Hants.
29th September 1914.

GENERAL STAFF.

1. DIVISIONAL OPERATIONS.

The Division will carry out field operations tomorrow 30th September. The leading troops will start at about 6 a.m. Operation orders will be issued this afternoon. All units will turn out as far as possible at War Establishment. Haversack rations and feeds will be carried. Rifles are not to be loaded.

At the conclusion of operations units will close and await orders for the return march.

Skeleton force. Each Infantry Brigade will detail one Officer and 40 men to act as skeleton force. The Officers Commanding these Brigade detachments will report to Major G.N.B. Forster, Royal Warwickshire Regiment at the 22nd Infantry Brigade camp at 5 p.m. for orders.
Each Brigade detachment will take out 12 signalling flags: the 21st Brigade detachment will, in addition, take out 6 red flags. The skeleton force will not carry packs or ammunition.

H. MONTGOMERY,   Colonel,
General Staff.

ADMINISTRATIVE STAFF.

2. DUTIES.

Brigade for duty tomorrow 30th instant - 20th Infantry Brigade.

3. DEFICIENCIES.

With reference to After Order No: 10 of the 26th instant, a 'Return of Deficiencies' completed on the form issued with todays Orders is to reach Divisional Headquarters by 6 p.m. today.

This return will be rendered daily by 6 p.m. on the form being issued daily with orders.

4. MOBILIZATION ORDERS.

With reference to the "Instructions for the Mobilization of Units of the 7th Division returning from abroad", the following further instructions have been received from War Office.
(a). DETAILS LEFT AT HOME.
  (i). These details will remain at Lyndhurst.
  (ii). 2 Officers per infantry battalion, 2 Officers for R.A. units and 1 Officer for A.S.C. units will report at Lyndhurst on Thursday October 1st to take charge of these details. These Officers are instead of those mentioned in para: 4 "Instructions for Mobilization &c."
  (iii). Details of other arms and branches will be attached to the details of the infantry battalions in their respective Brigade Areas.
  (iv). Further instructions as to the movement of these details to join reserve units will be issued later.
(b). DETAILS LEFT AT THE BASE.
  (i). Instructions for the despatch of these details oversea will be issued later. Pending further instructions these details will remain at Lyndhurst.

Orderly-room

Orderly-room-Sergeants and R.A.Clerks will proceed with their units to the Adjutant General's office at the base.

5. INSTRUCTIONS FOR ENTRAINMENT AND EMBARKATION.

Orders have been received from the War Office that the 'Landing Return' referred to in the latter part of para: 3, Part 1 of the above instructions shall be rendered in duplicate. The instructions should be amended accordingly.

The following amendments will also be made in Part 1 "Instructions for entrainment &c.", para: 5, delete from "carry" in line 4 to "mobilization" in line 5 and substitute "be provided with 3 days preserved rations by the Embarkation Commandant, Southampton."

Para: 5, page 3, delete last three lines of para: and substitute "3 days forage for each horse for the voyage will be provided by the Embarkation Commandant, Southampton"

6. BOOTS.

Repairs to boots must be arranged locally by Officers Commanding Units under similar conditions to those laid down for the Territorial Force in Army Order 335 dated 1st September 1914. (W.O.telegram 203 Q.M.G.7 d/- 28th September 1914.)

7. INTERPRETERS.

With reference to Routine Order No: 9 of the 26th instant, the following Officers have been posted as Interpreters.

```
Divl.HdQrs..........Lt:Col: Sir F.Ponsonby, K.C.V.O., C.B.
Northumberland Hrs.2/Lts Whitehurst, Mears, Lingeman, McQueen.
Cyclist Coy........2/Lieut Sutcliffe.
21st Infty Bde.....       Lieut: Underwood.(attd: from Divn H.Qrs)
14th Bde R.H.A.....2/Lieut Lloyd.
22nd Bde R.F.A.....Major The Master of Belhaven.
35th Bde R.F.A.....2/Lieut Herbert.
Ammn. Column.......2/Lieut Wiseman.
Divl.Train.........2/Lieut Appleyard.
```

J. L. J. CLARKE, Lieutenant Colonel,
A. A. & Q. M. G., 7th Division.

N O T I C E S.

LOST. A Black case, about 4 feet cube, containing Saddlery addressed in white to O.C., 35th Bde Ammunition Column R.F.A. This was seen at Lyndhurst Road Station on the evening of 27th instant and had been removed by someone before the following morning. If any unit has removed this in error will they please cause it to be forwarded to the O.C., 35th Bde Amm Col. R.F.A.

STRAPS, EXTENDING, PICKETING PEG.
2 (or 4 ?) sets of above have been delivered or left Divisional Headquarters.
Unit for which intended should make early application same.

FOUND. During Field operations on the morning of the 28th on Stoney Cross Plain, clip containing five live cartridges one single blank cartridge. In present possession of O.C. Field Ambulance, No: 4 Brigade Area.

7th DIVISION ROUTINE ORDERS No: 22,

Grand Hotel,
LYNDHURST. Hants.
29th September 1914.

AFTER ORDER.

8. SURPLUS BAGGAGE.
Any baggage and stores, not authorized to be taken oversea, that has not yet been sent away from Camp, should be despatched under regimental arrangements forthwith.

J. L. J. Clarke, Lieutenant Colonel,
A. A. & Q. M. G., 7th Division.

7th DIVISION ROUTINE ORDERS No: 23.

Grand Hotel,
LYNDHURST. Hants.
30th September 1914.

1. DUTIES. Brigade for duty tomorrow 1st Octbr: 1914 - 21st Infantry Brigade.

2. GUARDS. The Field Officer of the day of the Brigade on duty will inspect the guards found by his Brigade daily.

3. REVOLVER AMMUNITION. All Mark III, IV and V Revolver Ammunition in possession of Units should be withdrawn at once and returned to Ordnance Officer, Lyndhurst Road Station. Indents to replace that withdrawn should be submitted at the same time.

4. ALLOTMENTS OF PAY. Os C.Units are to call upon all their men to state whether any object to making the standard allotments to their wives and children, and, if so, at what reduced rate they wish to allot.
    Lists showing Regimental number and rank of men refusing standard allotment stating reduced rate offered, should be sent to reach Paymasters not later than 3rd October. In cases not so notified, stoppages will continue at the previous rates.

5. FUEL ALLOWANCES. Owing to the difficulty in obtaining sufficient supplies of wood for Camps, fuel should be issued at the rate of 1 lb of wood and 1 lb of coal, under para:240 and 184 Allowance Regulations, until further notice. (Southern Command Order No: 1191 of 29/9/14.)

6. PICQUET. The following picquet will be mounted daily at 6-30 p.m. by the Brigade on duty:-
1 N.C.O. and 5 men at the gate of the field N.E. of the Grand Hotel in which the spare horses are turned out. This picquet will see that no horses are taken from the field without proper authority.
    The picquet will come off duty at 6-30 a.m.

7. LEAVE. Leave on medical certificate is granted to the following officers for the periods stated:-
Lieutenant Colonel Lord Ridley, Northumberland Hussars for 3 months from 29th September 1914.
Lieutenant Colonel H.W.Coates,D.S.O., 2/Bedford Regiment for 6 months from 22nd September 1914.

8. HORSES. Civilian horses, when considered serviceable, should be used with civilian transport.
    All harness, civilian and military, poles swingle-trees &c. surplus to establishment will be sent to the Ordnance Depot and handed over to the Ordnance Officer as soon as harness has been fitted.
    Units are requested to comply with this order as soon practicable in order that an issue may be made to those short of such equipment.

9. INTERPRETERS. In continuation of Order No: 7 of Routine Order of 29th instant, the following Officer has been posted Interpreter as under:-
   Infty Bde - 2/Lieut Thick (attached from Divl HdQrs.)

10. DRESS.

7th Division Routine Orders No: 23 (continued).
****

10. DRESS.   Units will report by 6 p.m. today whether all men are in possession of one good suit of service dress, one good pair of boots and necessaries.

        Attention is drawn to para: 17 "Instructions for Mobilization of Units of 7th Division". The kit bags left at the base will contain the articles laid down in the Field Service Manuals with the exception of the suit of service dress and the pair of boots which will be packed separately.

                J. L. J. CLARKE, Lieutenant Colonel,
                    A. A. & Q. M. G., 7th Division.

N O T I C E S.
****

FOUND. During Field Operations on 28th instant at Castle Malwood, a canvas bucket. At present in possession of O. C., 23rd Field Ambulance.

BICYCLE. On Tuesday 29th Sept:1914, outside Lyndhurst Post Office a Government Bicycle No: 5406 was left. This bicycle appears to have been taken away by mistake as a machine No: 5654 with blue and white bands of paint and figures 8-7 on rear mud guard was found in its place. Will person in possession of machine No: 5406 communicate with Headquarters, 20th Infantry Brigade as early as possible.

FOUND. The following packages &c. were received into A.O.D. store ex- S.S."Briton" on arrival at Southampton from Cape Town on 19th instant. Owners should apply to Storeholder i/c A.O.D. Southampton, viz:-
Kit Bag. No: 17381 Sergt A.Gray. On label, R.A.M.C.,Military Hospital, Wynberg,Cape Town. (Rest Camp,Southampton)in pencil.
Case (large). Captain Ponsonby . On label is written - Belongs to an Officer of the Oxford & Bucks Yeomanry recently on Governor's Staff in South Africa and returned home to rejoin his Regiment.
Case. No name. "South Stafford Regt" stencilled thereon.
Box. No name. "Stafford Regt" written on a label. Has two D shaped rings at back and rope handles.
Kit-box small. No name. Empty. Painted red inside, no handles, and hinges fitted upon outside of lid.

DEFICIENCIES.

UNIT......................................

Officers.	Other Ranks.	Horses.	Guns.	Vehicles.	
				Four wheeled.	Two Wheeled.

REMARKS.

(Signature).

7th DIVISION ROUTINE ORDERS No: 25 (Continued)

Grand Hotel,
Lyndhurst. Hants.
30th September 1914.

AFTER ORDER.

11. AMMUNITION.

Commanding Officers will render a certificate to Brigade Headquarters by 10 a.m. tomorrow 1st October to the effect that they are in possession of the ammunition laid down in Army Form G. 1098 for their Units.

A similar certificate will be rendered by G.Os.C. Infantry Brigades, Divisional Artillery and Os.C. R.E., Cyclist Coy, and A.S.C. to Divisional Headquarters by 10 a.m. the 2nd October 1914.

J. L. J. CLARKE, Lieutenant Colonel,
A. A. & Q. M. G., 7th Division.

Issued 6 p.m.

SPECIAL 7th DIVISIONAL ORDER.
~*~*~*~*~*~*~*~*~*~

                                      Grand Hotel,
                                           LYNDHURST. Hants.
                                        1st October 1914.

LEAVE.

     It is regretted that owing to orders received from the War Office, all furloughs must be cancelled and all Officers and men must be at once recalled from leave.

     Acknowledge receipt and report to this Office when personnel is complete.

                                 J. L. J. CLARKE, Lieut:Colonel,
                     A. A. & Q. M. G., 7th Division.

Issued at 5-35 p.m.

7th DIVISION ROUTINE-ORDERS No: 24.
****

Grand Hotel,
LYNDHURST. Hants.
1st October 1914.

GENERAL STAFF.

1. DIVISIONAL OPERATIONS. The Division will carry out Field Operations tomorrow 2nd October. The leading troops will start about 6 a.m. Operation Orders will be issued this afternoon.

All units will turn out as far as possible at War Establishment with the exception of such transport and personnel as may be required for Administrative purposes in connection with the Mobilization of the Division.

Haversack rations and feeds will be carried. Rifles are not to be loaded.

The principal object of the operations will be to practice the entrenchment of a Defensive Position; the full war equipment of entrenchment tools should therefore be carried as far as the available transport permits.

At the conclusion of operations units will close and await orders for the return march.

H. MONTGOMERY, Colonel,
General Staff.

ADMINISTRATIVE STAFF.

2. STATIONERY. To avoid delay, requisitions for
(a). Numbered Army Forms and Books,
(b). Stationery.
(c). Printing
should be made on separate forms or separate sheets of paper.
(Authority:- War Office memo dated 21/9/14.)

3. DUTIES. Brigade for duty tomorrow 2nd October '14 - 22nd Infantry Brigade.

4. REVOLVERS. Officers (actually under orders for the front) requiring revolvers, should apply through their Commanding Officers to the local Ordnance Officer. Telegraphic money orders in prepayment should not be used. Two money orders (No: 1548 Ashurst and No: 159 Lyndhurst) having been sent to Woodon without sufficient address, further details should be sent by post to identify those Orders.

5. INTERPRETERS. All the Interpreters attached to Units in the Division will report themselves to Lieutenant-Colonel Sir F.Ponsonby,K.C.V.O., C.B., at the Headquarters Camp this afternoon at 4 p.m.

J. L. J. CLARKE, Lieut: Colonel,
A. A. & Q. M. G., 7th Division.

NOTICES.
****

LOST. Bicycle No: 5444 with No: 7 and Blue and White band on rear mudguard.
FOUND. In lines of 2/R.Scots Fus, Field Telephone instrument. Enquire 21st Infty Bde Headquarters.
LOST. On Wednesday's Field Operations, a colt revolver in holster. Would finder kindly return to Orderly Room 2/Bedford Regt.

7th Division Routine Orders No: 24 (Continued).

****

>Grand Hotel,
>LYNDHURST. Hants.
>1st October 1914.

AFTER ORDERS.

6. FIELD DRESSINGS.

With reference to Routine Order No: 21 (7) dated 28th ultimo, Units can now obtain the field dressings indented for, from the Ordnance Officer, Lyndhurst.

Early application should be made.

7. HORSES.

With reference to para: 3 of Circular Memorandum dated 29th September 1914 on the subject of Horses, sick horses will be retained by Units until instructions are issued by the Assistant Director of Veterinary Services as to their disposal.

>J. L. J. CLARKE, Lieutenant Colonel,
>A. A. & Q. M. G., 7th Division.

Issued at 2 p.m.

7th DIVISIONAL ROUTINE ORDERS No: 25.
****

                                Grand Hotel,
                                  LYNDHURST. Hants.
                              2nd October 1914.

1. DUTIES.   Brigade for duty tomorrow, 3rd October - 20th Infantry Brigade.

2. BLANKETS.   One blanket per man will be taken oversea from those now in possession of Units. Surplus blankets will be handed in to Ordnance Officer, Lyndhurst Road Station.

                         J. L. J. CLARKE, Lieutenant Colonel,
                         A. A. & Q. M. G., 7th Division.

N O T I C E S.
****

L O S T.   On evening of 28th September 1914, a Heavy Draught mare, no number, might be with 2 Crupper Galls on back and gall from throat lash on gullet. Finder please report to O.C., 2nd Border Regiment.

L O S T.   Government Bicycle Mark 1V No: 5959 with 1/R.W.F. painted on front mud guard taken from Camp on 1st instant. Person in possession of same should return it forthwith to O.C., 1st Royal Welsh Fusiliers.

7th Division Routine Order No 25 (continued)

Lyndhurst,
2nd October, 1914.

AFTER ORDER.

GENERAL STAFF.

3. Standing Orders.

Divisional Standing Orders are being issued to all concerned. All Officers will make themselves acquainted with their contents and will be responsible that their men understand those portions which concern them.

Amendments required to complete or correct the Directory (pp 11-16) should be notified to Division Head Quarters without delay.

With reference to paras 8 and 9, the alteration in the rule of the road will only come into force on arrival abroad.

The following paras will only become operative on arrival abroad:- 2 (a), 14, 17, 35(b) & (c), 36.

In para 37(a) for "999" read "99".

H. MONTGOMERY, Colonel,
General Staff.

PRELIMINARY ORDERS FOR EVACUATION OF LYNDHURST AND

ASHURST CAMPS.
****

1.   Before departure Officers Commanding Units will
have all tents struck with the exception of those
required for details left behind and marquees in which
tents and camp equipment will be stacked. Brigade Area
Commanders and Officers Commanding Units are responsible
that their Camp sites are left thoroughly clean prior
to departure.

2.   Officers Commanding details left behind will
detail guards over all Government property in their
charge. The senior officer left behind in each Brigade
area will be responsible for all details and camps in his
Brigade area.

3.   The Ordnance and Supply depots will remain as
at present.

Lyndhurst.   J. L. J. CLARKE, Lieut:Colonel,
1/10/14.   A. A. & Q. M. G., 7th Division.

7th DIVISIONAL ROUTINE ORDERS No: 26.

Grand Hotel,
LYNDHURST. Hants.
3rd October 1914.

GENERAL STAFF.

1. TACTICAL NOTES.

Copies of a letter received from the front dealing with certain tactical points in the field is being circulated for the information of Units.

H. MONTGOMERY, Colonel,
General Staff.

ADMINISTRATIVE STAFF.

2. DUTIES.

Brigade for duty tomorrow, 4th October - 21st Infantry Brigade.

3. VOYAGE RATIONS.

All Units and drafts proceeding to join the Expeditionary Force, will be provided with rations for the voyage by the Embarkation Commandant at Southampton, who will also provide forage for the voyage for all horses embarking at that port.

Units and drafts will continue to take with them the unexpired portion of their rations for the day of entrainment, and 10 lbs of oats will be carried in the nose-bag of each horse for the journey to Southampton.

4. CAMP EQUIPMENT ACCOUNTS.

With reference to the "Preliminary Orders for evacuation of Lyndhurst and Ashurst Camps" - Camp equipment accounts on A.F.G.973 should be completed as far as possible and handed over, with all supporting vouchers, to the Officers Commanding details left at Home. This Officer will see that the balance of stores, as shown in the Army Form G.973 agrees with the stores actually taken over, as the responsibility for their correctness when handed over to incoming units, will rest with him.

5. CHURCH PARADE.

Church parades will be held tomorrow under arrangements to be made by Brigade Area Commanders.

The Reverend C.H. Compton, Vicar of Lyndhurst, will conduct the Church of England service in No: 1 Brigade Area at 10 a.m.

The Reverend J. Holley will conduct a Roman Catholic service near the Wilts camp at 9-30 a.m.

The Reverend Henderson will conduct a Presbyterian service in the 20th Brigade lines at 9-30 a.m.

6. EQUIPMENT.

Bags, ration will be drawn oversea.

7. KITS.

No kit beyond that carried on the man is to accompany troops proceeding overseas.

All surplus kit is to be handed over to O.C. details left at Home. (W.O. wire M.72 d/- 2/10/14.)

J. L. J. Clarke, Lieut Colonel,
A. A. & Q. M. G., 7th Division.

7th DIVISIONAL ROUTINE ORDERS No: 27.

Grand Hotel,
LYNDHURST. Hants.
4th October 1914.

GENERAL STAFF.

1. DIVISIONAL ROUTE MARCH.

The Division will carry out a route march on Monday under peace conditions. Each unit will parade and march in "Train Loads", (vide Table 'A' Instructions for Entrainment and Embarkation, Part 1). Orders will be issued later as to the order of march, route and times of starting. "Train Loads" will parade complete with all transport loaded as laid down in Field Service Manuals.

As the Column passes the Divisional General, at a point which will be named in orders, each "Train Load" Commander will fall out and report complete or otherwise.

The Officer Commanding any Unit which is unable to take part in this march will report the reason immediately.

H. MONTGOMERY, Colonel,
General Staff.

ADMINISTRATIVE STAFF.

2. DUTIES.

Brigade for duty tomorrow 5th Oct:'14 - 22nd Infantry Brigade.

3. SPARE KITS.

(i). No kit will be taken oversea beyond that carried by the man.

(ii). Units in possession of a second service dress suit and pair of boots will have them packed and despatched forthwith to the Army Ordnance Depot, Portsmouth.

(iii). The remainder of the spare kit mentioned in para: 2 of War Office letter No: 79/Stores/15 dated 21/8/14 issued herewith will also be despatched forthwith to Army Ordnance Depot, Portsmouth.

(iv). All other surplus baggage will be handed over to the Officer in charge details left at Home.

4. HORSES: SURPLUS.

No more horses are to be turned out in the field near the Grand Hotel.

Units will be able to dispose of surplus horses, before embarkation to the Remount Depot at Southampton: Until such time they must be retained in the Units lines.

5. PICQUET.

With reference to Routine Order No: 23 (6), the picquet therein ordered is no longer required.

J. L. J. CLARKE,
Lieutenant Colonel,
A. A. & Q. M. G., 7th Division.

7th DIVISIONAL ROUTINE ORDERS No: 29.

16th September 1914.

1. RETURNS AND STATES.

With reference to paragraphs 151 and 152 Field Service Regulations, Part 11, states of all casualties, killed, wounded, missing and sick will be furnished through the usual channels to Divisional Headquarters as soon as possible after the casualties occur.

Returns will be rendered direct by Units to the Adjutant General's Office at the base.

2. TRANSPORT.

Officers Commanding Units will take steps to ensure that only authorized loads are carried on wagons and carts.

3. CAPTURED HORSES.

Owing to prevalence of Glanders amongst German horses, all those captured from the enemy are to be inspected by a Veterinary Officer before being brought into the lines.

4. TRANSPORT ANIMALS, DEFICIENCIES IN.

Officers Commanding Units will report as soon as possible their deficiencies in transport animals.

5. ORDERS AND PAMPHLETS.

The undermentioned Orders and Pamphlets are issued herewith, viz:-
"4th Army Corps Routine Orders of 15/10/14."
"Extracts from Routine Orders, Adjutant General's Dept. G.H.Q."
"Extracts from Routine Orders, Quartermaster General's Dept."
"Miscellaneous information published with Routine Orders &c."
"Special memorandum re supplies".

6. WAR ESTABLISHMENTS.

Copies of War Establishments, 7th Division dated Oct: 1914 are also issued herewith.

C. J. PERCEVAL, Lieutenant Colonel,
A. A. & Q. M. G., 7th Division.

7yh DIVISIONAL ROUTINE ORDERS No: 28.
****

YPRES.
14th October 1914.

1. BILLETING.
(a). When occupying concentrated billets, regimental billeting parties of 1 Officers and 1 N.C.O. per Squadron, Battery, and Company, will march immediately in rear of the main guard.

(b). Brigade billeting areas will be indicated to troops before they enter those areas.
Staff Captains will arrange for all units and trains to be met at the point where they diverge from the line of march of the column and to be conducted to their respective billets without halt.

(c). While troops are moving into billets care must be taken not to block the line of march.

(d). The positions of Brigade Area H.Q. will be notified to Divisional Headquarters immediately they are fixed.

2. TRAINS.
Supply wagons should not be used to carry baggage and should arrive empty at the refilling point.
Supply, Baggage, and Blanket wagons form part of the Divisional Train. These vehicles should be ready to join their affiliated train companies at the starting point in the order of march of the Units.
Attention is drawn to paragraphs 24 and 25 Standing Orders 7th Division.

3. CASH.
Requirements in Cash for Officers and or men are to be notified through the ordinary channel. A demand will then be made by Divisional Headquarters.

4. MAILS.
Units will send a wagon tonight to Divisional Headquarters for Mails.

5. REMOUNTS.
If it is necessary to requisition for Horses this must be done through Headquarters.

C.J.PERCEVAL, Lieutenant Colonel,
A. A. & Q. M. G., 7th Division.
NOTICES.

LOST. 1 Officers green canvas valise. If found please return to Headquarters, 7th Division.

FOUND. A British warm coat with Captain's stars. Apply to 14th Horse Artillery Brigade.

7th DIVISIONAL ROUTINE ORDERS No: 50,

17th October 1914.

1. DISCIPLINE.

(i)   The General Officer Commanding holds every Officer responsible for preserving discipline in the field and requires every Officer to assist in the Regulations being adhered to, whether the troops are directly under his orders or not.

(ii).   Transport is to be kept closed up. Wagons breaking down are to be pulled to one side and are not to cause the Column to be stopped.

No man other than the Driver is to be allowed to ride on Wagons unless in possession of a written order from an Officer.

Wagons are to be kept on the RIGHT of the hard portion of the Road.

All men and horses must invariably be marched in the Column and not in the fairway, which must be kept perfectly clear when the Column is on the march and at the halt.

When off duty, all men will salute Officers as in peace time.

Guards, (as opposed to outposts) are expected to pay compliments.

Officers Commanding Units are to arrange for men to have steady drill daily even if for five minutes only.

Troops are to march at attention for the first five minutes after starting, for five minutes after every halt and when coming into billets and bivouac.

2. POST-CARDS.

Several cases having occurred of post cards having been despatched without any address of the person to whom they are sent being written on them, it must be clearly explained to the men that while the address from which the post cards are written must in no case be stated, all correspondence must naturally have the address of the person for whom it is intended plainly written on it.

3. BILLETING.

Brigade Area Billeting Officers when selecting billets for troops should always decide on a suitable spot as a place of assembly for train vehicles. They should allot Billets to the Army Service Corps Company in the Brigade Area as near to this place of assembly as possible. Units in the Brigade Area should be informed of the exact position of this place of assembly.

The Headquarters Company of the Train will when possible be billetted near Divisional Headquarters.

Units are responsible for conducting their own vehicles to and from this place of assembly.

C. J. PERCEVAL, Lieutenant-Colonel,
A. A. & Q. M. G., 7th Division.

N O T I C E.

LOST.   A Brown leather dispatch case
"Adjutant,
    King Edwards Horse,
        Duke of Yorks H.Qrs,
            Chelsea"
stamped on it.   Finder please return same to Divisional Hdqrs.

7th DIVISIONAL ROUTINE ORDERS No: 31.

18th October 1914.

1. ORDNANCES SERVICES.

(i) No Stores or Vehicles are to be purchased or requisitioned, except under very special circumstances, by anyone but the D.A.D.O.S.,

When Stores are requisitioned by an Officer other than the D.A.D.O.S., he will forward the duplicate and triplicate receipt notes to that Officer, together with an Indent for the Stores, if an Indent has not already been put forward.

When an Officer other than the D.A.D.O.S., makes minor purchases, he must forward a list of the articles purchased with a receipt of the amount paid to the D.A.D.O.S. This list must bear a certificate that the articles have been received and are fit for the Service. The D.A.D.O.S., will satisfy himself that the transaction is correct, will certify to that effect and return the document to the Officer who effected the purchase.

Repayment of the money thus expended will, be made by the Field Cashier on production of this certified document.

A similar procedure will be adopted in the case of all repairs for which payment is made.

(ii) Indents to replace unserviceable Stores, losses and upkeep to be rendered to the D.A.D.O.S., by 7.a.m. the 20th instant.

Indents will be rendered in triplicate on the proper form.

It is published for information that, except in case of urgency, replenishment of Equipment and Stores will be made periodically at intervals and dates to be ordered by D.O.S., G.H.Q.

Equipment and Stores are sent to the Railhead from the Ordnance Advanced Base, these are conveyed in lorries to the Rendezvous or Refilling Point, where C.Os will make arrangements for representatives to take over consignments of Stores for their Units from the D.A.D.O.S., these stores will be loaded in the Supply Section of the Train for delivery to Units.

As Troops cannot march and fight without Boots, Horse Shoes, Clothing, etc., it is imperative that Commanding Officers forsee the wants of the Units under their Command and put forward Indents in good time to meet all requirements.

2. WEEKLY RETURNS.

In future Army Form B.213 (in duplicate) will be rendered to Divisional Headquarters by 12 noon on Fridays and not direct to the Adjutant General's Office at the Base.

3. MEMORANDUM.

Attention is directed to "Instructions regarding the Services of Maintenance for the guidance of the 3rd Cavalry Division and 4th Corps", copies of which are circulated herwith.

C.J.PERCEVAL, Lieut:-Colonel,
A. A. & Q. M. G., 7th Division.

Instructions regarding the Services of Maintenance for the
Guidance of the 3rd Cavalry Division and 4th Corps.
****

SUPPLIES. 1.   Troops when on the march will be in possession of the
following rations :-
    (a). On the man.   The Iron Ration and any portion of the
                              current days ration not carried in the
                              vehicle for cooks.

    (b). In the Cooks') The current days food less any portion
         vehicle.   ) carried on the man.

    (c). In the Supply)
         Section of   ) Food for the following day.
         the train.   )
         (7th Divn.)   )

2.   Divisional Supply Columns will have allotted to them
transport on the following scale :-
    For Supplies......................27 lorries.
    For the conveyance of)
       Ordnance Stores   )
       from the railhead)......... 3   "
       for the day.   )
    For Postal Services............. 1 lorry.
    For Petrol...................... 1   "
    Workshops and Stores............ 4 lorries.
    Spare for reliefs............... 4   "
                         TOTAL......... 40 lorries.

3.   Supply Columns will be regarded as Corps Troops - or as
Divisional Troops in the case of Divisions acting independently -
and Corps, or Divisions, as the case may be, will, unless orders
are issued by G.H.Q. to the contrary, be responsible for all
movements of these columns between railheads and the troops,
and will accordingly fix their own rendezvous.

4.   Hay, wood and vegetables should be purchased whenever
possible. Requisitioning should only be resorted to when -
    (a).The vendor is unwilling to sell.
    (b).The price cannot be agreed upon, in which case the
        price demanded by the vendor and the estimated fair
        price will be clearly stated on the requisitioning
        note.
    (c).When the amount of money required to complete the
        purchase is so large that the necessary sum is not
        available.
    In all cases initials, name and rank of the requisitioning
officer should be plainly recorded.

5.   Rum will be issued twice weekly on Mondays and Thursdays.
A more frequent issue can be arranged for on demand to A.D.S.,
G.H.Q.. Tobacco will be issued once a week on Saturdays.
    A stock of medical comforts will be kept at Railheads and
can be drawn upon as required.

AMMUNITION: 6. Each Corps and each Cavalry Division in the Army is
definitely allotted one Ammunition Park, and the latter will be
controlled and dealt with in the same way as the Supply Columns.
Unallotted Divisional Ammunition Parks constitute a reserve
under the control of G.H.Q. They are used to replace
                                            casualties

casualties in the Cavalry Divisional and Corps Parks, and are available to be drawn upon in case of urgency if the Cavalry Divisional and Corps Parks are unable to replenish from Ammunition railhead. The usual procedure, however, will be to replenish from the ammunition railhead and not from the Reserve Ammunition Parks.

ORDNANCE STORES. 7. The three lorries allotted to each Divisional Supply Column to convey Ordnance Stores from Supply railheads are to be used for that purpose alone.

8. All indents for stores must be sent to the Divisional Ordnance Officer concerned. Indents from Corps Headquarters and Army Troops must be sent to the Ordnance Officer, 7th Division.

9. All purchases or requisitioning of stores should be affected through the Ordnance Officer. All stores should be paid for on the spot, and requisitioning only resorted to in cases of extreme urgency when purchase is clearly impossible.

10. All surplus stores, including those which owing to loss of personnel or horses can no longer be made use of, will be returned to railhead under Divisional arrangements and handed over to the R.T.O. for conveyance to the Advanced Base.

11. A store of barbed wire, sandbags, entrenching tools and demolition explosives are kept with the ammunition train, and can be drawn upon when required.

12. The issue of a blanket per man has been authorized, and transport for the conveyance of the same in infantry units may be provided from local sources on the scale of 2 vehicles per battalion, if government transport is not available.

VETERINARY. 13. Sick horses which have to be despatched to the veterinary hospitals on the L. of C. should be sent to the Supply railhead for entrainment in the empty Supply Railway trains.

(Signed) W. R. ROBERTSON.

Q. M. G.

14th October 1914.

7th DIVISIONAL ROUTINE ORDERS No: 33.
****

23rd October 1914.
****

1. AMMUNITION BOXES.

Units will make every endeavour to return empty Ammunition Boxes of all natures which are in a serviceable condition as soon as possible to Refilling Point from whence they will be forwarded by empty Supply Train to Base.

2. VEHICLES.

Spare and serviceable parts of all vehicles abandoned owing to break-down or damage should be recovered as far as possible and sent to Supply Column to take to Railhead, the Railway Transport Officer to be notified. This Officer will forward all spare stores &c. to the Ordnance Advanced Base.

3. HORSES.

The General Officer Commanding wishes the greatest attention paid to Horsemanship as to neglect of this is attributable a large proportion of horse wastage. Whenever possible men must dismount and so rest their horses.

Officers Commanding Units are responsible that unfit horses are not left about the country. These cases are to be reported to the Veterinary Officer who will arrange for their disposal.

4. TRAIN VEHICLES.

In future the Train Vehicles of the Northumberland Hussars are to be considered part of Divisional Headquarters and when on the march will march with Divisional Headquarters.

5. S T O R E S.

The following articles are in 7th Division Ammunition Park, viz:- 100 picks, 200 shovels, 1000 Sandbags, 30 coils Barbed wire.

R.F.A.HOBBS,   Captain,

D. A. A. & Q. M. G., 7th Division.

7th DIVISIONAL ROUTINE ORDERS No: 34.
****

27th October 1914.

1. DISCIPLINE.

Numerous cases having occurred in which houses occupied by British Troops have been ransacked and much other damage done, it must be remembered that at present our Troops are operating in the country of our Allies and Commanding Officers must take the necessary steps to prevent any damage being done.

If there is any recurrence of the state of affairs already reported, ks the General Officer Commanding will take the strongest disciplinary measures.

2. SANITATION.

The General Officer Commanding wishes to draw the attention of all concerned to the necessity of exercising the strictest supervision over the sanitary condition of their respective areas.

Water to be used for drinking purposes should invariably be boiled or made into Tea. Water bottles should be filled as far as is possible in the evening.

3. RETURNS.

Awards of punishment should not be shown on the reverse of Army Form B.213 but cases of detention and imprisonment should be shown on the reverse of Army Form B.2069.

Appointments to Lance Corporal should not be shown on the reverse of Army Form B.213.

Army Form B.213 must be rendered as punctually as circumstances admit.

4. AIRCRAFT.

All obviously hostile aircraft will be fired at. No aircraft will be fired at without the order of an Officer. Officers must make quite sure they have identified Aircraft as hostile before giving the order to fire. Aeroplanes observing for our own Artillery signal by dropping Lights which might be mistaken for Bombs.

Cases having recently occurred where our own Troops have fired on British Aeroplanes, Commanding Officers are responsible that this order is communicated to every man under their Command

5. ORDNANCE SERVICES.

Indents are to be rendered to the D.A.D.O.S. by the 10th proximo for the following articles:-

Undervests, woollen.)	
Drawers, woollen.)	
Gloves, worsted.)	For all troops.
Belts, flannel.)	
Scarves, woollen.)	
Boots, Canadian.	For mounted troops only at the rate of 10 per cent.
Gloves, large without fingers.	For Infantry Only.
Shoes.)	
Spats.)	
Stockings, worsted.)	For Cyclists only.
Coats, British warm.)	
Capes, mackintosh.)	

(7th Divisional Routine Orders No: 34. Continued Sheet 2.)

Gloves, leather, wool lined)	For Motor Drivers and
Gauntlets.)	Cyclists.
Sweaters.	For Motor drivers only.

6. SUPPLIES.
a.   All Units will make a demand to the Senior Supply Officer to complete their Iron Rations.
b.   Frequent cases have occurred where supply wagons have not reached their Unit and the men in charge say they have been turned back by an Officer. In future a written order must be obtained from this Officer that he has turned the wagon back and no other excuse will be accepted. This does not of course mean that wagons are to pass the outpost line. When a wagon cannot find its Unit the N.C.O. or Man in charge should report at once to his Brigade Headquarters or to Divisional Headquarters.

7. CENSOR STAMPS.
    Personal receipts for 'passed by censor' stamps have not been sent to the War Office as requested when the original issue was made.

    Units issued with such stamps are requested to report at once direct to Divisional Headquarters the number of their stamp.

R.F.A.HOBBS,   Captain,

D. A. A. & Q. M. G., 7th Division.

7th DIVISIONAL ROUTINE ORDERS No. 35.

28th October 1914.

1. CASH.

Cash can be drawn at any time from the Field Cashier, 4th Army Corps, Hotel de Ville, Ypres.

2. APPOINTMENTS.

Lieutenant-Colonel C.M.Ryan, D.S.O., Army Service Corps, now commanding 7th Divisional Train, to be A.A. Q.M.G., 7th Division, vice Lieutenant-Colonel C.J. Perceval, D.S.O. (wounded). Dated 23rd October 1914.)
(Army Routine Order No: 246.(iii) dated 26th Oct: 1914.)

3. REINFORCEMENTS.

Owing to the notifications from Units of deficiencies in their personnel having reached the D.A.G. 3rd Echelon, G.H.Q. at the Base by various methods and often only after a long lapse of time, overlapping of demands and delay in replacement have been caused.

The last two sentences in paragraph 1 of the memorandum issued with Army Routine Orders of September 23rd will be deleted and the following substituted:-

"Demands to replace casualties and normal wastage
"due to sickness, etc., will be submitted by formations
"in the first instance, to the Adjutant General,
"General Headquarters, by whom they will be passed
"to the D.A.G., 3rd Echelon, G.H.Q. at the Base.
"Units on the L. of C. will submit demands for
"personnel due to normal wastage direct to D.A.G.
"3rd Echelon, G.H.Q. at the Base."
(Army Routine Order No: 248 dated 26/10/14.).

4. PRISONERS OF WAR.

Any communications which German Prisoners of War in the hands of the Corps at the front may request permission to make to their relatives in Germany (prior to their being despatched to the Lines of Communication) should, if approved, be forwarded officially under cover to the D.A.G., 3rd Echelon, G.H.Q. at the Base for transmission, in due course, to the War Office.
(Army Routine Orders No: 249 dated 26/10/14.)

5. REQUISITIONING.

Requisition Order Books and Requisition Receipt Books are now available for issue. Application should be made to the Senior Supply Officer. Para: 2 of Instructions is on no account to be complied with except on the Duplicate Copy. The number on the outside of each book should be entered on each form for purposes of reference. The name of the Officers to whom these books are to be issued will accompany the application.

6. ORDNANCE SERVICES.

Any of the following stores which may become damaged beyond local repair are to be returned to the Railhead as early as possible for conveyance to the Advanced
P.T.O.

Advanced Base:-
    Dial Sights No: 7.
    Carriers - do -
    Directors No: 3.
    Carriages 15 & 18 pr.

7. CLOTHING &c. ON REPAYMENT TO OFFICERS.
    a.   Anything can be obtained on payment.
    b.   Officers who have lost Equipment at the Front and not in a position to pay cash can obtain without payment, but a list of names and articles issued must be recorded and sent to Ordnance, Advanced Base.
            This record is required to enable the Chief Paymaster to either demand payment later on or to check claims for compensation which may be preferred later on.

                        R.F.A.HOBBS, Captain,
                        D. A. A. & Q. M. G., 7th Division.

7th DIVISIONAL ROUTINE ORDERS No: 36.
****

4th November 1914.

1. ACQUITTANCE ROLLS.
    In rendering Acquittance Rolls, Officers should be careful to see that the Rolls sent to the Base are legible. The mens' signatures must be taken, and the whole distinctly written. In the case of the Royal Artillery, Royal Engineers and Army Service Corps, the battery or company must be stated.
(Army Routine Order No: 251 of 29th October 1914.)

2. TELEGRAPHIC ADDRESS.
    The telegraphic address of Headquarters Requisition Office, I.G.C. is "REQUISITION, c/o COMMUNICATIONS" and that of the Central Requisition Office is "REQUISITION BASE".
(Army Routine Order No: 232 of 29th October 1914.)

3. HORSE SHOES.
    Horse Shoes and Nails will be supplied by Ordnance, Advanced Base in bulk. Commanding Officers will make arrangements for representatives to draw these from the Rendezvous or Refilling Point. Indents are not required.
    It will be notified in orders when the first consignment, which is on its way, will arrive.

4. ORDNANCE SERVICES.
    Number twelve wheels should be used for sixty pounder and four point seven carriages and number ten wheels for the limbers as far as possible.

5. BOOKS - DEVOTIONAL.
    The War Office has authorized the issue of a Prayer Book for Jewish Soldiers. These can be obtained through Chaplains from the Principal Chaplain, 3rd Echelon, to whom a consignment has been sent for distribution.

R. F. A. HOBBS,   Captain,
D. A. A. & Q. M. G., 7th Division.

7th DIVISIONAL ROUTINE ORDERS No: 57.

BAILLEUL.
7th November 1914.

1. PASSES.

(i). Passes for inhabitants of BAILLEUL who work or live just outside the town have the name 'BAILLEUL' in red ink written at the top. These passes are to be accepted without the signature of the A.P.M.

(ii). Passes for HAZEBROUCK and other places to the West of the line POPERINGHE - BAILLEUL - ESTAIRES will be signed by the Major and do not require an additional signature unless they are passes to return to BAILLEUL or are passes authorizing bearer to proceed by motor, carriage or bicycle.

(iii). Passes to proceed in any other direction will require the countersignature of an A.P.M.

(iv). All civilians must be within the area of their villages or towns by 6 p.m. and within their houses by 8 p.m. where they must remain until 6 a.m. unless in possession of a pass signed by an A.P.M.

2. SHOPS.&c.

All Cafes, Estaminets and Shops are to be cleared and closed by 8-30 p.m. and all men except those on duty are to be in their billets at that hour.

3. LIGHTS.

The lights in all houses occupied by Civilians are to be masked by shutters or blinds.

4. WATER.

The Town Water supply is only turned on between the hours of 6 a.m. and 9 a.m., and 5 p.m. to 7 p.m.

5. COMMISSIONS

When Warrant or Non-commissioned Officers are granted Commissions in any other Army Corps they should proceed to the Railhead, if known, of their new Corps and thence to their new Unit by Supply Columns. When the Railhead is not known they should be directed to report to G.H.Q. for instructions.

6. PERIODICAL RETURNS.

7th Divisional Routine Order No: 32(1) of 19th October 1914 is republished for information, viz:-
" The following periodical returns will be rendered by
"G.Os.C. and Os.O. concerned on the dates &c. specified, viz:-

"A.F.B.213.	Field Return.	Every Friday by 12 noon & after an action (in duplicate).
"A.F.B.2069.	Offence Report.	Every Friday by 12 noon.
"A.F.B.158.	Nominal Roll of Officers.	Last day of each month by 12 noon.(in duplicate).

"M.S.

"M.S. " " "	Daily return	By 12 noon daily.	)Officers by)name, other)ranks by No:)in Regiments.
"M.S. " " " " "	Report of enemy's casualties & prisoners, vehicles, animals &c. captured.	Daily report by 12 noon.	
"A.F.B.231. " " " " "	Field State.	5 p.m. on Sundays. (vide para: 56 Standing Orders for 7th Divn.)."	

Efforts must be made to ensure that these returns are rendered with greater punctuality.

7. REVOLVERS.

It has been brought to notice that some Officers have proceeded on Active Service armed with Colts .45 Calibre Automatic Pistols for which ammunition is not available in the A.O.D.

Provided the numbers of Officers in possession of these pistols is not excessive, endeavours will be made to arrange to send out that quantity of Webley & Scott Revolvers for issue to Officers on repayment.

The names of Officers requiring revolvers should be submitted to the Divisional Ordnance Officer as early as possible, who will demand the numbers required from the Advanced Base.

R. F. A. Hobbs, Captain,

D. A. A. & Q. M. G., 7th Division,

7th DIVISIONAL ROUTINE ORDERS No: 38.

BAILLEUL.
8th November 1914.

1. CENSOR STAMPS.

Units will report at once the serial number of Censor stamps in their possession.

If any stamps have been lost, this fact must be reported at once giving the serial number.

2. REINFORCEMENTS.

Units will report the arrival of all reinforcements giving names of Officers and numbers of other ranks.

3. CASH.

Until other arrangements are made, Units will obtain cash from the nearest Cashier.

4. COURT MARTIAL.

No: 5919 Private Edward Tanner, 1st Battalion, The Wiltshire Regiment, was tried by a Field General Court Martial for "Desertion".

The sentence of the Court was to suffer "Death by being shot."

The sentence was duly carried out at 7.10 a.m. on 29th October 1914.
(Army Routine Order No: 284 dated 5th November 1914.)

5. SIGNAL SERVICE - DESPATCH RIDERS.

When messages in closed envelopes are handed in at a Signal Office and marked "URGENT", it means that a Despatch Rider is to be sent with the message at once, whether by day or night. To check the number of messages so sent, they must be signed on the outside of the envelope by an Officer who is authorized to send "Priority" messages. Messages which are marked "Ordinary" will be sent as opportunity offers, which is usually in daylight, within a few hours.
(Army Routine Order No: 285 dated 5th November 1914.)

6. REFILLING POINT.

Refilling Point for the 9th November 1914 is at the same place and time as that on the 8th instant.

7. REQUISITION RECEIPT NOTES.

Reference Field Service Regulations, Part II, Appendix IV, para: 7, in future, officers signing requisition forms will give their rank as well as their name on the original requisition receipt note.

The unit or force of the requisitioning officer will, in no circumstances, be shown on the original requisition note, but will be inserted by him on the duplicate and triplicate notes.

Consequently, this information will not be given in the Belgian Army Forms when used by the British Forces, and Forms 3, 8, and 11 should be amended by deleting "Footnote 1" and the word "Corps" from footnote 2.

R.F.A. Hobbs, Captain,
D.A.A. & Q.M.G., 7th Division.

7th DIVISIONAL ROUTINE ORDERS No: 38.

BAILLEUL.
9th November 1914.

1. APPOINTMENTS.

Major A.B.E.Cator, Scots Guards is granted the temporary rank of Lieutenant-Colonel while acting in Command of the 20th Infantry Brigade.

2. PERIODICAL RETURNS.

With reference to Routine Order No: 37 (3) of the 7th November 1914, for "Daily Return" substitute "Daily Return of deaths, injuries, missing &c., together with statement showing detail of reinforcements received."

3. HORSES.

The Mobile Veterinary Section will take over sick horses daily at 10 a.m. on the Menin Road just outside Bailloul. Distinguishing flag of Mobile Section: Red with White inverted triangle.

4. CASH.

(a) The Field Cashier will attend at Divisional Head Quarters to-morrow at 10 a.m. Units requiring cash should send representatives to Divisional Headquarters at that hour to draw same.

(b). Advances of cash cannot be made to Officers through Imprest Accounts.

Officers requiring cash advances should either draw same personally from the Field Cashier or where a number of Officers is involved, one Officer may draw the total amount in bulk on presentation of a <u>receipted</u> form as detailed below, viz:-

Rank & Name.	Corps.	Agents.	Amount. £ s d	Receipt.

5. GLANDERS AND FARCY.

A report has been received to the effect that a serious outbreak of glanders exists amongst the horses of certain units of the German Army.

It is, therefore, necessary that measures should be taken to safeguard the horses of our Army.

The danger will be greater when an advance is made over territory previously occupied by the German Forces.

The usual sources of infection, and precautionary measures to be taken are given below:-

(1). <u>Abandoned or Stray Horses</u>:- These are frequent subjects of the disease, and should not be picked up and made use of until inspected by a Veterinary Officer, and Mallein Test applied.

(2). <u>Captured Horses</u>:- (Paragraph 117, Field Service Regns, Part II). Even though apparently in good health should be similarly dealt with before being drafted to Units.

(3). <u>Enquiry from Local Authorities</u>:- This should always be done to determine if the disease is known to exist, or has existed in their areas.

(4). <u>Billeting</u>:- Whenever the situation admits, it is better to picket horses in the open, avoiding dirty stables, cow-sheds

P.T.O.

cow-sheds and locations showing evidence of occupation by the enemy, and probable contamination.

(5). Feeding:- The mangers and racks of such stables are most dangerous, and should be left severely alone. It is not practicable to clean them. Feeding should be from nose-bags (corn) and from the ground (hay).

(3). Watering:- The common water troughs of villages and towns and of stable yards are fruitful sources of danger, and should be avoided. If their use is absolutely necessary, they should be thoroughly cleaned and disinfected. Advantage should constantly be taken of streams, and, when none are available, watering by bucket should be resorted to as much as possible. (Army Routine Order No: 289 of 6th November 1914.)

R. F. A. HOBBS, Captain,

D. A. A. & Q. M. G., 7th Division.

7th DIVISIONAL ROUTINE ORDERS No: 40.

BAILLEUL.
10th November 1914.

1. Ordnance Stores.

It has been brought to notice that Units have demanded special stores and articles in excess of the authorized scales of equipment laid down in Mobilization Store Tables.

As provision and supply in above cases will not be proceeded with by Lines of Communication without approval having been previously obtained from G.H.Q., it is necessary that such special requirements should be referred to G.H.Q. through Divisional Headquarters for decision of Q.M.G. before indents are submitted by Units to Divisional Ordnance Officer.

2. Harness and Saddlery.

It is observed that Units are in the habit of demanding small component parts of Harness and Saddlery. In view of the fact that considerable quantities are being delivered daily by Units at Refilling Point for return to Base, Units prior to formulating demands as above should instruct their representatives to make enquiries at the Refilling Point, as it may frequently be possible to make up the deficiencies of one unit from the surplus of another.

3. Arms and Equipment.

A very considerable and, with proper supervision, quite avoidable wastage having taken place in the matter of Arms and Equipment &c. belonging to Units, the following procedure will be adopted, viz:-

(a). The arms and equipment of sick and wounded will be taken with them to Hospital.
(b). Arms and equipment left in the trenches or on the field will be collected by Units, cleaned and re-issued.
(c). Equipment surplus to Unit requirements will be sent in empty supply wagons to Refilling Point. Thence it will be conveyed to Base per arrangements to be made by Ordnance Officer.

4. Horses.

All Units in possession of horses captured from the enemy will report numbers to the A.D.V.S. as soon as possible so that the horses may be subjected to the Malloin Test for Glanders.

5. Appointments.

(i). Captain L.C.Jackson, Adjutant 1st Divisional Engineers to be G.S.O., 3rd Grade, 7th Division, vice Captain W.S.Douglas (severely wounded). Dated 3rd November 1914.
(ii). Major C.K.Morgan, R.A.M.C. joined the 7th Division on the 7th instant for duty as Deputy Assistant Director of Medical Services vice Lieutenant-Colonel S.Guise Moores, R.A.M.C. transferred to the 1st Division as Assistant Director of Medical Services.

6. Discipline.

Attention is directed to Circular Memorandum re Discipline, copies of which are issued herewith.

R. F. A. HOBBS, Captain,

D. A. A. & Q. M. G., 7th Division.

7th DIVISIONAL ROUTINE ORDERS No: 41.
****

BAILLEUL.
11th November 1914.

1. MEDICAL.

A dentist has been sent to each Clearing Hospital. Officers requiring dental services should be enabled to attend.
(4th Army Routine Order No: 71 dated 10th Nov:14.)

2. FUEL.

1. Fuel for offices which are stationary is hereby authorized at the scale of 125 lbs coal per fireplace per week.

2. Fuel for General and other Headquarter Offices and Signalling Offices with the troops, is authorised at the scale of 18 Kilos of coal per fireplace per day.

3. A certificate as to the number of fireplaces for which fuel is demanded will be given on the requisition for fuel.

4. Fuel wood may be drawn in lieu of coal at the equivalent of 2 lbs Wood for 1 lb coal (vide para: 240 Allowance Regulations).
(Army Routine Order No: 271 of 1st Nov: 1914.)

3. ARMS.

The attention of Officers Commanding Units is drawn to the necessity for seeing that the rifles of the Unit under their Command are kept in good condition.

If mud and grit are allowed to remain on the rifles, the action is bound to suffer and jams may occur.
(Army Routine Order No: 273 of 1st November 1914.)

4. ORDNANCE SERVICES.

Until further orders Ordnance stores will be issued at No: 5 Rue St Jacques between the hours of 8 a.m. and 4 p.m. All Quartermasters will attend to draw stores for their Units. In the case of Units who have not Quartermasters, the Quartermaster Sergeants will attend.

R. F. A. HOBBS, Captain,
D. A. A. & Q. M. G., 7th Division.

7th DIVISIONAL ROUTINE ORDERS No: 42.

BAILLEUL.
12th November 1914.

1. TRAFFIC.

In consequence of a change of Railheads the following instructions for regulating the traffic between HAZEBROUCK and BAILLEUL are issued:-

Transport going WEST to East will use the road) HAZEBROUCK - BORRE - STRAZEELE.

Transport returning from EAST to WEST will use the road) METEREN - FLETRE - CAESTRE - HAZEBROUCK.

Transport returning from MERRIS NEUF BERQUIN will use the road) South of the Railway by PETIT SEC BOIS.

2. RETURNS.

Officers Commanding Units will render to the "D.M.S., Communications" direct, a return giving strength in Officers and other ranks and showing the numbers in each class who have been inoculated against Enteric Fever.

3. PROMOTION.

The following extract from Army Routine Order No: 295 of 9th November 1914 is published for information.

X   X   X   X   X

" The undermentioned Non-commissioned Officers (Motor "Cyclists, Royal Engineers) to be temporary Second Lieutenants. "Dated 1st November 1914.:-
"   INFANTRY.
"2nd Bn Nottinghamshire and Derbyshire Regiment.:-
"   No: 28754 Sergeant C. Triscott.   "

X   X   X   X   X

4. CENSORS.

With reference to Army Routine Order No: 217 of the 20th October 1914, giving a revised list of persons to whom "Passed by Censor" stamps are to be issued, any Units therein mentioned who have not yet received their Censor stamps should apply by wire to the Base Stationery Depot for one to be sent.
(Army Routine Order No: 296 of 9th November 1914.)

5. RATIONS.

When meat and vegetable rations are issued in lieu of bacon, the issue will be at the rate of one tin for four rations of bacon.
(Army Routine Order No: 299 of 9th November 1914.)

6. PASSES - UNAUTHORIZED PERSONS.

Unauthorized persons of both sexes continue to land in this country and to proceed into the zone occupied by the British Army in the Field.

In future, any person not subject to military law who is not in possession of a pass signed personally by the Adjutant General, British Army in the Field, or the Inspector General of Communications, and who is found in the zone occupied by the British Army in the Field, or East of a line drawn from Calais to Paris, will be arrested and detained until

P.T.O.

instructions are received from General Headquarters as to disposal.

No passports, safe-conducts, "laisser-passer" or documents of any description will be recognised.
(Army Routine Order No: 281 of 5th November 1914.)

7. MILITARY PRISON IN THE FIELD.

A Military Prison has now been established at Havre, and men under sentence of Penal Servitude or Imprisonment should be committed there when more convenient than Nantes.
(Army Routine Order No: 282 of 5th November 1914.)

8. RATION ALLOWANCE - French Interpreters.

An allowance of 1.50 fr. per meal for French soldier-interpreters accompanying officers on motor journeys is authorized.

Authority:- W.O. letter No: 121/621 (A.M.G.F.a.) dated 25th October 1914.

The amounts should be claimed by the Officers concerned, and included on their own travelling claim.
(Army Routine Order No: 283 of 5th November 1914.)

9. RETURNS.

Some misunderstanding appears to exist as to the correct method of making out the Field States.

The numbers shown on the fighting strength should include all ranks with the exception of sick men, men actually detailed to march with the Train and Train drivers.

10. ORDNANCE SERVICES.

With reference to Routine Order No: 54(5) dated 27th October 1914, supply of Shoes, Stockings and Spats for Cyclists is not approved. Supply of the remaining articles with the exception of flannel belts will not be made until ordered by Q.M.G.

11. REFILLING.

Until further orders refilling will take place at 8 a.m.

12. ISSUE OF FROST COGS FOR HORSE SHOES.

During the Winter months, shoes horse, which have been tapped with screw holes for Frost Cogs will entirely replace the ordinary shoes.

Frost cogs will be enclosed in all boxes containing horse shoes which have been tapped with screw holes, and will be packed in canvas bags in the correct proportions to allow all the shoes with which packed to be fitted with one set of cogs and in addition, a few spare.

The fitting of the cogs will be carried out regimentally, and for this purpose the following will be supplied:-

Taps 3/8 inch = 1)
" ½ " = 1) For each Farrier and Shoeing-Smith.
Wrenches = 1)

In addition the following proportions will be supplied for 25% of the strength of the horses (to be carried by the man):-

Cavalry horses..	R.A., R.E., A.S.C. & Infty Tpt Horses
Taps 3/8 inch)	Taps 3/8 inch 25%
" ½ ") 100%	" ½ " 75%
Wrenches.)	Wrenches. 100%

The

Sheet 2.

The wrenches are suitable for either size of cogs. In shoes horse, size 1 to 7 inclusive, the holes are to be tapped to 5/8" pitch, and in all other sizes to ½" pitch.

Indents for shoes, horse, with frost cogs, should be submitted to Ordnance Advanced Base through the channels referred to in Routine Order No: 278 as early as possible.

Shoes fitted with cogs, together with taps, and wrenches can be carried in the shoe cases, or as may be found convenient.
(Army Routine Order No: 301 of 10th November 1914.)

Reference above, Indents should be submitted to Divisional Ordnance Officer for transmission to Ordnance Advanced Base as early as possible.

12. RATIONS.

It has been observed in checking Field States that the demands for Rations are in some cases in excess of these numbers. As a rule there should be no difficulty in indenting for the correct number but if Units find they have indented for too many rations the matter must be adjusted when putting in the next demand.

13. GENERAL COURT MARTIAL.

The detail of Officers as mentioned below will assemble at 9 Rue de Lille, BAILLEUL at 11 a.m. on the 13th day of November 1914, for the purpose of trying by a General Court Martial ▓▓▓▓▓▓▓▓▓▓▓▓▓▓▓▓▓▓▓▓▓▓▓▓▓▓▓▓▓▓▓▓▓ and such other person or persons as may be brought before them.

PRESIDENT.

Colonel (Temporary Brigadier General) R.J.Pinney, Commanding 23rd Infantry Brigade, is appointed President.

MEMBERS.

Four members to be detailed by the G.O.C. 8th Division, not to be under the rank of Field Officer.

JUDGE ADVOCATE.

Major A.C.Daly, West Yorkshire Regiment, A.A. & Q.M.G. 7th Division, is appointed Judge Advocate.

The accused will be warned and all witnesses duly required to attend.

14. APPOINTMENTS.
(a).   Major A.C.Daly, West Yorkshire Regiment, has been appointed A.A. & Q.M.G., 7th Division and assumed his duties on 11th instant.
(b).   Captain H.Sponder Clay has been appointed A.D.C. to G.O.C., 7th Division and assumed his duties on 5th instant.

R. F. A. Hobbs, Captain,

D. A. A. & Q. M. G., 7th Division.

7th DIVISIONAL ROUTINE ORDER No: 42. (Continued).

BAILLEUL.
12th November 1914.

AFTER ORDER.

15. GENERAL COURT MARTIAL.

(1). Routine Order No: 13 of today is cancelled.

(2). The detail of Officers mentioned below will assemble at 9 Rue de Lille, BAILLEUL, at 11 a.m. on the 13th day of November 1914, for the purpose of trying by a General Court Martial, ▇▇▇▇▇▇▇▇▇▇▇▇▇▇▇▇▇▇ ▇▇▇▇▇▇, and such other person or persons as may be brought before them.

PRESIDENT.

Colonel (temporary Brigadier General) F.C.Carter, C.B., Commanding 24th Infantry Brigade, is appointed President.

MEMBERS.

Four members to be detailed by the G.O.C., 8th Division, not to be under the rank of Field Officer.

JUDGE ADVOCATE.

Major A.C.Daly, West Yorkshire Regiment, A.A. & Q.M.G., 7th Division is appointed Judge Advocate.

The accused will be warned and all witnesses duly required to attend.

R.F.A.HOBBS, Captain,
D.A.A. & Q.M.G., 7th Division.

7th DIVISIONAL ROUTINE ORDERS No: 45.

BAILLEUL.
15th November 1914.

1. APPOINTMENTS.

Colonel A.R.Hoskins, D.S.O. has been appointed General Staff Officer, 1st Grade, 7th Division, vice Colonel H.Montgomery transferred to 8th Division, and assumed his duties on 12th instant.

2. COURTS-MARTIAL.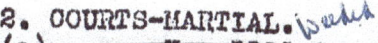

3. ORDNANCE SERVICES.

It must be clearly understood that Ordnance stores are to be demanded from the D.A.D.O.S. by indent or message only. Cases have occurred where lists of deficiencies of stores have been rendered to the D.A.D.O.S. and indents submitted afterwards for the same stores, causing duplication of supplies. When stores have once been demanded they should not be re-demanded, but may be hastened, a reference to the number and date of indent or message being quoted.

4. COMMISSIONS.

Commanding Officers of Royal Artillery and Regular Infantry Units will submit through the usual channels the names of any Non-commissioned Officers and men whom they recommend for attachment as probationary 2nd Lieutenants to Infantry battalions of this Division.
Those probationers, if favourably reported on will be recommended for promotion to the rank of 2nd Lieutenant.

R. F. A. HOBBS, Captain,
D. A. A. & Q. M. G., 7th Division.

N O T I C E.

LOST near BAILLEUL a dark brown gelding, marked I A.S.C. (clipped) on off hind quarter. Branded 39 on off hind hoof. Will finder kindly communicate with Headquarters 7th Divisional Train.

7th DIVISIONAL ROUTINE ORDERS No: 44.

16th November 1914.

1. PAY.

(a). Officers advances. Officers may have advances of £5 at a time and up to a maximum of £15 per month. These amounts must be drawn personally by officers from the Field Cashier, 4th Corps. In cases where it is found impossible for Officers to attend personally, a list of those requiring advances showing Rank, Name, Unit, Agent, Amount, and Receipt may be brought to the Field Cashier by an Officer who will be able to draw the amount in bulk.

(b). Requisition for cash by Units. Pay of Non-Commissioned Officers and Men must be requisitioned for by Units, care being taken that the distribution by Companies is shown, also Rank and Name of Company Commander. One officer can then draw the money.

The method of accounting by Imprest holders is clearly defined in supplement to Field Service Regulations, Part 11, who will be held responsible for all money so advanced to them, until it has been satisfactorily accounted for.

Requisitions for cash will be brought to the Field Cashier, 4th Corps, who will be with the Corps Headquarters, but on occasions he will visit Headquarters of Divisions, due notice being given beforehand.

2. CASH.

The Field Cashier, 4th Corps will be with Divisional Headquarters, to-morrow the 17th instant, from 10 a.m. till 1 p.m.

3. SANITATION.

Water Closets in billets are not to be used by the Troops. Latrines are to be dug and these only are to be used. Otherwise congestion and insanitation will occur, as ordinary methods are suspended and the demand is much too great for existing arrangements.

R.F.A.HOBBS, Captain,
D. A. A. & Q. M. G., 7th Division.

7th DIVISIONAL ROUTINE ORDERS N0: 44. (Continued).
****

13th November 1914.

AFTER ORDER.

4. CLOTHING & SUPPLIES.

(a)   Those Units who have not drawn all their clothing &c. should do so to-morrow from the Ordnance Store at 5 Rue St Jacques, BAILLEUL. The following are available for issue, viz:-

    Great Coats.
    Boots.
    Caps, Service Dress.
    Jackets, ,, ,,
    Pantaloons, ,, ,,
    Trousers. ,, ,,
    500 Gaiters for Gordon Highlanders.
    Shirts.
    Socks.
    Drawers.
    Puttees,

and sundry other stores.

(b).   Coke can be drawn on application to Senior Supply Officer. Experiments should be made in the manufacture of charcoal in accordance with circular memorandum issued, as the supply of coke is limited.

    Units requiring further supplies of straw should make application to the S.S.O.

                      R.F.A. HOBBS, Captain,
        D. A. A. & Q. M. G., 7th Division.

7th DIVISIONAL ROUTINE ORDERS No: 45

17th November 1914.

1. PROMOTION.

Conductor P.G.Ling, from Army Ordnance Corps to be Assistant Commissary of Ordnance, with Honorary rank of Lieutenant. Dated 31st October 1914.

2. MEDICAL.

All cases of sickness in Units occupying trenches must report to the Medical Officer at their Battalion Aid Post, who will decide as to their disposal.

3. TRANSPORT.

A representative from all 12 Battalions, 3 Brigade Headquarters, Field Companies and Field Ambulances will attend at the Headquarters of the Train near the wrecked church in SAILLY at 10 a.m. tomorrow the 18th instant.

Those representatives must be prepared to give full information as regards their transport horses, harness and vehicles. They will then be told where they can obtain horses to replace the greater part of their deficiencies.

4. COURTS-MARTIAL. Deleted

5. STRAGGLERS &c.

Each brigade will send a Military Mounted Policeman daily at 3 p.m. to the Office of the A.P.M. to take over stragglers, &c.

The Office of the Assistant Provost Marshal has been established opposite to the church at SAILLY.

(Continued)

6. BLANKETS:

If not already done, Units will send for th[e]
blanket wagons, and issue the blankets to the troops
in order that they may be aired.

R.F.A. HOBBS, Captain,
D. A. A. & Q. M. G., 7th Division.

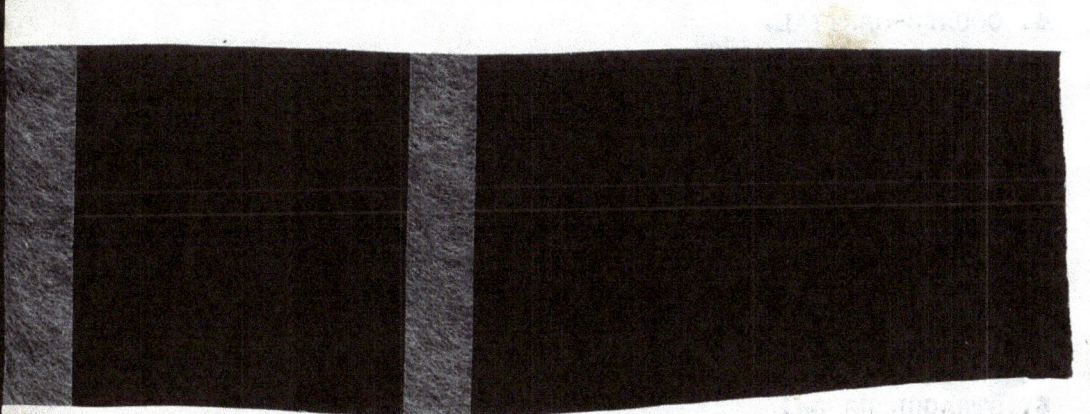

7th DIVISIONAL ROUTINE ORDERS No: 46.
****

18th November 1914.

1. HORSES:
Attention is drawn to the following circular issued to-day, viz:- "Care of Horses and Stable Management in the Field".

The General Officer Commanding holds Officers Commanding units personally responsible that every effort is made to instil the instructions contained therein.

Veterinary Officers are on no account to be diverted from their proper duties for such purposes as conducting remounts &c.

Officers Commanding units will furnish, each Saturday, to Divisional Headquarters, a return of their horse casualties, under the following headings:-

Died.	Destroyed.	Transferred to Mobile Vet.Section.	Cured.	Remaining under Treatment	Total strength of horses.

2. CLOTHING AND NECESSARIES.

Units will submit requisitions for total requirements of Cap badges and Regimental numerals. It is not expected that the new indents can be complied with to the full extent, but proportions per unit will be issued when bulk has been received.

3. OBSERVATION APPLIANCES.

A supply of optical appliances for observation in trenches is being sent out from Home and will shortly be issued to Units of this Division.

A report on these appliances will be forwarded will be forwarded to these Headquarters as soon as possible by Units stating whether they have received the issue of further supplies and if so whether a folding or rigid pattern is preferred. Any points which would assist the War Office in modifying the design should be included in this report.

R.F.A.HOBBS, Captain,

D. A. A. & Q. M. G., 7th Division.

7th DIVISIONAL ROUTINE ORDERS No: 46 (Continued).

18th November 1914.

AFTER ORDER.

4. TRANSPORT.

Those representatives of Units who neglected to comply with Divisional Routine Order No: 45 (3) of yesterday's date will meet the D. A. Q. M. G. at the Headquarters of 7th Divisional Train at SAILLY Bridge at 10 a.m. to-morrow the 19th instant.

R.F.A.HOBBS, Captain,
D. A. A. & Q. M. G., 7th Division.

CARE OF HORSES AND STABLE MANAGEMENT IN THE FIELD.
****

It is obvious that a considerable proportion of horse wastage is attributable to defective horse-mastership, and general supervision on the part of those responsible. Only the most careful attention to detail will enable horses to undergo the hardships to which they must necessarily be subjected under existing conditions. The following points which require special attention are circulated for the guidance of those concerned.

1. (a). **WATERING.** Horses must be watered as regularly as circumstances permit and not less than three times a day. They will not drink much in the early morning during cold weather so it must not be concluded that they are not thirsty and can go without water for a considerable length of time. They should, of course, never be watered immediately after feeding.

(b). **FEEDING.** Care must be taken that the full ration of forage is drawn for horses of different classes. The following is the scale allowed:-

	Oats.	Hay.
Heavy draught (Shires & Clydesdales)	19 lbs.	15 lbs.
Heavy draught.	15 lbs.	16 lbs.
Light draught & others.	12 lbs.	12 lbs.

(c). It is most important that every advantage should be taken of procuring Hay. Bulky food is most essential to the well-being of horses and no amount of Oats in excess of the scale laid down will compensate for want of Hay. Oat Hay can frequently be obtained and, in the absence of Hay, is the best substitute.

(d). The practice of placing oats on the ground for horses to eat is both wasteful and dangerous. Horses can only obtain a small proportion of their food and that is mixed with dirt, the result being frequent attacks of colic. Deficiencies in nose-bags should at once be made good and nose-bags improvised when necessary.

(e). Regularity of feeding is most important and should be strictly carried out as far as is consistent with nature of duty. Two pounds of Bran is procurable in lieu of that amount of Oats and should be taken advantage of especially when Hay is not obtainable.

(f). When military operations permit, it is the greatest advantage to horses to be turned loose to graze and roll. They should not be turned loose in a clover field, however, where they can gorge themselves with grass, but ordinary pasture should always be taken advantage of.

(3). **NATURE OF WORK.** Heavy draught horses are not meant for fast work. They will not stand it under the most favourable conditions, much less with heavy coats and standing in the open. As far as is consistent with duty, fast work must be avoided with all classes of horses. When horses with heavy coats sweat they cannot be dried for hours and the result of standing wet during the night is disastrous.

(4). When horses come in wet with rain or sweat, a layer of straw should always be placed under the blanket. Horses

P.T.O.

Horses then   dry more quickly and obtain more warmth.

(5). Sore backs are frequently caused by the use of the surcingle without pads. They are put on loosely, but rain contracts them and they cut into the back. Two small pads of straw can always be substituted for a pad.

(6). <u>GENERAL REMARKS.</u> (a). The practice of tieing several horses closely together in a bunch should be avoided: they do not rest and in wet weather the place becomes a quagmire. This is particularly noticeable amongst Infantry Transport. Advantage is not taken to spread the horses out and move them about to fresh ground frequently. Horses are allowed to stand on the same bit of ground day after day when fresh ground is easily procurable.

(b). <u>DRIVING.</u> Carelessness on the part of drivers is largely responsible for loss of condition amongst horses. Frequently the lead horses, and very often one of them only, does the whole of the work. This should be carefully controlled as it is responsible for a good deal of waste.

(c). During the cold weather horses should be exercised as early as possible in the morning, particularly when it is wet.

(d). It is most important for the control of the general health of the animals that cases of illness should be reported at once. Units without a Veterinary Officer will find one at the Headquarters of the Brigade Area in which they are located. The A.D.V.S. will be grateful if units will apply to him if they cannot get into touch with a Veterinary Officer immediately.

18/11/1914.   A. C. DALY,   Major,
                                  A. A. & Q. M. G., 7th Division.

7th DIVISIONAL ROUTINE ORDERS No. 47.

19th November 1914.

1. HORSES - Exercising of.

Horses will on no account be exercised on the roads, but in the adjacent fields.

2. DESPATCH RIDERS.

Despatch riders or orderlies leave 7th Division Signal Office as follows:-

To all units at 9 a.m., 2 p.m. and after issue of Operation Orders.
To 4th Corps and 8th Division at 10-30 a.m. and 4 p.m.

Notes:- 4th Corps sends a despatch rider to G.H.Q. Report Centre at 8 a.m.

G.H.Q. Report Centre sends despatch riders to General Headquarters at 10 a.m. and to 1st Corps, 3rd Corps, Cavalry Corps &c. at 1-30 p.m.

This means of communication with above Units is much quicker than by post.

F. R. A. HOBBS, Captain,
D. A. A. & Q. M. G., 7th Division.

7th DIVISIONAL ROUTINE ORDERS No: 48.

20th November 1914.

GENERAL STAFF.

1. HORSES - Exercising of.

It is important that horses should be exercised so that they are not easily observed by Aircraft. Care must be taken that they are not exercised in the vicinity of batteries in action or Infantry formations.

2. ORDERS - Distribution of.

It has been noticed that orders from this Office which should be communicated to the Troops do not get to them. Officers Commanding must take steps to ensure that all orders which concerns those under their Command are rapidly and regularly communicated.

3. AEROPLANES.

Troops are forbidden to fire on any Aircraft unless ordered to do so by a General Officer.

4. ENTRY OF HOUSES BY TROOPS.

No Troops are to enter any house unless they have been billetted there by a responsible officer or unless they do so in the course of any action.

The Assistant Provost Marshal will see that the empty houses are locked up as far as possible.

A. R. HOSKINS, Colonel,
General Staff.

ADMINISTRATIVE STAFF.

5. FUEL FOR DRYING CLOTHES.

Where it is possible to arrange for drying-rooms in cottages or other buildings, the Lieutenant-General Commanding 4th Corps is prepared to recommend an issue of fuel for the purpose of drying the clothing of the troops. (4th Corps Routine Order No:106 dated 18th November 1914.)

6. HORSE RUGS - Issue of.

The issue of Horse rugs on a scale of one per horse is sanctioned for the horses of all Units, except the riding horses of Cavalry. (Army Routine Order No: 320 dated 14th November 1914.

7. WARM CLOTHING.

Issue of the Warm Clothing referred to in Routine Order No: 328 of 15th instant (4th Corps Routine Order No: 101 dated 13th November 1914)will now be made as supplies become available. Indents should, in accordance with Routine Order No: 278 of 3rd November 1914, be at once sent to Ordnance Officers concerned.

The following articles will be considered public clothing, and whenever possible, should be recovered from casualties and re-issued to meet deficiencies:-
Coats lined fur.
Coats British warm linings to knees.
Coats British warm.

Waistcoats

P.T.O.

Waistcoats fur.
Jackets leather.
Capes mackintosh.
Boots Canada or Elcho pattern or ski boots.

Units or individuals receiving coats lined fur or coats British warm of either pattern will at once return the Greatcoats in possession, which will be collected regimentally and conveyed to railhead where they will be handed over to the Railway Transport Officer for conveyance to the Ordnance Officer, Base. (Army Routine Order No: 332 dated 16th Nov: 1914.)

A. C. DALY,   Major,
A. A. & Q. M. G., 7th Division.

7th DIVISIONAL ROUTINE ORDERS No: 49.
****

21st November 1914.

GENERAL STAFF.

1. RANGE - Testing machine guns.

It is notified for information that a 30 yards range for the testing of machine guns and training of detachments has been selected in a brick field on the S. side of the SAILLY - BAC St MAUR road about B of BAC St MAUR. The range will be allotted as follows:- 20th Infantry Brigade, 10 a.m. - 12 noon; 21st Infantry Brigade, 12 noon - 2 p.m.; 22nd Infantry Brigade, 2 p.m. - 4 p.m.

2. SUSPICIOUS OCCURRENCES.

In the event of any sniping of trenches from the rear, cutting of cable wire, signalling, suspicious lights, suspicious loitering in rear of the lines, or any other occurrences which give rise to suspicion being observed, a written report should be submitted to the A.P.M. as early as possible giving full details and stating accurately the time and place of the occurrence.

A. R. HOSKINS, Colonel,
General Staff.

ADMINISTRATIVE STAFF.

3. CASH.

The Field Cashier, 4th Army Corps, will be at 7th Divisional Headquarters from 10 a.m. till 2 p.m. tomorrow the 22nd instant.

4. SICK HORSES.

The Mobile Veterinary Section is at "Ferme Seingler" Croix du Bac (immediately N. of BAC St MAUR Bridge and on the West side of the road.), and will receive sick horses between the hours of 8 a.m. and 10 a.m. daily.

A. C. DALY, Major,

A. A. & Q. M. G., 7th Division.

7th DIVISIONAL ROUTINE ORDERS No: 50.

22nd November 1914.

GENERAL STAFF.

-- Nil --

A.R.HOSKINS, Colonel,
General Staff.

ADMINISTRATIVE STAFF.

1. MEMORANDUM.

Attention is drawn to (a) Circular re clearance of inhabitants, (b) Circular re sanitation in billets, issued to all Units to-day.

2. HORSES.

During the present vigorous weather Units will draw 2 lbs Bran and a proportion of straw per horse (in lieu of same extra quantity of oats) to supplement the hay ration of 8 lbs. Bulky food is indispensable for the health of horses during cold weather.

3. FROST BITE.

(a). As a precaution against frost bite men are recommended to wrap their legs and feet in straw, which should be put either under the puttees or tied round with string.

(b). When a man feels his hands and feet getting numb with cold he should get a comrade to apply brisk friction to restore the circulation.

(c). When in Brigade or General Reserve men should be made to take off their wet socks and dry them thoroughly.

4. DRUMS, OIL &c.

All drums issued to Units, containing paraffin, motor grease, &c. should be returned to Refilling Point for conversion into braziers.

A. C. DALY, Major,
D. A. & Q. M. G., 7th Division.

NOTICE.

A wrist watch sent to be mended by an Officer of the Division when the Division was at Lyndhurst, can be had on application to Divisional Headquarters.

(Issued with 7th Divl Routine Orders of 22/11/14.)

CLEARING AREAS OF INHABITANTS.

G. H. Q. Instructions.

Proviso. (1). As regards clearing areas of inhabitants, unless presence of inhabitants who are permanent residents interferes directly with tactical operations, they will not be disturbed.

Refugees. (2). Refugees or inhabitants of other districts who are being housed by residents may be removed if they occupy accommodation required for troops, but this will be undertaken by French or Belgian Authorities through representatives at Corps Headquarters.

Absentees. (3). Inhabitants who are absent from their house when British Troops enter an area will not be allowed to enter into residence without permission of G.O.C. Corps.

Sniping or Cutting of wires. (4). If sniping or cutting of wires occurs in areas in rear of trenches all inhabitants may be removed but only through the French or Belgian representatives at Corps Headquarters.

Procedure. (5). In every case in which action in regard to inhabitants is necessary it will be taken through the medium of the representatives of the country concerned, and if such action does not meet the case, the matter must be reported to the Provost Marshal, G.H.Q.

A. C. DALY,   Major,

22nd November 1914.   A. A. & Q. M. G., 7th Division.

(Issued with 7th Divl Routine Orders of 22/11/14.)

SANITATION.

SANITARY. There is a lack of sanitary organization in billets, more especially amongst detached bodies such as Machine Gun Sections, Transport details &c.
The Regimental personnel for sanitary duties should be so allotted that detachments have a due proportion for work in all billets occupied by the Unit.

WATER. In farms the source of supply is generally a shallow well situated under a dung heap. All water is unsafe and must be boiled before use.

WATER BOTTLES. Units when in Divisional reserve will arrange to "scald" all bottles at least once a week. This can be done individually by boiling water in canteens.

ABLUTION PLACES. These should be provided some distance from the source of water supply, and waste water run on to land or into a soakage pit. At present men are washing around the pumps and soiled water drains immediately into the wells.

COOKING places must be kept scrupulously clean and all cooking confined to them.

STRAW when used in billets should be renewed once a week and oftener in wet weather. Floors of occupied rooms should be swept out frequently.

DRYING ROOMS. A room should be set apart for drying clothing in wet weather and charcoal braziers provided.

VERMIN. In most billets 'flat irons' are available and when hot are very effectual in destroying vermin. Special attention should be given to the seams of clothing.

Attention is drawn to Field Service Regulations, Part 1, Section 53 and Part 11, Section 84.

A. C. DALY, Major,
A. A. & Q. M. G., 7th Division.

22nd November 1914.

7th DIVISIONAL ROUTINE ORDERS No: 50 (Continued).

****

22nd November 1914.

ADMINISTRATIVE STAFF.

AFTER ORDERS.

5. FORAGE.

Owing to the difficulty of transport the following scale of forage is ordered :-

Horses.	Oats.	Bran.	Hay.
Riding and Draught.	12 lbs.	2 lbs.	8 lbs.
Heavy Draught.	15 lbs.	2 lbs.	8 lbs.
Clydesdale & Shire.	19 lbs.	2 lbs.	8 lbs.

The balance of the Hay ration must be made up in Straw procured locally, or, if no local supply available arrangements will be made by the Senior Supply Officer for Units to draw from other localities.

When Bran is not available 2 lbs Oats will be issued in lieu of 2 lbs Bran.

6. SACKS.

All empty sacks will be returned in empty supply wagons for use in carrying coke &c.

A. C. DALY,   Major,

A. A. & Q. M. G., 7th Division.

7th DIVISIONAL ROUTINE ORDERS No: 51.
----coooooooo*oooooooop----
23rd November 1914.

GENERAL STAFF.

1. ROADS - Responsibility for.

With reference to Operation Order No: 35/1 dated 16th November 1914, the responsibility for the road on the right of the Centre Section now rests solely with the Officer Commanding the Centre Section.

A. R. HOSKINS, Colonel,
General Staff.

ADMINISTRATIVE STAFF.

2. DUTIES.

Two troops Northumberland Hussars and the Cyclist Company are employed to patrol the 7th Division Area S.E. of the R.LYS. Their duties are to observe the civil population, get acquainted with those in their area and to assist the military police in enforcing discipline and preventing looting. They should be given every facility to carry out their duties by the troops billitted in the Area.

3. ORDNANCE SERVICES.

(a). Units are to return at once to Railhead all surplus and repairable wagons, limbered, G.S. or portions fore and hind of same. They are urgently required.

(b). Except when specially ordered no issues in excess of War Establishments will be made. Brigadiers will take such steps as they think necessary to ensure that Units of their Brigades demand Equipment &c. strictly in accordance with the xxx authorized scale for war.

4. BRAZIERS.

A test has been made to light coke in a brazier without any coal whatever.

The Brazier was lighted with helf a side of a 'Bacon' box, and about one sheet (single) of newspaper. It was found that the coke caught without any difficulty.

This experiment was done in the open. Only a little smoke was made, in fact a smoke was caused for only about three minutes.

The coke should be at first broken into small pieces a little larger than a chestnut. This is most important if it is to be lighted easily. The holes in the brazier were enlarged and a better result was at once obtained.

5. FIELD GENERAL COURTS-MARTIAL.

(a). Attention is directed to extracts from Rules of Procedure relative to F.G.C.M., copies of which have been issued to all concerned this day.

(b). When officers below the rank of Field Officer are appointed Presidents of Field General Courts-Martial, a certificate to the effect that an Officer of Field rank was not available to sit as president should form part of the proceedings.

6. GLANDERS AND FARCY.

Attention is drawn to Divisional Routine Order No: 39(5) dated 9th instant, relative to Glanders and Farcy and the precautions to be taken to guard against same.

Disinfectants can be obtained on application to the Senior Supply Officer.

A. C. DALY, Major,
A. A. & Q. M. G., 7th Division.

7th DIVISIONAL ROUTINE ORDERS No: 52.

24th November 1914.

GENERAL STAFF.

1. PARADES.

The G.O.C. will see the 2nd Bn "Queens" and 2nd Bn Royal Scots Fusiliers on parade tomorrow 25th instant at 2-30 p.m. and 3 p.m. respectively, at places in their billetting areas to be selected by Brigadier Generals Commanding 21st and 22nd Infantry Brigades and intimated to this Office.

2. HOSTILE FUZE.

In the case of a hostile fuze being picked up, the exact reading should be reported, and any clue as to the direction from which the shell came should be added; the direction of the noise of passage through the air and the direction of the marks on graze give indications of this.

A. R. HOSKINS,
Colonel,
General Staff.

ADMINISTRATIVE STAFF.

3. BRAZIERS.

The result of a continuous 24 hours test was to show that an ordinary "bucket" brazier when full burns approximately 40 lbs of Coke during the time mentioned.

This works out at an average of 5 tons daily for 300 "bucket" braziers (100 per infantry brigade) and is as much as can be handled.

In future Coke will be reserved for men in the trenches and in Reserve in the open.

The remainder of the troops will be issued with Coal and Wood on a scale which will be published.

A scale for issue of Candles and Oil will also be published.

4. SUPPLIES & ORDNANCE SERVICES.

Misunderstandings have frequently occurred when drawing supplies and ordnance stores owing to inexperienced representatives being sent on behalf of Units. The Quartermaster or Quartermaster Sergeant (or in times of emergency the official drawer) should invariably attend when issues are made. No other representatives will be recognised.

5. INQUIRY OFFICE.

An Inquiry Office for Army Service Corps and Ordnance Services will be established from tomorrow at the SAILLY cross Roads.

The position will be clearly indicated by a Notice board. Representatives of Units detailed to draw supplies or stores, if in doubt on any point will address themselves to the Inquiry Office either by day or night.

6. SHOEMAKERS.

A number of shoemakers are required at Base for repair of boots being returned from the Front. Units &c. will render a report to Divisional Headquarters by 5 p.m. tomorrow stating whether they have any Shoemakers serving under their Command who could be spared for this duty.

7. HORSES.

It is noticed that horses are being crowded into dirty dark buildings, notwithstanding instructions to the contrary, vide Army Routine Order No: 289 of 6th November 1914 (7th Divl Routine Order No: 30(5) dated 9th November 1914.)

Apart from the risk of contracting contagious disease, horses will not thrive under these conditions. They will do much better in the open.

Commanding Officers must see that attention is given to this order.

8. RETURNS.

As there still appears to be some misunderstanding in the method of reporting casualties the correct method is republished herewith.

Units will report daily to Divisional Headquarters through the usual channels, the names of Officers and total number of other ranks killed, wounded and missing and reinforcements received on the previous day. These reports must reach Divisional Headquarters by 5 p.m. daily.

Units report direct to D.A.G., G.H.Q., 3rd Echelon, Base, by the quickest method (by wire if possible) the regimental numbers of dead or missing (vide Army Routine Order dated 29/8/14 in 'Extracts from Routine Orders'). Medical Units send to D.A.G., Base a nominal roll of all ranks treated for wounds. Units show on the back of A.F.B.213 all casualties, reinforcements &c. which have occurred since the last A.F.B.213 was rendered, thus verifying the casualties reported by other methods.

Army Forms B.213 should be rendered in duplicate through the usual channels so as to reach Divisional Headquarters by 12 noon on Fridays. One copy is then forwarded direct to D.A.G. Base and one copy is filed.

Army Form B.2069 should be rendered with Army Form B.213. Army Form B.231 (Weekly State) should be furnished through the usual channels so as to reach Divisional Headquarters by 5 p.m. on Sundays.

Attention is drawn to Field Service Regulations, Part 11, para:

(Sheet 2.)

para: 133 (3), (4), (5), 134, and 'Notes on clearing of a battlefield' (issued with extracts from Routine Orders) paras 5 & 6.

Every effort must be made to render these returns punctually so that arrangements may at once be made to send up reinforcements and to notify relations of casualties which have occurred.

9. WATER CARTS.

All demands for Water Carts should state if required to replace unserviceable filtering apparatus or to replace lost or totally unserviceable.

Those with defective filtering apparatus only should be retained and used if tanks are in good order.

10. HORSE CASUALTIES.

A statement showing in detail horse casualties in the 7th Division during the week ending 21st November 1914 is issued with Routine Orders of today.

A. C. DALY,   Major,

A. A. & Q. M. G., 7th Division.

7th DIVISION,

RETURN OF HORSE CASUALTIES FOR WEEK ENDING 21st NOVEMBER 1914.

Unit.	Died.	Destroyed.	Transferred to Mobile Vet: Sect:	Cured.	Remaining under treatment.	Total strength.
Divl Hdqrs.	-	-	1	-	3	69 *
7/Sig: Coy.	-	1	-	-	2	51
N.Hussars.	1	2	8	15	26	477 ø
7/Cyclist Co:	-	-	-	-	-	2
Hdqrs R.A. & Pom-Pom Det:	-	-	-	1	-	33
14th H.A.Bde.	-	1	-	-	-	-
22nd F.A.Bde.	1	2	12	12	16	438
35th F.A.Bde.	-	-	12	-	26	768
Div.Ammn.Col.	2	3	5	19	33	777
Hdqrs R.E.	-	-	9	14	22	572
54th F.Coy,R.E.	-	-	-	-	1	13
55th -do-	1	-	-	-	7	79
20th I.Bde.	2	2	-	-	2	78
21st I.Bde.	-	-	-	2	23	287
22nd I.Bde.	-	-	4	-	8	382
Div. Train.	2	1	6	6	19	242
21st F.Amb.	-	-	3	3	11	477
22nd F.Amb.	-	-	2	-	2	61
23rd F.Amb.	1	-	-	-	2	65
12/M.Vet.Sec.	-	-	-	-	2	67
						14.
Total.	10	12	62	74	205	4852

* Does not include 29 attached.

ø Includes 29 attached to Divisional Headquarters.

7th DIVISIONAL ROUTINE ORDERS No: 53.
25th November 1914.

GENERAL STAFF.
NIL

A.R. HOSKINS, Colonel,
General Staff.

ADMINISTRATIVE STAFF.

1. SICK &c.

The following is the percentages of sick, wounded &c. in the 3 Infantry Brigades of the 7th Division for the 24th instant:—

20th Infantry Brigade.
Admitted to Hospital sick 14, wounded 4.
Percentage of sick and wounded to strength of Brigade = .57%
Admitted for Frost bite 5 (all in 1st Grenadier Guards).
Percentage of Frost bites to strength in Trenches = .28%

21st Infantry Brigade.
Admitted sick 2 Offrs & 12 men. Wounded 3 men.
Percentage of sick & wounded to strength of Brigade = .62%
Admitted for Frost bite 2.(2nd beds R. 1,2nd Yorks R. 1.)
Percentage of Frost bites to strength in Trenches = .18%.

22nd Infantry Brigade.
Admitted sick 1 Offr & 31 Men. No wounded.
Percentage of sick & wounded to strength of Brigade = .95%.
Admitted for Frost bite 5.(2/R.War.R. 2,1/R.W.Fus: 3.)
Percentage of Frost bites to strength in trenches = .29%.

Total admissions from 7th Division :—
Sick 4 Offrs & 69 men. Wounded 9 men. Frost bite 12.

2. BATHS.

A Bath-house for N.C.Os and Men has been established in the building at the back of the 7th Divisional Headquarter Offices.
The Bath-house will be allotted to Units daily in orders.

26th instant. 8-30 a.m. to 11 a.m. 22nd Infantry Brigade (to 2/Queens Regiment).
11 a.m. for remainder of day 21st Infantry Brigade.
27th instant. 20th Infantry Brigade. 8-30 a.m.

The following points should be noted :—
(i). About 50 men can have hot baths at a time, each party should take about 35 minutes.
(ii). The Unit to whom the Bath-house is allotted will arrange for an Officer or responsible N.C.O. to be on duty during the time the Baths are being used.
(iii). Rules for men bathing are on a board at the Bath-house and will be read to each party before entering the building.
(iv). Soap will be provided if required but must not be taken away. Men must bring their own towels.
(v). Men should bring a change of clothing with them, if they have one.
(vi). Greatcoats will invariably be brought to save unnecessary chills.

3. HORSE MANAGEMENT.

The circular on Horse Management issued with Routine Orders of the 18th November 1914 emphasized the fact that heavy draught horses were not to be driven at a trot. This order is not being observed. Officers Commanding Units will take steps to ensure that the instructions contained in the circular mentioned are made known to all under their command who are concerned with the care of horses.

4. HORSE RUGS.

Horse Rugs when drawn will be carried under Regimental arrangements.

5. BILLETTING AREAS.

The following additional billetting area has been allotted to the 7th Division, viz:- The Rectangle ROUGE de BOUT - SAILLY - RUE de la LYS - road junction just above the second E of LAVENTIE including the roads bounding this rectangle.

Billetting areas for the reserve battalions of the three brigades are reallotted as follows and will be taken up next time the battalions are relieved.

20th Brigade. RUE du QUESNOY from the SAILLY - FROMELLES road to the U of RUE BATAILLE.

21st Brigade. Roads running S.E. from RUE de la LYS and PT de la JUSTICE to the cross road just S.E. of the railway.

22nd Brigade. RUE BATAILLE from the U of RUE to the FLEURBAIX road.

The other allotment of areas and roads remains the same. Royal Artillery will be billetted as required by the position of the guns.

A. C. DALY,
Major,
A.A. & Q.M.G., 7th Division.

7th DIVISIONAL ROUTINE ORDERS No: 54.
****

ADMINISTRATIVE STAFF.   26th November 1914.

1. VETERINARY CHESTS.

A Unit Veterinary Chest has been provided for each Infantry Battalion. They will send representatives to the Mobile Veterinary Section, at "Ferme Seingier" Croix du Bac (¼ mile N. of Bac St Maur Bridge on W. side of road) to collect them as soon as possible.

2. WASTE OF STRAW.

There is a great waste of straw going on in various Units. It is being used as bedding on wet ground in large quantities and at the present rate the supply cannot last long. This must be guarded against as a reserve of dry straw for use under the blanket in wet weather is essential.

3. HORSE LINES.

To ensure frequent change of ground it is advisable to establish a regular system of picketing horses. They can then be systematically moved from time to time subject to tactical requirements and concealment from aeroplanes. This will ensure better stable management. At present horses are spread about indiscriminately and cutting up large areas of ground.

4. SICK.

The following is the percentages of sick, wounded &c. in the 3 Infantry Brigades of the Division for the 25th instant:-

20th Infantry Brigade.
Admitted to Hospital sick 2 Offrs & 26 men, Admitted wounded 3 men.
Percentage of admissions to Brigade strength   = 1.6%

21st Infantry Brigade.
Admitted to Hospital sick 9 men. Admitted wounded 2 men.
Percentage of admissions to Brigade strength   = .4%

22nd Infantry Brigade.
Admitted to Hospital sick 14 men, Admitted wounded 1 man.
Percentage of admissions to Brigade strength   = .45%

Total admissions from 7th Division :-
Sick 2 Offrs, 49 men. Wounded 6.

5. HORSE RUGS - Issue of.

Divisional Routine Order No: 46 (6) dated 20th instant is cancelled and the following substituted:-
"The issue of horse rugs on a scale of one per horse is sanctioned for the horses of all units."
(Army Routine Order No: 359 dated 23rd November 1914.)

6. WARM CLOTHING.

The last paragraph of Divisional Routine Order No: 46 (7) dated 20th instant relating to the return of greatcoats is cancelled.

Units may, if they so desire, retain the greatcoats in addition

P.T.O.

7TH DIVISIONAL ROUTINE ORDER No: 54.

1. VETERINARY CHARTS.

A Unit Veterinary Chart has been provided for each Infantry Battalion. They will send representatives to the 7th Div. Veterinary Section, at "Ferme Sotogise" Croix au Bac (½ mile N. of one ¼ mile Inlage on N. side of road) to collect them as soon as possible.

2. WASTE OF STRAW.

There is a great waste of straw going on in various Units. It is being used as bedding on the ground in large quantities and at the present rate the supply cannot last long. This must be guarded against as a reserve of dry straw for use under the blanket in wet weather is of enormous importance.

3. HORSE LINES.

To ensure frequent change of ground it is advisable to establish a regular system of picketing horses. They can then be systematically moved from time to time subject to tactical requirements and conditions from aeroplanes. This will ensure better stable management. At present horses are spread about indiscriminately and cutting up large areas of ground.

4. SICK.

The following is the percentage of sick, wounded &c. in the 3 Infantry Brigades of the Division for the 28th instant:-

20th Infantry Brigade.
Admitted to Hospital sick 2 Offrs & 29 men. Admitted wounded 3.
Percentage of admissions to Brigade strength   = 1.0%

21st Infantry Brigade.
Admitted to Hospital sick 9 men. Admitted wounded 2 men.
Percentage of admissions to Brigade strength   = .4%

22nd Infantry Brigade.
Admitted to Hospital sick 14 men. Admitted wounded 1 man.
Percentage of admissions to Brigade strength   = .65%

Total admissions from 7th Division :-
Sick 2 Offrs, 52 men. Wounded 6.

5. HORSE RUGS – Item at

Divisional Routine Order No: 46 (5) dated 20th instant is cancelled and the following substituted:-

"The issue of horse rugs on a scale of one per horse is sanctioned for the horses of all units."
(Army Routine Order No: 353 dated 23rd November 1914.)

6. WARM CLOTHING.

The last paragraph of Divisional Routine Order No: 46 (7) dated 25th instant relating to the return of greatcoats is cancelled.

Units may, if they so desire, retain the greatcoats in addition to the Coats lined fur or Coats British Warm.
(Army Routine Order No: 353 dated 23rd November 1914.)

A. C. DALY,
Major,
A. A. & Q. M. G., 7th Division.

7th DIVISIONAL ROUTINE ORDERS No: 54 (continued).

26th November 1914.

ADMINISTRATIVE STAFF.

After Orders.

7. **HORSE RUGS.**

With reference to Divisional Routine Order No: 54 (5) of to-day's date, the rugs issued are to be used for draught horses, other requirements will have to be met by G.S.Blankets for the present. Units will put forward demands on the D. A. D. O. S. for numbers required.

8. **RATIONS.**

In future Iron Rations must only be consumed by order and the fact that they have been so consumed must be immediately reported.

A. C. DALY,   Major,

A. A. & Q. M. G., 7th Division.

7th DIVISIONAL ROUTINE ORDERS No: 55.

27th November 1914.

ADMINISTRATIVE STAFF.

1. SICK.
The following is the percentages of sick, wounded &c. in the 3 Infantry Brigades of the Division for the 26th instant:-

20th Infantry Brigade.
Admitted to Hospital sick 28, Admitted wounded 3.
Percentage of admissions to Brigade strength = 1.0%

21st Infantry Brigade.
Admitted to Hospital sick, 1 Offr 7 men, Admitted wounded 2 men.
Percentage of admissions to Brigade strength = .36%

22nd Infantry Brigade.
Admitted to Hospital sick 1 Offr 20 men, Admitted wounded 7 men.
Percentage of admissions to Brigade strength = .83%

Total admissions for 7th Division = 3 Officers and 66 men sick and 15 men wounded.

2. BATHS - ALLOTMENT OF.
The Bath-house is allotted as follows:-

28th instant	-	22nd Infantry Brigade at 8-30 a.m.
29th instant	-	21st Infantry Brigade at 8-30 a.m.
30th instant	-	20th Infantry Brigade at 8-30 a.m.
1st December	-	7th Divl Train 8-30 a.m. to 12 noon.
		Divl Engineers.12-15 p.m. to 3-30 p.m.
		R.A.M.C. 3-45 p.m. to 7 p.m.
2nd December	-	Royal Artillery.
3rd December	-	Royal Artillery.

Hot water will be ready at 8-30 a.m. daily and Officers Commanding Units will ensure that their men arrive punctually in parties of 50.

3. CASH.
The Field Cashier, 4th Army Corps will be at Divisional Headquarters at 11 a.m. on Sunday 29th instant. All pay should be drawn then.

4. WATER CARTS.
Owing to the recent frost water carts must be thoroughly overhauled and defects made good without delay.

5. R.E.STORES.
Applications for barbed wire, sandbags, loopholes and other R.E. stores should be made by Brigades to their affiliated R.E.Company.

6. HORSE SHOES.
Units will render a return to the D.A.D.O.S. by noon the 29th instant, giving an estimate by sizes of the horse shoes they would like weekly.

7. LEAVE.

Officers proceeding on leave and requiring bus accommodation from Corps Headquarters to Boulogne should notify their Brigade or formation headquarters. G.O.Cs Brigades, Royal Artillery and Officers Commanding Divisional Troops should then notify 4th Corps Headquarters the number of officers requiring accommodation. Such notification should be rendered to reach Corps Headquarters at least 24 hours before the accommodation is required.

With regard to Non-commissioned Officers proceeding on short furlough, notification of bus accommodation required should be forwarded to Divisional Headquarters at least 36 hours before such time as the accommodation is actually required.

8. MEDICAL.

The following Medical Officers will report at the Office of the A.D.M.S.7th Division at 11 a.m. on Sunday the 29th instant:-
Lieutenants DRUMMOND, GANTLIE, FREEMAN, HARDIE, LUKER, WARBURTON, BALLINGALL and CHRISTIE.

A. C. DALY, Major,

A. A. & Q. M. G., 7th Division.

7th DIVISIONAL ROUTINE ORDERS No: 56.

28th November 1914.

GENERAL STAFF.

1. AEROPLANES.

When an aeroplane passes overhead all troops are to get under cover, and are not to leave their positions or billets to gaze skywards at the aircraft.

2. CABLE LINES – Protection of.

The attention of all troops is directed to Standing Order No: 4 of which the following is an extract:- "Every care will be taken to protect lines laid by Signal Companies (or by the Artillery). If a cable is found to be exposed, dragged from the side of the road, or liable to damage, it will be put back."

Cases have recently occurred of Artillery cables having been apparently destroyed by working parties cutting brushwood &c., great inconvenience being caused thereby.

A. R. HOSKINS, Colonel,
General Staff.

ADMINISTRATIVE STAFF.

3. ORDERS – DISTRIBUTION OF.

It has been brought to notice that many orders concerning horse management, scale of forage &c. are not seen by Regimental Transport Officers. To obviate this a separate copy of Routine Orders will henceforth be issued to each Regimental Transport Officer provided an orderly is sent to 7th Divisional Headquarters Offices to fetch them. Back orders on this subject can also be seen at 7th Divisional Hdqrs Office but there are not sufficient spare copies to issue.

4. LEAVE.

Transport as required will leave 7th Divisional Train Hdqrs at PONT TOURNANT, SAILLY at 6 a.m. daily until further orders to convey Warrant Officers and Non-commissioned Officers proceeding on furlough to MERVILLE in time to catch the 8-30 a.m. bus from 4th Corps Hdqrs.

Officers proceeding on leave may avail themselves of this mode of transit if they so desire.

Complete lists of those proceeding by this route must reach the A.S.C. Enquiry Office at SAILLY cross roads not later then 10 p.m. the previous evening.

5. COURTS-MARTIAL.

Proceedings of Field General Courts Martial must be distinctly and legibly written. Whenever possible proceedings should be recorded in Ink.

P.T.O.

6. BATH-HOUSE.
A separate bathroom with hot water for the convenience of Officers has now been established at the Divisional Bath-House and can be used by Officers between the hours of 9 a.m. and 5 p.m. daily.

7. HARNESS.
Any Unit requiring Harness should apply to Ordnance Stores, SAILLY where a small quantity is now available.

8. HOOKS G.S. WAGON - FORE PORTION.
It having been brought to notice that the hooks on fore portion of G.S. Limbered Wagons are wearing thin, Units are to submit to the D.A.D.O.S. the number of hooks that require replacing as early as possible in order that repairs may be carried out locally.

9. INTERPRETERS.
General and other Officers concerned will submit a return to these Headquarters by 5 p.m. on 30th instant showing all Interpreters they have attached to Units under their Command.

10. LEAVE.
The second paragraph of Routine Order No: 55 (7) of yesterday's date is cancelled.

Notification of bus accommodation required by N.C.Os proceeding on furlough will be sent direct to 4th Corps Headquarters in the same manner as that of Officers.

11. BILLETS.
FLEURBAIX and other large villages under shell fire will not be used as permanent billets.

A. C. DALY,   Major,

A. A. & Q. M. G., 7th Division.

7th DIVISIONAL ROUTINE ORDERS No: 57.
****

29th November 1914.

ADMINISTRATIVE STAFF.

1. HONOURS AND REWARDS.

The Field-Marshal Commanding-in-Chief has been pleased to award the medal for Distinguished Conduct in the Field to the following Non-commissioned Officers and Men of the 7th Division :-

No: 29520 Sergeant G.Spain, "F" Battery, Royal Horse Artillery.
" On the 25th October 1914 Sergeant Spain was detached with a
"single gun while his Battery was at KRUISEIK Hill, in order to
"support the Gordon Highlanders. He brought his gun into action
"and worked it with great coolness in a very exposed position, and
"at very close range from the enemy. The action of this well
"commanded and handled gun had a great effect."

No: 53934 Bombadier R.Arney, "F" Battery, Royal Horse Artillery.
" During the fighting before YPRES, Bombdr Arney successfully
"maintained telephonic communication between Battery Headquarters
"and the Battery in spite of such a heavy fire that two stations
"in which he was placed were destroyed about him by gun and maxim
"fire. The result of his gallant and persistant efforts was that
"the Battery were able to maintain an effective fire on the enemy,
"which otherwise would have been impossible."

No: 21652 Sergeant W.C.Warr, 106th Battery, Royal Field Artillery
"was in charge of a sub-section and found himself left alone at the
"gun, all his men being killed or wounded. He was joined by

No: 21652 Corporal J.Holmes, 106th Battery, Royal Field Artillery
"who came up under heavy fire from the reserve ammunition wagon and
"together they worked the gun until ordered to leave."

No: 4867 Coy Sergt Major R.Lovatt, 2nd Battalion, Yorkshire Regt:
No: 6632 Sergeant W.Hitch, 2nd Battalion, Yorkshire Regiment,
" On October 26th, the Commanding Officer called for
"volunteers and these Non-commissioned Officers led them with the
"result that the trench was retaken under very heavy fire from the
"enemy who were 150 yards away.

No: 9495 Private F.Norfolk, 2nd Battalion, Yorkshire Regiment.
" On 22nd October, Private Norfolk continued to work a machine
"gun with great effect after the rest of the team had been killed
"or wounded."

No: 8275 Sergeant A.Stuart, 2nd Battalion, Yorkshire Regiment.
" On 20th October this Non-commissioned Officer left the
"trenches under a heavy fire to give information to the Royal
"Artillery in order to correct their fire. On another occasion
"he attacked by himself three Germans who had penetrated our lines,
"killing one and driving the other two into our trenches where they
"were captured."

No: 19225 Lance Corporal F.Cole, Royal Engineers.

On the evening of October 22nd, No: 1 Section of the 55th Company, R.E. was detailed for work in the trenches in the vicinity of REUTEL. Owing to heavy Artillery fire on the 23rd the section was confined to its trenches. One trench was blown up by a High Explosive shell with the result that the occupants were completely buried. Lance Corporal Cole saw the occurrence and called out No: 19908 Sapper R.Blackie, No: 19205 Sapper W.Burgess, and No: 19430 Sapper T.McCreddin. These men proceeded to the exploded trench across the open and under a heavy shrapnel fire, dug with their hands until they extracted the two occupants who were unconscious. They then carried them under cover.

The Commander-in-Chief regrets that he is unable to award the Distinguished Conduct Medal to all these three Sappers and No: 19908 Sapper R. Blackie has been selected for the honour.

2. SICK.

The following is the percentages of sick, wounded &c. in the 3 Infantry Brigades of the Division for the 28th instant:-

20th Infantry Brigade.
Admitted to Hospital sick 29 men, wounded 4 men.
Percentage of admissions to Brigade strength = 1.06 %.

21st Infantry Brigade.
Admitted to Hospital sick 1 Offr, 12 men, wounded 4 men.
Percentage of admissions to Brigade strength = .61 %

22nd Infantry Brigade.
Admitted to Hospital sick 1 Offr, 11 men, wounded 2 men.
Percentage of admissions to Brigade strength = .41 %

Total admissions from 7th Division = 2 Officers 61 men sick, 10 men wounded.

3. LEAVE.

All applications for leave must state **distinctly**
(i) Date applicant arrived in country and (ii) how his duties will be provided for in his absence.

4. DEFICIENCIES.

Attention is called to the weekly return of deficiencies in horses, harness, carts, wagons &c. which is due in this Office not later than noon on Monday 30th instant.

5. RECTIFIERS.

Rectifiers issued with Detonators No: 8 should be kept. There are no more available at present.

6. BARBERS SHOP.

A Barbers shop for the men has been arranged in the same building as the Baths and will be at the disposal of the Unit to whom the Bath-house is allotted for the day.

The.

The Barbers shop will be open at 8 a.m. daily so that first party can be ready to use the Baths at 8-30 a.m.

A. C. DALY,   Major,
A. A. & Q. M. G., 7th Division.

7th DIVISIONAL ROUTINE ORDERS No: 58.
30th November 1914.

1. HONOURS AND AWARDS.

(a). The Field Marshal Commanding-in-Chief has awarded the Distinguished Conduct Medal to the following Warrant Officer;-
Sergeant Major BAKER, 1st Battalion, South Staffs Regiment.
"On Oct 31st, Sergt Major Baker behaved with conspicious gallantry under heavy fire in rallying and collecting his men during the evacuation of KLEINKILLEBERG. He had previously been recommended for a commission for his good services."

(b). With reference to recent awards for distinguished service in the Field, the G.O.C. 7th Division desires to say that these have been selected by the Field Marshal Commanding-in-Chief from the names sent in. Others are reserved for future lists which may be called for later.

Officers who may, at a later date, get retrospective information of meritorious and gallant acts are to bring them to notice as they become aware of them, since, during the fighting before YPRES and owing to the loss of Officers and other ranks it has not always been possible to get information of such deeds at the time.

The Divisional General is well aware that in every corps most gallant deeds have been done and he is grieved to think that any of these deeds may be lost to record through the death or absence of those who would otherwise have brought them to notice.

2. SICK.

The following is the percentages of sick and wounded in the 3 Infantry Brigades of the Division for the 29th instant:-

20th Infantry Brigade.
Admitted to Hospital, sick 13 men, wounded 1 man.
Percentage of Admissions to Brigade strength = .47%

21st Infantry Brigade.
Admitted to Hospital, sick 15 men, wounded 1 man.
Percentage of Admissions to Brigade strength = .52%

22nd Infantry Brigade.
Admitted to Hospital, sick 18 men.
Percentage of admissions to Brigade strength = .51%

Total admissions from 7th Divn = 1 Offr 36 men sick, 2 men wounded.

3. NEWSPAPERS.

While the Division remains stationary, Mails should be ready for delivery about 12 noon daily; this hour may vary according to the punctuality of the railway trains. A limited number of English papers of the previous days date will be available at the Post Office for issue. These papers will be sorted out, divided up in proportion to establishments, and bound up in rolls addressed to the different Head Quarters and Units.

The representatives detailed to receive mails should be instructed to collect these papers. If these papers are not received a report should be sent to this Office.

4. LEAVE.

Attention is directed to this Office circular letter of to-day's date, relative to applications for leave, copies of which have been issued to all concerned.

P.T.O.

5. APPOINTMENTS.

Captain E.G.L.Thurlow, Somerset Light Infantry to be Brigade Major 22nd Infantry Brigade, vice Captain G.H.Janes. Dated 20th November 1914.

Lieutenant E.A.Osborne, Royal Engineers, from Section Officer, to command 7th Divisional Signal Company, and is granted the temporary rank of Captain whilst so employed, vice Major F.S.Garwood. Dated 18th Nov:14.

Captain E.A.Parker, Royal Welsh Fusiliers to be Aide-de-Camp (temporary) to G.O.C.7th Division, vice Captain J.E.V.Issac. Dated 25th October 1914.

Captain B.S.Moss-Blundell, 2nd Bn Yorkshire Regt is granted the temporary rank of Major whilst commanding the Battalion. Dated 22nd November 1914. (G.H.Q.List No: 2, Appointments, commissions and rewards, dated 28th November 1914.)

A. C. DALY, Major,

A. A. & Q. M. G., 7th Division.

NOTICE.

LOST. November 25th from Railway Station LA GORGUE Officer's kit bearing name 2/Lieut LEGGE, Wiltshire Regt. If found please send to D.A.Q.M.G., Headquarters, 7th Division.

7th DIVISIONAL ROUTINE ORDERS.

1st December 1914.

SPECIAL EARLY ORDER.

1. HONOURS AND REWARDS.

Under instructions from Military Secretary, G.H.Q. all Officers and Other Ranks of 7th Division and attached troops who have been awarded Victoria Crosses, D.S.O's and Distinguished Conduct Medals will be assembled at 7th Divl Headquarters by 1 p.m. today. A presentation of Medals will take place.

In addition to rewards already notified the following have been awarded Distinguished Service Orders :-

Lieutenant Lord C.N.Hamilton, Grenadier Guards.
Major A.B.Cator, 2nd Scots Guards.
Captain C.B.Paynter, Scots Guards.
Captain G.V.Fox, Scots Guards.
Lieutenant H.W.V.Stewart, Royal Scots Fusiliers.
Lieutenant H.EM. Kreyer, 2nd Yorkshire Regiment.
Lieutenant C.Lamb, 2nd Border Regiment.
Captain J.E.V.Issac, Rifle Brigade (Reserve of Officers).

No: 9939 Private Burns, R.A.M.C. has been awarded the Distinguished Conduct Medal.

A. C. Daly,   Major,
A. A. & Q. M. G., 7th Division.

7th DIVISIONAL ROUTINE ORDERS No: 59.
****

1st December 1914.

ADMINISTRATIVE STAFF.

1. BARBERS SHOP AND BATH HOUSE.
(a). In future each Unit will detail two men with, if possible, some knowledge of hair cutting, to assist in the Barbers Shop during the time their Unit is using the Bath-House.

These men should arrive with the first party and report to the Non-commissioned Officer in charge Bath-House.

Tools will be supplied. Although there is a limited number of razors in the Barbers shop, men who are in possession of their own razors are advised to bring them with them.

(b). The Bath-House is allotted as follows:-
Dec: 4th ... ... 22nd Infantry Brigade.
Dec: 5th ... ... 21st Infantry Brigade.
Dec: 6th ... ... 20th Infantry Brigade.

There is no objection to Brigades interchanging dates if desired.

2. HORSE CASUALTIES.
A Statement showing in detail horse casualties in the 7th Division during the week ending 28th November 1914 is issued with Routine Orders of today.

3. HORSES - DISEASES.
Owing to the prevalence of Ringworm amongst the horses the following precautions will be taken by Units.

Every case which is in the least suspicious will be isolated and reported to the Veterinary Officer at once.

Harness, saddlery, brushes &c. which have been in contact with affected cases will be thoroughly scrubbed with disinfectant before being used again.

Owing to long coats the outbreak is difficult to control and can only be checked by the most careful inspections and co-operation with Veterinary Officers.

A. C. DALY, Major,
A. A. & Q. M. G., 7th Division.

7th DIVISION.

RETURN OF HORSE CASAULTIES IN 7th DIVISION DURING WEEK ENDING 28th Nov:1914.

Unit.	Died.	Destroyed.	Transferred to Mobile Vet: Sect:.	Cured.	Remaining under Treatment.	Total strength
Divl.Hdqrs.	–	–	–	3	1	83
7th Sig.Coy.	–	–	1	1	1	53
N.Hussars.	–	–	–	14	33	480
7th Cyclist Co:	–	–	1	–	–	2
R.A.Hdqrs & Pom-Pom Det.	–	–	–	–	–	33
14th H.A.Bde.	1	–	–	7	29	440
22nd F.A.Bde.	–	3	7	13	25	768
35th F.A.Bde.	1	2	3	26	68	771
3rd Hy A.Bde.	1	1	9	7	11	256
Div.Amn.Col.	2	–	5	24	29	527
H.Q.,R.E.	–	–	1	–	–	12
54th Coy.R.E.	–	–	1	2	24	81
55th Coy,R.E.	1	–	1	–	3	76
20th I.Bde.	–	–	1	14	38	262
21st I.Bde.	–	2	4	5	39	281
22nd I.Bde.	2	1	6	4	19	263
Divl.Train.	–	2	3	13	26	445
21st F.Amb.	–	–	–	–	4	61
22nd F.Amb.	–	–	–	3	–	65
23rd F.Amb.	–	–	–	–	8	63
12/M.Vet.Sect.	–	–	–	–	2	18
Total	8	11	43	136	360	5040

7th DIVISIONAL ROUTINE ORDERS No: 60.

2nd December 1914.

ADMINISTRATIVE STAFF.

1. CASH.
The Field Cashier, 4th Army Corps will be at Divisional Headquarters to-morrow from 10 a.m. till 1 p.m.

2. FIELD PUNISHMENT.
All men undergoing Field Punishment will, when their Units are in General Reserve, be handed over to the A.P.M.

3. APPOINTMENTS – TEMPORARY WARRANT OFFICERS.
Non-commissioned Officers temporarily performing the duties of a Warrant Officer, who is wounded, a prisoner of war, or missing, may be given the acting Warrant Rank, with pay.

Permanent promotion to Warrant rank will continue to be dealt with according to the procedure laid down in King's Regulations, Para: 287. (Authority:- W.O. letter 121/1385 (A.G.4a.) dated 19th November 1914. 4th A.C.No: 292(A) dated 1/12/14.)

4. HORSES.
The hair on horses heels is on no account to be removed.

5. COURTS-MARTIAL.
In cases of offences against the inhabitants of a country application should, whenever practicable, be made for trial of such offences by General Court-Martial.

6. SICK.
(i). The following is the percentages of sick and wounded in the 3 Infantry Brigades of the Division for the 30th November 1914:-

20th Infantry Brigade.
Admitted to Hospital, sick 10, wounded 4 men.
Percentage of admissions to Brigade strength = .47%

21st Infantry Brigade.
Admitted to Hospital, sick 6 men, wounded 1 man.
Percentage of admissions to Brigade strength = .23%

22nd Infantry Brigade.
Admitted to Hospital, sick 12 men, wounded 'Nil'
Percentage of admissions to Brigade strength = .34%

Total admissions from 7th Division = 41 men sick, 6 wounded men.

(ii). The following is the percentages of sick and wounded in the 3 Infantry Brigades of the Division for the 1st instant.:-

20th Infantry Brigade.
Admitted to Hospital, sick 8 men, wounded 1 Offr, 1 man.
Percentage of admissions to Brigade strength = .33%

21st Infantry Brigade.
Admitted to hospital, sick 1 Offr, 14 men, wounded 'Nil'.
Percentage of admissions to Brigade strength = .46%

22nd Infantry Brigade.
Admitted to Hospital, sick 6 Offrs, 17 men, wounded 'Nil'
Percentage of admissions to Brigade strength = .57%

Total admissions from 7th Division = 5 Offrs, 53 men sick, 1 Offr, 1 man wounded.

A. C. DALY, Major,
A. A. & Q. M. G., 7th Division.

7th DIVISIONAL ROUTINE ORDERS No: 61.

3rd December 1914.

ADMINISTRATIVE STAFF.

1. HONOURS AND REWARDS.
(a). With reference to Special Routine Order of the 1st instant, the following Officer has also been awarded the Distinguished Service Order :-
  Lieutenant E.A.Osborne, Royal Engineers.
(b). With reference to Routine Order No: 57 (1) of the 29th November 1914, for "No: 21652 Corporal J.Holmes" substitute "No:4309 Corporal T.W.Holmes".

2. PAYMENT OF TROOPS.
Until further orders the Field Cashier, 4th Corps will be at Divisional Headquarters from 10 a.m. till 1 p.m. on Sundays, Tuesdays and Thursdays.
His Office at Divisional Headquarters is situated on the first floor.

3. HORSES.
The clipping of horses heels is forbidden as they are bound to get cracked heels if not protected by hair.

4. ANTI-TYPHOID INOCULATION.
Enteric Fever is reported to be rife in the enemy's lines.
Anti-Typhoid inoculation has been found very effective in preventing the disease, and an opportunity is now given for receiving this treatment when Units are in billets in general reserve.
A Company at a time can receive treatment, and a second injection will be given 10 days later. The day following each injection the man will be relieved from duty as far as the exigencies of the service permit.
It is very important that Officers and men who have not yet been inoculated, should take this opportunity of being done, so that the efficiency of the Army may not be reduced through Enteric Fever.
The A.D.M.S. will allot time and dates and will make all arrangements direct with Officers Commanding Units.

SICK.
The following are the percentages of sick and wounded in the Infantry Brigades of the 7th Division for the 2nd instant:-
20th Infantry Brigade.
Admitted to Hospital, sick 12 men, wounded 3 men.
Percentage of admissions to Brigade strength = .53%
21st Infantry Brigade.
Admitted to Hospital, sick 12 men, wounded 2 men.
Percentage of admissions to Brigade strength = .46%
22nd Infantry Brigade.
Admitted to Hospital, sick 24 men, wounded 3 men.
Percentage of admissions to Brigade strength = .77%
Total admissions from 7th Division = 58 men sick, 8 men wounded.

A. O. DALY, Major,
A. A. & Q. M. G., 7th Division.

7th DIVISIONAL ROUTINE ORDERS No: 62.

ADMINISTRATIVE STAFF.

4th December 1914.

1. SANITATION IN TRENCHES.

Complaints have been made by Units going into the trenches of the insanitary state in which they have been left by the Unit going out. The same system should be adopted by all Units. Although the biscuit tin is not an ideal substitute for the latrine bucket, yet if not allowed to be more than two thirds filled it can be made to answer its purposes. It might be strengthened by fitting battens of wood round it.

2. FUEL WOOD.

The practice of indiscriminately cutting down trees for firewood must cease.

Wood and fuel in ample quantities is being issued every day in the ordinary course. The attention of Regimental Transport Officers is especially directed to this matter.

3. ELECTRIC TORCHES.

With reference to the electric torches issued for experimental purposes, a report from each Brigade will be rendered to this Office by 9 a.m. on 5th instant.

4. MONTHLY STRENGTH RETURN.

With reference to this Office circular letter No: 292(A) dated 2nd instant, Units will show no Army Service Corps Drivers attached to them belonging to the 7th Divisional Train, as that Unit includes all these in its state.

5. CLEANLINESS OF ROAD DITCHES.

It has been noticed that in some cases troops have cleaned the mudd off the road in front of their billets by scraping it into the roadside ditch, thereby blocking the ditch. Mud taken off the road should be placed on the field side of the ditch.

In other places roadside ditches have been filled in to make an entrance to a bivouac or similar purpose, resulting in the collection of water in the ditch. Such barriers should be made good by laying agricultural drain pipes under them at the level of the bottom of the ditch.

All roadside or other ditches in the immediate vicinity of billets or bivouacs should be kept clean by the troops.

6. SICK.

The following are the percentages of sick and wounded in the 3 Infty Brigades of the Division for the 3rd instant:-

20th Infantry Brigade.
Admitted to Hospital, sick 2 Offrs, 31 men, wounded 2 men.
Percentage of admissions to Brigade strength = 1.23%

21st Infantry Brigade.
Admitted to Hospital, sick 10 men, wounded 4 men.
Percentage of admissions to Brigade strength = .46%

22nd Infantry Brigade.
Admitted to Hospital, sick 1 Offr, 43 men, wounded 2 men.
Percentage of admissions to Brigade strength = 1.3%.

Total admissions from 7th Division, sick 3 Offrs, 99 men, wounded 11 men.

P.T.O.

7. HORSES.

Attention is called to the prevalence of injuries to horses backs caused by surcingles. A supply of surcingle pads has been wired for and Officers Commanding Units should at once make good their deficiencies. When rugs or blankets are taken off, men should be instructed to pass the hand along the surface of the skin where the surcingle has rested and to report any indication of hardening, swelling or tenderness. If detected in this early stage, treatment is more or less simple, but if allowed to go on, it results in serious injury and very often necessitates destruction of the horse.

A. C. DALY,
Major,
A. A. & Q. M. G., 7th Division.

7th DIVISIONAL ROUTINE ORDERS No: 63.
------ooooo*ooooo------

5th December 1914.

GENERAL STAFF.

1. TROOPS ON THE MARCH.
Small bodies of troops marching on narrow roads will form two deep when necessary so as not to impede traffic.

A. R. HOSKINS, Colonel,
General Staff.

ADMINISTRATIVE STAFF.

2. BATHS - ALLOTMENT OF.
The Bath-House is allotted as follows :-
December 7th - 8 a.m. to 10 a.m. Transport details 21st Infty Bde.
10 a.m. to 12 noon. " " 20th Infty Bde.
12 noon to 2 p.m. " " 22nd Infty Bde.
2 p.m. to 4-30 p.m. Royal Engineers.
4-30 p.m. to 6-30 p.m. Army Service Corps.
December 8th. 22nd Infantry Brigade.
December 9th. 21st Infantry Brigade (but from 12 noon to 2 p.m. reserved for R.A.M.C.)
December 10th. 20th Infantry Brigade.
December 11th. Royal Artillery (for details who could not get baths on previous dates).
Above hours can be interchanged by mutual arrangement if desired
As there still appears to be misunderstanding about the connection between the Barber's Shop and Bath-House, the following itinerary is re-published -
1st party arrives at 8 a.m. and uses the Barber's Shop till 8-30 a.m. when the Bath-House is open for them. 2nd party arrives 8-30 a.m. goes to Barber's Shop and succeeds 1st party at Bath-House and so forth.

3. SICK.
The following are the percentages of sick and wounded in the 3 Infantry Brigades of the 7th Division for the 4th instant:-
20th Infantry Brigade.
Admitted to Hospital, sick 1 Officer 10 men, wounded 2 men.
Percentage of admissions to Brigade strength = .43%
21st Infantry Brigade.
Admitted to Hospital, sick 12 men, wounded 4 men.
Percentage of admissions to Brigade strength = .53%
22nd Infantry Brigade.
Admitted to Hospital, sick 12 men, wounded 1 man.
Percentage of admissions to Brigade strength = .37%
Total admissions from 7th Division = sick 1 Offr, 44 men, wounded 7 men.

4. BILLETING AREAS.
With reference to Divisional Routine Order No: 53(5) dated 25th November 1914, the roads running S.E. from Pt. de la Justice and thence to the Rue de QUESNOY is now allotted to the 20th Infty Brigade. The billetting area for the 21st Infantry Brigade Reserve Battalion is the road running S.W. from the Pt de la Justice to Rue de la LYS, thence S.E. to the railway and thence N.E. to the 20th Brigade road.

P.T.O.

5. COURTS-MARTIAL.

Attention is again drawn to Divisional Routine Order No: 56(5) dated 28th November 1914. Proceedings of Courts-Martial are frequently so faintly and badly written as to be almost illegible. More care should be exercised in this respect. The proceedings should be written in ink whenever possible or at least with a sharp pointed indelible pencil.

A. C. DALY,
Major,
A. A. & Q. M. G., 7th Division.

NOTICES.

LOST. From 8th Royal Scots billet at Bac St Maur on the morning of the 3rd instant, an Officer's military bridle, almost new. "J.F.CROMBIE, 8 R.S" marked on inside of each head band. Maker "Watt," Edinburgh. Any information regarding same should be communicated to Divisional Headquarters.

FOUND. Black Gelding. Two white socks behind. White stare and nose, and white saddle mark. Nos: 158/5.B.G. 95.G. Owner should communicate with 7th Divisional Artillery Headquarters.

7th DIVISIONAL ROUTINE ORDERS No: 64.

7 6th December 1914.

ADMINISTRATIVE STAFF.

1. SICK.

The following are the percentages of sick and wounded in the 3 Infty Bdes of the Division for the 5th instant:-

20th Infantry Brigade.
Admitted to Hospital, sick 16 men, wounded 2 men.
Percentage of admissions to Brigade strength = .6%

21st Infantry Brigade.
Admitted to Hospital, sick 1 Offr, 6 men, wounded 'Nil'
Percentage of admissions to Brigade strength = .23%

22nd Infantry Brigade.
Admitted to Hospital, sick 9 men, wounded 1 man.
Percentage of admissions to Brigade strength = .28%

Total admissions from 7th Division = Sick 1 Offr, 43 men, Wounded 3 men. Percentage of sickness to Division strength = .3%

2. BILLETS.

Many complaints have been received recently as to the state in which Units in General and Corps Reserve leave their Billets. In future the Officer Commanding outgoing Battalion will arrange for the Quartermaster to attend at Divisional Headquarter Office with a written certificate that the billets have been left in a clean and sanitary state. The certificate should include an acknowledgement by the Commanding Officer of incoming Battalion that he is satisfied.

3. LEAVE - BUS ACCOMMODATION.

Commencing from to-night, conveyance for Officers and N.C.Os returning from leave will be provided by the Officer Commanding 7th Divisional Train to connect with the Bus which stops at 4th Corps Headquarters at MERVILLE. Officers Commanding Units will notify direct to Army Service Corps Enquiry Office, SAILLY CROSS ROADS by 12 noon daily the numbers returning from leave that date, specifying whether Officers or Non-commissioned Officers (as per pro-forma):-

"To A.S.C. Enquiry Office.
"2 Officers, 2 N.C.Os 1st Grenadier Guards arrive MERVILLE
"to-night on return from leave.
"date .... Signature........................"

Officers and Non-commissioned Officers in the Infantry will proceed to the 1st line Transport of their Units where orders should be sent to them.

4. HORSES - CASUALTIES.

A statement showing Horse Casualties in 7th Division during week ended 5th December 1914 is issued with Routine Orders of to-day.

A. C. DALY,
Major,
A. A. & Q. M. G., 7th Division.

(Issued with 7th Divl Routine Orders d/t 6/12/1914.)

RETURN OF HORSE CASUALTIES IN 7th DIVISION DURING WEEK ENDED 5th DEC: 1914.

UNIT.	Died.	Destroyed.	Transferred to Mobile Vet:Section	Cured.	Remaining under Treatment.	Total Strength.
Divl:Hdqrs.	-	-	-	1	6	83
7th Sig:Coy.	-	-	-	1	19	55
N.Hussars.	1	1	2	9	43	477
7th Cyclist.	-	-	-	-	-	2
Hdqrs R.A. & Pom-Pom Det:	-	-	-	-	-	33
14th H.A.Bde.	-	1	-	15	47	660
22nd F.A.Bde.	-	3	13	13	47	761
35th F.A.Bde.	1	1	-	34	75	736
3rd Heavy Bde.	1	1	1	16	18	280
Div:Ammn:Col:	-	-	-	23	84	515
Hdqrs R.E.	-	-	-	-	2	8
54th Coy, R.E.	2	-	-	-	35	80
55th Coy, R.E.	-	-	-	-	6	74
20th I.Bde.	-	-	2	13	41	262
21st I.Bde.	-	-	-	7	53	238
22nd I.Bde.	-	1	-	7	33	255
Divl.Train.	4	3	-	16	21	464
21st F.Amb.	-	-	-	2	5	61
22nd F.Amb.	-	-	-	-	-	65
23rd F.Amb.	1	-	1	-	17	62
Mob:Vet:Sect:	-	-	-	-	2	18
TOTALS.	10	11	19	187	554	5219

7th DIVISIONAL ROUTINE ORDERS No: 35.

7th December 1914.

ADMINISTRATIVE STAFF.

1. DESIGNATION - Change in.

In future the Anti-Aircraft Section of the 7th Division will be designated "No: 7 Pom Pom Section".

2. SICK.

The following are the percentages of sick and wounded in the 7th Division for the 5th instant:-

20th Infantry Brigade.
Admitted to Hospital, sick 1 Offr, 5 men, wounded 1 Offr 3 men.
Percentage of admissions to Brigade strength = .28%

21st Infantry Brigade.
Admitted to Hospital, sick 10 men, wounded 3 men.
Percentage of admissions to Brigade strength = .44%

22nd Infantry Brigade.
Admitted to Hospital, sick 10 men, wounded 1 man.
Percentage of admissions to Brigade strength = .28%

Royal Artillery.
Admitted to Hospital, sick 3 men.
Percentage of admissions to R.A. strength = .09%

Army Service Corps.
Admitted to Hospital, sick 1 man.
Percentage of admissions to A.S.C. strength = .24%

Royal Army Medical Corps.
Admitted to Hospital, sick 3 men.
Percentage of admissions to R.A.M.C. strength = .41%

Details
Admitted to Hospital, sick 1 man.

Total admissions from 7th Division = Sick 1 Offr, 33 men, wounded 1 Offr 7 men. Percentage of admissions to Division strength = .26%

3. BATHS - Allotment of.

With reference to Divisional Routine Order No: 63(2) dated 5th instant, the allotment of the Bath-House to the Royal Artillery on the 11th instant is cancelled and the following is substituted:-

December 11th - 20th Infantry Brigade.
December 12th - 21st Infantry Brigade.
December 13th - 22nd Infantry Brigade.
December 14th - Royal Artillery.

4. SURPLUS TRANSPORT.

With reference to 4th Army Corps Routine Order No: 196 dated 6th instant, the certificates referred to therein will be rendered to this Office by Officers concerned by 12 noon on 9th instant.

5. HORSES.

Owing to the prevalence of skin disease of a serious nature in various parts of the country the following precautions will be taken :-

All remounts will, on arrival at their Units, be inspected by the Veterinary Officer and will, as far as conditions permit be isolated for a period to be determined by him. The same will apply

P.T.O.

to horses arriving from other formations such as those with blanket wagons &c. &c.

Skin eruptions occurring in any horse will be immediately reported to the Veterinary Officer.

Officers Commanding Units will inform their men of the danger of their horses coming into contact, directly or indirectly, with those of other formations and will thus as far as is consistent with operations, maintain a system of isolation.

A. C. DALY,
Major,
A. A. & Q. M. G., 7th Division.

7th DIVISIONAL ROUTINE ORDERS No. 38

ADMINISTRATIVE STAFF.

8th December 1914

1. **SICK.**

The following are the percentages of sick and wounded in the 7th Division for the 7th instant:-

20th Infantry Brigade.
Admitted to Hospital, sick 9 men, wounded Nil.
Percentage of admissions to Brigade Strength = .25%

21st Infantry Brigade
Admitted to Hospital, sick 16 men, wounded 2 men.
Percentage of admissions to Brigade Strength = .61%

22nd Infantry Brigade
Admitted to Hospital, sick 14 men, wounded 4 men.
Percentage of admissions to Brigade Strength = .46%

Royal Artillery
Admitted to Hospital, sick 2 men, wounded Nil.
Percentage of admissions to R.A. Strength = .06%

Royal Engineers
Admitted to Hospital, sick 1 man, wounded Nil.
Percentage of admissions to R.E. Strength = .16%

Army Service Corps
Admitted to Hospital, sick 5 men, wounded Nil.
Percentage of admissions to A.S.C. Strength = .73%

R.A.M.C.
Admitted to Hospital, sick 1 man, wounded Nil.
Percentage of admissions to R.A.M.C. strength = .15%

Total admissions from 7th Division = Sick 46 men, Wounded 6 men.
Percentage of admissions to Division Strength = .32%.

2. **LEAVE.**

Officers proceeding on leave will on arrival in England at once, notify the Adjutant General, WAR OFFICE, in writing as per pro forma.

Rank ... ...
Name ... ...
Regiment ... ...
Brigade ... ...
Division ... ...
Corps ... ...
Period of Leave ... ...
Address ... ...

3. **CASH.**

The office of the Field Cashier is now established at a house, about half-way between the SAILLY cross roads and the 7th Divisional Hd Qr Office and on the same side of the road. The House is clearly marked by a sign board.

4. **CASUALTY REPORTS**

With reference to Field Service Regulations, Part 11, Section 133. Units will report direct to D.A.G. 3rd Echelon, Base, by letter, (motor cyclist post whenever possible) the regimental numbers and names of dead & missing.

A.C.Daly
Major
A.A. & Q.M.G., 7th Division.

P.T.O

AFTER ORDER.

5. HORSES.
(a) An outbreak of Mange has been discovered amongst the transport horses of the 6th Battalion, Gordon Highlanders which has just joined the Division. These horses have been placed in isolation and the horses of other units must on no account come into contact with them, either directly or indirectly.
(b). Dandy brushes are now an authorized issue and can be obtained on indent from the Ordnance Officer.

          A. C. DALY,   Major,
   A. A. & Q. M. G., 7th Division.

7th DIVISIONAL ROUTINE ORDERS No. 37

9th December 1914.

ADMINISTRATIVE STAFF

1. SICK.

The following are the percentages of sick and wounded in the 7th Division for the 8th instant:-

20th Infantry Brigade.
Admitted to Hospital, sick 10 men, Wounded 8 men.
Percentage of admissions to Brigade Strength = .5%

21st Infantry Brigade
Admitted to Hospital, sick 9 men, Wounded Nil.
Percentage of admissions to Brigade Strength = .3%

22nd Infantry Brigade
Admitted to Hospital, sick 6 men, Wounded 2 men.
Percentage of admissions to Brigade Strength = .2%

Northumberland Hussars
Admitted to Hospital, sick 1 man, Wounded Nil.
Percentage of admissions to Regtl Strength = .22%

Royal Artillery
Admitted to Hospital, sick 3 men, wounded Nil.
Percentage of admissions to R.A. strength = .093%

Army Service Corps.
Admitted to Hospital, sick 2 men, Wounded Nil.
Percentage of admissions to A.S.C. strength = .48%

Total admissions from 7th Division = Sick 51 men, Wounded 10 men.
Percentage of admissions to Division Strength = .25%.

2. RUM - ISSUES OF.

With reference to 4th Army Corps Routine Order No.44 (190) of 5th instant, the following will be the scale of rum issue to all Units not provided for in above mentioned order.
R. E. For men employed in work on trenches in defensive line Daily Issue.
INFANTRY. (a) Full issue for each complete day in trenches - this does not include day of going into trenches.
(b) Days spent in Brigade, Divisional or Corps Reserve, No Issue.
ALL OTHER TROOPS. 2 Issues a week.

Officers Commanding Units are responsible that all issues of rum are made and consumed by daylight.

3. CLOTHING.

Units having men in possession of dark overcoats should put forward demands on the D.A.D.O.S. to replace.

4. ROADS.

The private road leading through the White Chateau Grounds & over the Pontoon Bridge is not to be used for normal traffic except when the tactical situation demands it.

5. TRAFFIC.

The Drawbridge over Canal 700 metres due south of first N. in St QUENNELLE, reference map St OMER, sheet 4, FRANCE 80000, is to be closed for traffic for 24 hours, commencing 7 a.m. Thursday 10th December 1914.

A. C. Daly   Major.
A. A. & Q. M. G., 7th Division.

7th DIVISIONAL ROUTINE ORDERS No. 38

10th December 1914.

ADMINISTRATIVE STAFF

1. SICK.

The following are the percentages of sick and wounded in the 7th Division for the 9th instant:-

20th Infantry Brigade
Admitted to Hospital, sick 12 men, Wounded 2 men.
Percentage of admissions to Brigade Strength:- .39%

21st Infantry Brigade
Admitted to Hospital, sick 5 men, wounded 1 man.
Percentage of admissions to Brigade Strength = .2%

22nd Infantry Brigade
Admitted to Hospital, sick 14 men, Wounded 1 Officer
Percentage of admissions to Brigade Strength = .38%

Royal Artillery.
Admitted to Hospital, sick 9 men, wounded Nil.
Percentage of admissions to R.A. Strength = .27%

Army Service Corps.
Admitted to Hospital, sick 1 men, Wounded Nil.
Percentage of admissions to A.S.C., strength = .24%

R. A. M. C.
Admitted to Hospital, sick 5 men, Wounded Nil.
Percentage of admissions to R.A.M.C. strength = .4%

----
1 Officer
Total admissions from 7th Division = Sick 45 men, Wounded 3 men.
Percentage of admissions to Division strength = .3%

2. UNIFORMS - FRENCH TROOPS.

Attention is directed to Memorandum circulated this day on issue of gray-blue uniforms to French Troops.

3. BATH HOUSE.

The shed on the right immediately outside the entrance to the Bath House is now fitted with pegs on which men may hang their great-coats. The outer room of the building can be used as a waiting room by men waiting their turn for Bath and Barbers Shop. Seats and newspapers will be provided but the latter are on no account to be taken away.

4. FIREWOOD

No hop poles are to be purchased or requisitioned for firewood.

5. BUS ACCOMMODATION.

Attention of Brigade and Formation Head Quarters is directed to 7th Divisional Routine Orders No.55 (7) dated 27/11/14, and 34 (3) dated 6/12/14 - 4th Corps Head Quarters to be notified regarding accommodation between MERVILLE and BOULOGNE, and 7th Divisional Train between MERVILLE and SAILLY.

6. CLOTHING.

Commanding Officers will render a return by 9 a.m. 12th inst, shewing the number of undercoats fur, gloves, mufflers & mittens in their possession and the number of these articles they still require to complete the requirements of their respective units.

7. MEDICAL

Attention is directed to 4th Army Corps Order 211 dated 9th inst.

A.C.Daly   Major
A. A. & Q. M. G., 7th Division.

7th DIVISIONAL ROUTINE ORDERS No. 69

11th December 1914

ADMINISTRATIVE STAFF

1.— SICK

The following are the percentages of sick and wounded in the 7th Division for the 10th instant:—

20th Infantry Brigade
Admitted to Hospital, sick 10 men, Wounded 1 man.
Percentage of admissions to Brigade Strength = .3%

21st Infantry Brigade
Admitted to Hospital, sick 5 men, Wounded Nil.
Percentage of admissions to Brigade Strength = .17%

22nd Infantry Brigade.
Admitted to Hospital Sick, 15 men, Wounded 2 men.
Percentage of admissions to Brigade Strength = .43%

Royal Engineers.
Admitted to Hospital, sick 1 man, Wounded 2 men.
Percentage of admissions to R.E. Strength = .49%

Army Service Corps
Admitted to Hospital, sick 2 men, Wounded Nil.
Percentage of admissions to A.S.C. strength = .48%

R. A. M. C.
Admitted to Hospital Sick 3 men, Wounded Nil.
Percentage of admissions to R.A.M.C. strength = .4%

Total admissions from 7th Division = Sick 36 men, Wounded 5 men.
Percentage of admissions to Division strength = .25%

2. BATH HOUSE

The Bath House is allotted as follows:—
- 20th Infantry Brigade ... ... 15th December 1914
- 21st Infantry Brigade ... ... 16th December 1914
- 22nd Infantry Brigade ... ... 17th December 1914

1st party of 50 in each case to arrive at 8 a.m. and if possible should be in charge of an Officer. 2 Assistant Barbers (to help for the day only) should, in addition, accompany this party. Men **must** bring great coats.
Barbers Shop opens at 8 a.m. Bath House opens at 8.30 a.m.

3. HORSES — GENERAL CONDITION OF.

The general condition of riding and light draught horses is suffering materially from unnecessary fast work. It is noticed that mounted fatigue and exercising parties returning to their lines late in the afternoon proceed at a fast pace.

There is nothing more wasting to the general condition and more injurious to the health of horses than standing in cold and rain after sweating into a thick coat which it is impossible to dry. No amount of care and management will counteract the ill effects of this.

When mounted fatigue parties or in fact any mounted party are returning to their lines in the evening they should do so at a slow pace. There is no economy in time getting back quickly as it involves hours of extra work if the horses receive the attention which their sweating condition requires.

4. EMPTY SACKS.

Units are directed to return all Empty Chaff and Bran Sacks on hand to Supply Stores at once. It must be borne in mind that issues of forage are seriously interfered with if Sacks are not returned immediately when emptied.

P. T. O.

5. LEAVE

Officers and men arriving at MERVILLE from BOULOGNE by the Midnight Bus can remain in the Verandah Convent School until the conveyance arrives from here to bring them back.

6. VEHICLES

Approval has been given for a one horse vehicle for Officers Mess of each Infantry Battalion provided it can be procured locally by Units concerned.

7. BOOTS REPAIR OF

All Boots worth repairing will, when replaced be collected under arrangements to be made by Officers Commanding Units and returned to Supply Railheads for conveyance to Advanced Base.

If possible, they should be tied in pairs by the laces and packed in the sacks in which supplies are forwarded to the troops.

A. C. Daly   Major.
A. A. & Q. M. G., 7th Division.

7th DIVISIONAL ROUTINE ORDERS No. 70

12th December 1914

ADMINISTRATIVE STAFF

1. SICK.

The following are the percentages of sick and wounded in the 7th Division for the 11th instant:-

20th Infantry Brigade.
Admitted to Hospital, sick 14 men, Wounded 2 men
Percentage of admissions to Brigade Strength = .44%

21st Infantry Brigade.
Admitted to Hospital, sick 1 Officer, 9 men, Wounded 3 men.
Percentage of admissions to Brigade Strength = .44%

22nd Infantry Brigade.
Admitted to Hospital, sick 2 Officers, 9 men, Wounded 1 man.
Percentage of admissions to Brigade Strength = .3%

Northumberland Hussars
Admitted to Hospital, sick 1 man, Wounded Nil.
Percentage of admissions to Regtl Strength = .22%

Royal Artillery.
Admitted to Hospital, sick 5 men, Wounded Nil.
Percentage of admissions to R.A. strength = .15%

Army Service Corps.
Admitted to Hospital Sick 1 man, Wounded Nil.
Percentage of admissions to A.S.C. Strength = .24%

Total admissions from 7th Division = Sick 3 Officers, 39 men, Wounded 6 men.
Percentage of Admissions to Division strength = .29%.

2. BATH HOUSE.

Men <u>must</u> bring their own towels - Soap is provided.

3. PRISONERS

All prisoners for commitment to a Military Prison should be sent under escort to the Assistant Provost Marshal.
Both Army Form C.355 and Army Form C.385 must accompany them.

4. BILLETS.

It is to be distinctly understood that men not on duty are on no account to go outside their own billetting area unless provided with a pass signed by an officer.

General Officers Commanding R. A., and Infantry Brigades and Officers Commanding Divisional Troops will take steps to enforce this order - at present, it is not being enforced in certain Units.

A. C. Daly   Major
A. A. & Q. M. G., 7th Division.

P.T.O

AFTER ORDER

5. VERY PISTOLS - RIFLE BOMBS - Etc.

Demands for Very Pistols, Very Cartridges, Hales' rifle bombs, and Hand Grenades will be put forward in the same manner as for Small Arm ammunition through affiliated Artillery Brigade Ammunition Columns namely:-

20th Infantry Brigade through 35th Brigade A.C.
21st Infantry Brigade through 14th Brigade A.C.
22nd Infantry Brigade through 22nd Brigade A.C.

A maximum allowance of 15 Cartridges per week for Very pistol is sanctioned. Owing to the supply of these cartridges being limited, demands up to the full amount cannot be met at present.

A.C.Daly   Major

A.A. & Q.M.G., 7th Division.

7th DIVISIONAL ROUTINE ORDERS No. 71

13th December 1914.

ADMINISTRATIVE STAFF

1. SICK.

The following are the percentages of sick and wounded in the 7th Division for the 12th instant:-

20th Infantry Brigade
Admitted to Hospital, sick, 2 Officers, 25 men, Wounded 3 men.
Percentage of admissions to Brigade strength = .83%

21st Infantry Brigade
Admitted to Hospital, sick, 7 men, Wounded 1 man.
Percentage of admissions to Brigade strength = .27%

22nd Infantry Brigade.
Admitted to Hospital, sick, 11 men, Wounded 6 men.
Percentage of admissions to Brigade strength = .43%

Northumberland Hussars
Admitted to Hospital, sick, 1 man, Wounded Nil.
Percentage of admissions to Regtl strength = .22%

Royal Artillery.
Admitted to Hospital, sick, 3 men, Wounded Nil.
Percentage of admissions to R.A. strength = .09%

Royal Engineers
Admitted to Hospital, sick, 1 man, Wounded Nil.
Percentage of admissions to R.E. strength = .16%

Army Service Corps.
Admitted to Hospital, sick, 1 man, Wounded Nil.
Percentage of admissions to A.S.C. strength = .24%

R. A. M. C.
Admitted to Hospital, sick, 1 man, Wounded Nil.
Percentage of admissions to R.A.M.C. strength = .14%

Total admissions from 7th Division = Sick 2 Officers, 50 men.
Wounded 10 men.
Percentage of admissions to Division Strength = .58%

2. DUTIES

The Brigade on duty tomorrow 14th inst, 22nd Infantry Brigade.
Next for Duty:- 20th Infantry Brigade.

3. VEHICLE AND HORSE RETURN.

Units are reminded that the vehicle and horse return is due in tomorrow and every Monday by 12 noon. It is requested that this return may always be rendered on a form similar to that issued.

4. TRAFFIC.

The SAILLY bridge over River LYS will be closed for traffic from 8 a.m. to 12 noon on Tuesday 15th inst for an examination prior to repair.

5. BICYCLES COMPONENTS.

Units requiring components for repair to bicycles can obtain parts on application to Ordnance Refilling point.

6. COLLARS HORSE.

Cloth white for repair of collars horse is now available for issue.

A. C. Daly Major
A. A. & Q. M. G., 7th Division.

(Issued with 7th Divl Routine Orders d/- 13/12/14)
RETURN OF HORSE CASUALTIES IN 7th DIVISION DURING WEEK ENDED 12th Dec.1914.

UNIT	Died.	Destroyed.	Transferred to Mobile Vet:Section.	Cured.	Remaining under Treatment.	Total Strength
Divl.Hdqrs	-	-	2	6	6	81
7th Sig.Coy.	-	1	-	16	10	59
N.Hussars	-	2	2	28	41	480
7th Cyclist.	-	-	-	--	--	2
Hdqrs R.A. & Pom Pom Det.	-	-	-	--	--	33
14th R.A.Bde	-	1	3	15	40	655
22nd F.A.Bde.	1	2	2	10	64	756
35th F.A.Bde	1	1	2	36	57	763
3rd Heavy Bde.	2	-	3	16	12	276
Div:Ammu:Col:	1	-	-	85	35	515
Hdqrs,R.E.	-	-	-	2	--	8
54th Coy,R.E.	-	-	-	24	12	80
55th Coy,R.E.	-	-	-	3	5	80
20th I.Bde.	-	1	1	20	36	323
21st I.Bde	-	-	3	14	45	243
22nd I.Bde	1	-	1	21	25	268
Divisional Train.	3	1	5	12	17	495
21st F.Amb.	-	-	-	2	3	61
22nd F.Amb	-	-	-	-	-	64
23rd F.Amb.	1	-	-	6	12	62
Mob:Vet:Sect.	-	-	-	2	-	18
TOTALS	10	9	22	318	420	5322

7th DIVISIONAL ROUTINE ORDERS No. 72
14th December 1914
ADMINISTRATIVE STAFF

1. SICK.

The following are the percentages of sick and wounded in the 7th Division for the 13th instant:-

20th Infantry Brigade.
Admitted to Hospital, sick, 28 men, Wounded 1 man.
Percentage of admissions to Brigade Strength = .8%
21st Infantry Brigade.
Admitted to Hospital, sick 17 men, Wounded 1 man
Percentage of admissions to Brigade Strength = .61%
22nd Infantry Brigade.
Admitted to Hospital, sick 11 men, Wounded 5 men.
Percentage of admissions to Brigade Strength = .41%
Royal Artillery.
Admitted to Hospital, sick, 5 men, Wounded Nil.
Percentage of admissions to R.A. Strength = .09%
Army Service Corps.
Admitted to Hospital, sick, 3 men, Wounded Nil.
Percentage of admissions to A.S.C. strength = .75%

Total admissions from 7th Division = Sick 62 men, Wounded 8 men,
(includes 1 man of Details).

Percentage of admissions to Division strength = .45%

2. FIELD SERVICE POST CARD

There is no objection to the following being written on the Field Service Post Card:- "A merry Christmas" and "A Happy New Year".

3. BOOTS.

Hob Nails for Boots are now available and can be drawn by Units by applying at Ordnance Refilling Point.
Indents need not be submitted.

4. COURTS MARTIAL.

Officers Commanding Units will satisfy themselves that proceedings of Courts Martial are correctly made out, and completed in every respect before sending in to this office, otherwise unnecessary work is caused to all concerned.

A. C. Daly   Major
A. A. & Q. M. G., 7th Division.

7th DIVISIONAL ROUTINE ORDERS No. 75

15th December 1914

GENERAL STAFF

1. HAND GRENADES

A limited number of W.D. Pattern hand grenades and of Hale's hand grenades (which are somewhat similar to Hale's rifle [grenades]) are on charge of Brigade Ammunition Columns for issue to the Infantry Brigades to which they are affiliated.

Infantry Brigadiers will arrange with Officers Commanding affiliated Field Companies R.E. for 4 Sappers in each section of R.E. and for 8 men in each Infantry battalion to be thoroughly instructed in the use of these grenades.

It is suggested that the Infantry should be selected from men who have shown most aptitude in throwing improvised hand grenades, and that these men should be earmarked to form a Brigade bombing detachment.

The instruction should, if possible, be given at or near the billets of the Field Company concerned, who have been supplied with grenades for the purpose.

It is important that the instruction should be expedited so that these grenades may be used practically with as little delay as possible.

2. MAPS

In future only the following maps should be used in writing orders, reports, etc.
(a) For details of trenches the $\frac{1}{10,000}$ maps of Right, Left Centre and Left sections of the defence.
(b) For local tactics the $\frac{1}{40,000}$ "Country S.W. of ARMENTIERES" map.
(c) For general use the $\frac{1}{80,000}$ Sheets.

A. R. Hoskins   Colonel
General Staff.

ADMINISTRATIVE STAFF.

3. SICK.

The following are the percentages of Sick and Wounded in the 7th Division for 14th instant:-

20th Infantry Brigade
Admitted to Hospital Sick, 1 Officer, 15 men, Wounded 3 men.
Percentage of admissions to Brigade strength = .39%

21st Infantry Brigade
Admitted to Hospital, sick 11 men, Wounded 1 man.
Percentage of admissions to Brigade Strength = .39%

22nd Infantry Brigade
Admitted to Hospital, sick, 11 men, Wounded Nil.
Percentage of admissions to Brigade strength = .26%

Northumberland Hussars.
Admitted to Hospital, sick, 2 men, Wounded Nil.
Percentage of admissions to Regtl strength = .45%

Royal Artillery
Admitted to Hospital, sick, 5 men, Wounded 2 men.
Percentage of admissions to R.A. strength = .15%

Royal Engineers.
Admitted to Hospital, sick 1 man, Wounded Nil.
Percentage of admissions to R.E. strength = .18%

Army Service Corps
Admitted to Hospital, sick 2 men, Wounded Nil.
Percentage of admissions to A.S.C. strength = .5

R.A.M.C.
Admitted to Hospital, sick, 1 man, Wounded Nil.
Percentage of admissions to R.A.M.C. Strength = .15%

Total admissions from 7th Division = Sick 1 Offr, 46 men, Wounded 6 men.
Percentage of admissions to Division strength = .3%

P.T.O.

4. **CLAIMS - COMPENSATION AND REQUISITIONS.**
All claims for compensation and all requisitions
that cannot be traced are to be forwarded to this office.
It should be stated on compensation claims that the damage
inspected by an officer, and the name of the officer shou[ld be]
given for future reference if further information should [be]
required.

5. **BATH HOUSE**
The 20th Infantry Brigade will have the use of the Bath
House tomorrow.
17th & 18th December:- 22nd Infantry Brigade.

19th December:- 20th Infantry Brigade.

20th December:- 22nd Infantry Brigade.
O. C. Divisional Troops or detached units desiring use of the
Bath House will notify hours at which most convenient and dates
will be allotted.

A.C.Daly   Major
A. A. & Q. M. G., 7th Division.

7th DIVISIONAL ROUTINE ORDERS No. 74

16th December 1914

GENERAL STAFF.

1. MAPS

In Routine Orders No. 73, para 2, line 3, delete the word "Loft".

A. R. Hoskins   Colonel
General Staff.

ADMINISTRATIVE STAFF.

2. SICK.

The following are the percentages of Sick and Wounded in the 7th Division for 15th instant.

20th Infantry Brigade.
Admitted to Hospital, Sick, 1 Officer, 31 men. Wounded 5 men.
Percentage of admissions to Brigade strength = .84%

21st Infantry Brigade.
Admitted to Hospital, sick, Nil. Wounded 1 man.
Percentage of admissions to Brigade strength = ---

22nd Infantry Brigade.
Admitted to Hospital, sick, 8 men, Wounded 5 men.
Percentage of admissions to Brigade Strength = .3%

Royal Artillery.
Admitted to Hospital, sick, 7 men, Wounded 1 man.
Percentage of admissions to Brigade Strength = .21%

Royal Engineers.
Admitted to Hospital, sick Nil. Wounded 1 man.
Percentage of admissions to R.E. strength = .16%

R. A. M. C.
Admitted to Hospital, sick, 2 men. Wounded Nil.
Percentage of admissions to R.A.M.C. strength = .3%

Total admissions from 7th Division = Sick 1 Officer, 48 men, Wounded 13 men.
Percentage of admissions to Division strength = .46%

3. FUR UNDERCOATS.

In view of the possibility of the recurrence of severe weather, arrangements should now be made to collect and dry fur undercoats.

4. SHOEMAKERS

A report is required from all Units under headings as follows:-
1. Number of shoemakers at present with the Unit.
2. How employed and if any boots are being repaired under regimental arrangement.
3. The adequacy of the tools for the number of shoemakers that could be found by each unit.

5. OFFENCES - SLEEPING WHEN ON SENTRY.

Attention is directed to Circular issued today on this Subject.

6. MANGE.

A case of mange having been discovered amongst the horses of the Divisional Train, Units will keep Divisional Train Horses separate and take all precautions to protect their own horses from all sources of infection.

P. T. O.

7. SURCINGLE PADS & HORSE SHOES.

A large supply of surcingle pads and horse-shoes with frost cogs are now available at the Ordnance Store, and should be drawn without delay.

8. CASH.

With reference to Routine Order No.61 (2) dated 3/12/14, the Field Cashier will, in future visit his office near those Head Quarters on Tuesdays and Fridays commencing 18th inst. The Field Cashier will not attend tomorrow 17th inst.

9. REMOUNTS.

All Units requiring horses will send a representative with a knowledge of the requirements of their Unit to the field immediately E of Divisional Head Quarters on the N side of the SAILLY - ARMENTIERS Road, on Friday next December 18th at 9 a.m.

All horses above establishment will be sent to the above place at the same hour. If any Unit is not represented it will be concluded that this Unit is up to strength and not over establishment.

A. C. Daly
Major
A. A. & Q. M. G., 7th Division.

7th DIVISIONAL ROUTINE ORDERS No: 75.
------ooooo*ooooo------

17th December 1914.

GENERAL STAFF.

1. MACHINE GUN CLASS.

It is notified for information that the Machine Gun Class of the 20th Infantry Brigade will be firing to-morrow about 9-30 a.m. on the Testing Range South of BAC ST MAUR mentioned in 7th Divisional Routine Order No: 49 (1) of 21st November 1914.

A. R. HOSKINS.   Colonel,
General Staff.

ADMINISTRATIVE STAFF.

2. SICK.

The following are the percentages of sick and wounded in the 7th Division for the 16th instant :-

20th Infantry Brigade.
Admitted to Hospital, sick 1 Officer, 14 men, Wounded 5 men.
Percentage of admissions to Brigade strength = .45%

22nd Infantry Brigade.
Admitted to Hospital, sick 8 men, Wounded 2 men.
Percentage of admissions to Brigade strength = .24%

Royal Artillery.
Admitted to Hospital, sick 6 men.
Percentage of admissions to Royal Artillery strength = .18%

Royal Engineers.
Admitted to Hospital, wounded 1 man.
Percentage of admissions to R.E. strength = .17%

Army Service Corps.
Admitted to Hospital, sick 2 men.
Percentage of admissions to A.S.C. strength = .5%

Royal Army Medical Corps.
Admitted to Hospital, sick 1 man.
Percentage of admissions to R.A.M.C. strength = .15%

Details.
Admitted to Hospital, sick 1 man.

Total admissions from 7th Division = Sick 1 Officer, 32 men, Wounded 8 men. Percentage of admissions to Division strength = .23%.

3. SHOEMAKERS.

The report called for in Divisional Routine Order No: 74 (4) of 16th instant, should reach this Office by 9 a.m. 20th idem.

4. NATIONAL SERVICE LEAGUE FIELD GLASSES.

These Glasses are on charge of Units and not individuals. A record has been taken of the index number of the glasses already issued and similar action will be taken in regard to future issues. The record will be forwarded to the Secretary, National Service League and the hope has been expressed that as many glasses as possible may be returned after the War and restored to the original owners.

5. BATH HOUSE.

Parties attending at the Baths sometimes wait their turn in the field on the south side of the Bath House. This applies particularly to mounted parties. Such parties must not leave tins, paper, &c. lying about the field or in the ditch. All clothing to be burnt must be taken out to the fire near the latrine on the N. side of the Bath House and not left in any of the outhouses.

P.T.O.

6. COURTS-MARTIAL.

With reference to circular letter No: 449/A. of 15th instant, the Divisional Court Martial Room is now established at a house about 150 yards beyond the SAILLY cross Roads on the left hand side leading towards ESTAIRES. A sign-boards will be placed outside the house.

Major G. W. Duberly, 1st Bn Grenadier Guards is appointed standing President of Courts Martial till further notice. His own Quarters will be with the 1st line transport Grenadier Guards, BAC St MAUR. G.Os O., R.A, and Infantry Brigades and Os.C.Units Divisional Troops will arrange direct with Major Duberly for the trial of all accused men as laid down in circular quoted above.

7. BILLETS.

Officers Commanding Units will report to this Office by 9 a.m. 19th instant, the exact position of the billets occupied by the Quartermasters of their respective Units.

8. MEDICAL.

Several cases of Enteric Fever have occurred in the Division since its arrival in the present area. Inoculations for the prevention of the disease are now being carried out and all who have not been done are strongly advised to take advantage of the opportunity. One Battalion in the Division has every Officers and man inoculated and all should follow their example. Field sanitation must be zealously enforced.

Medical Officers i/c Units will at once inform their Commanding Officers of any suspected case of Enteric and, as far as is possible to arrange it, the remaining men of the platoon or formation should be kept together in billets and their blankets not used by other men.

A. C. DALY, Major,
A. A. & Q. M. G., 7th Division.

7th DIVISIONAL ROUTINE ORDERS No: 76.
------ooooo*ooooo------

18th December 1914.

ADMINISTRATIVE STAFF.

1. SICK.

The following are the percentages of sick and wounded in the 7th Division for the 17th instant:-

20th Infantry Brigade.
Admitted to Hospital, sick 22 men, Wounded 1 Officer 2 men.
Percentage of admissions to Brigade strength = .57%

22nd Infantry Brigade.
Admitted to Hospital, sick 2 offrs, 11 men, Wounded 6 men.
Percentage of admissions to Brigade strength = .45%

Northumberland Hussars.
Admitted to Hospital, sick 1 man.
Percentage of admissions to Unit's Strength = .23%

Royal Artillery.
Admitted to Hospital, sick 4 men.
Percentage of admissions to R.A. strength = .12%

Royal Engineers.
Admitted to Hospital, wounded 1 man.
Percentage of admissions to R.E. strength = .17%

Army Service Corps.
Admitted to Hospital, sick 1 man.
Percentage of admissions to A.S.C. strength = .25%

Royal Army Medical Corps.
Admitted to Hospital, sick 2 men.
Percentage of admissions to R.A.M.C. strength = .3%

Total admissions from 7th Division = Sick 2 Offrs, 41 men, Wounded 1 Offr, 9 men. Percentage of admissions to Division strength = .37%

2. SENTRIES.

The following will be added to the orders of all guards behind the advanced lines:-
"Sentries will halt all persons, motors and mounted men approaching their post between 4-30 p.m. and 7 a.m. All foreigners ^or suspicious persons^ who cannot give a satisfactory account of themselves or are not in possession of a green pass will be detained till seen by an Officer. If the Officer is not satisfied that they are really what they represent themselves to be, he will send them under escort to the A.P.M. for examination."

A. C. DALY,   Major,
A. A. & Q. M. G., 7th Division.

7th DIVISIONAL ROUTINE ORDERS No: 77.
****

19th December 1914.

ADMINISTRATIVE STAFF.

1. CHRISTMAS CARDS.

The Lieutenant-General Commanding, 4th Corps, realizing the difficulty of buying here, and on Active Service, Christmas Cards for friends at Home, has designed and had printed a Christmas Card.

As there are only Cards for about 50% of the total strength, it is hoped that no Officer or man will receive more than one.

The Lieutenant-General regrets that time prevented one card being printed for each man of the 4th Corps and it is hoped that as many as there are will prove useful.

These cards are now at the Headquarters Office and will be issued for distribution in proportion to strength to Headquarters of Brigades, Artillery, and Engineers, Cyclist Coy, Northumberland Hussars and Train.

Representatives from each of above named will attend at this Office to-morrow to take away cards.

2. SICK.

The following are the percentages of sick and wounded in the 7th Division, for the 18th instant:-

20th Infantry Brigade.
Admitted to Hospital, sick 55 men, Wounded 5 men.
Percentage of admissions to Brigade strength = .86%
21st Infantry Brigade.
Admitted to Hospital, sick 6 men,
Percentage of admissions to Brigade strength = .2%
22nd Infantry Brigade.
Admitted to Hospital, sick 2 Offrs, 9 men, Wounded 2 men.
Percentage of admissions to Brigade strength = .3%
Royal Artillery.
Admitted to Hospital, sick 3 men.
Percentage of admissions to R.A. strength = .09%
Army Service Corps.
Admitted to Hospital, sick 2 men.
Percentage of admissions to A.S.C. strength = .5%
Royal Army Medical Corps.
Admitted to Hospital, sick 1 man.
Percentage of admissions to R.A.M.C. strength = .15%.

Total admissions from Division = Sick, 2 Offrs, 56 men, Wounded 5 men.
Percentage of admissions to Division strength = .36%

3. DRUMS.

Officers Commanding Infantry battalions requiring any drums, side, brass, or bass, should put forward Indents at once to the Divisional Ordnance Officer.

P.T.O.

4. BATHS.

The Baths are allotted as under:-

December 21st – Royal Engineers (including Infantry details attached to them)
8 a.m. to 12 noon.
12 noon to 5 p.m. – Royal Army Medical Corps.
5 p.m. to 6-30 p.m. – Train and A.S.C. Drivers with Units.

The hours mentioned above must be adhered to.

December 22nd – Royal Artillery (but 10 a.m. to 11 a.m. reserved for Infantry details attached to R.E.)
December 23rd – 21st Infantry Brigade (but 10 a.m. to 11 a.m. reserved for Infantry details attached to R.E.)
December 24th – 22nd Infantry Brigade.
December 25th – 20th Infantry Brigade.

5. ALLOWANCES – Officers engaged in Active Operations.

Field Allowance and continuance of Lodging, Fuel and Light Allowances:-

Officers drawing British rates of pay, whether married or unmarried, of the Regular Army, the Special Reserve or the Territorial Force, will, while serving abroad with the Expeditionary Force on the continent of Europe, or in Egypt during the continuance of active operations in that country, draw allowances during the remaining period of the present war as follows:-

(a). Officers on consolidated pay will be eligible for Field Allowance in addition to the higher rate of consolidated pay, and may draw it under the same conditions as Regimental Officers.

(b). Officers not on consolidated pay will draw the Lodging, Fuel and Light Allowances of their rank continuously while so serving, irrespective of whether they were or were not previously occupying quarters or drawing these allowances.

(c). The allowances are issuable from 18th November 1914 in the case of officers then already serving abroad and from the date of arrival abroad in other cases.

(d). The allowances will not be issuable for any period during which the Officer's family is permitted to occupy public quarters free of charge, or the officer is in-receipt of Lodging Allowance for his family.

Special Army Order XXXVI, dy-29-11-14.

6. IRON RATIONS.

The Biscuit and Meat portions of the Iron Rations issued yesterday should be used up in lieu of preserved meat and biscuit rations. The grocery portion in tins is to be returned to the Senior Supply Officer by whom it will be retained.

A. C. DALY, Major,
A. A. & Q. M. G., 7th Division.

(Issued with 7th Divisional Routine Orders d/- 20/12/1914).

RETURN OF HORSE CASUALTIES FOR WEEK ENDING 19th December 1914.

UNIT.	Died.	Destroyed.	Transferred to Mob.V. Section.	Cured.	Remaining under Treatment.	Total strength.
Div:Hdqrs.	-	-	-	3	5	83
7/Signal Coy.	-	-	1	8	3	64
Northumberland H.	-	1	2	25	28	477
7/Cyclist Coy.	-	-	-	-	-	2
Hdqrs R.A. & Pom Pom Section.	-	-	-	-	2	33
14th Bde R.H.A.	-	-	-	18	33	657
22nd Bde R.F.A.	-	1	8	19	62	769
35th Bde R.F.A.	1	-	4	53	39	765
3rd Heavy Bde.	1	2	3	17	16	305
Div: Ammn: Col.	-	-	1	28	29	480
Div:Engineers H.Q.	-	-	-	-	-	8
54th Coy,R.E.	-	-	-	5	7	78
55th Coy,R.E.	-	-	2	4	3	80
20th Ifty Bde.	-	2	-	45	37	313
21st Ifty Bde.	1	1	4	6	36	246
22nd Infty Bde.	1	-	7	10	17	311
Div: Train.	-	3	7	6	13	494
21st Fd.Amb.	1	-	-	-	3	62
22nd Fd.Amb.	-	-	-	-	1	64
23rd Fd.Amb.	1	-	4	8	1	65
12/M.V.Sect.	-	-	-	-	-	18
TOTALS:-	6	10	36	225	335	5374

7TH DIVISIONAL ROUTINE ORDERS   No.78

20th December 1914

GENERAL STAFF

1. INFORMATION - FORWARDING OF.

There is more delay than necessary in sending information from the Firing Line to Divisional Headquarters. Any information of importance or which may at the time or might soon effect other sections should be sent immediately not only to Divisional Head Quarters but to both other Section Commanders and in the case of the right and left section to the Brigadier on their outer flank.

2. PRISONERS - RETICENCE OF.

If by any unfortunate chance any man or officer falls into the hands of the enemy he must reply to no questions but only give his rank and name. This must be impressed on each individual man.

Care must be taken that all men joining in the future in addition to those now serving with Units have this strongly impressed on them. It is of course to be understood that no man has any excuse for being taken prisoner unless incapacitated by his wounds from using his weapon.

        Sd   A.R.Hoskins   Colonel
           General Staff.

ADMINISTRATIVE STAFF.

3. BATH HOUSE.

Men attending for Baths are on no account to use the latrine of the 7th Signal Company. A Latrine for the special use of men coming for Baths has been prepared at the back of the Bath House. There is a notice to this effect in the Bath House and it is also on the Order Board which is read out to the men. There is therefore no excuse for any misunderstanding on this point.

4. TOOLS - ENTRENCHING - CARE OF.

Officers and all ranks are reminded that we are, and shall be, very dependent on having a sufficient supply of entrenching and digging tools. The G.O.C. is not satisfied that those in use are as well looked after as they might be, and that those not in use are collected until required again. This matter requires the closest possible supervision.

5. DRAFTS.

Officers taking over drafts from the Base, will, in future, see and initial the written instructions showing the personnel to be taken over, brought by Officers Conducting Parties.

6. TRAFFIC.

The SAILLY Road Bridge over the River LYS will be closed for 12 hours from 8 a.m. to 8 p.m. on Tuesday 22nd inst, for repairs. Foot Traffic will be permitted.

        A. C. Daly   Major
    A. A. & Q. M. G., 7th Division.

7th DIVISIONAL ROUTINE ORDERS.   No. 79

21st December 1914

ADMINISTRATIVE STAFF.

1. WIRE CUTTERS.

It is practically impossible at present to obtain the service pattern wirecutters in large numbers. Great care should be taken not to lose wirecutters as it will be impossible to replace them.

2. SERVICE DRESS.

There is at present a shortage in the supply from Home of Service Dress Jackets and Pantaloons, and therefore special care is required that the articles are not demanded unless really necessary, and as far as opportunity offers steps should be taken to have any repaired that can be done.

3. PRINCESS MARY'S GIFTS

All Units are to indent on Supply Officers for Princess Mary's Gifts.

A. C. Daly   Major
A. A. & Q. M. G., 7th Division.

7th DIVISIONAL ROUTINE ORDERS. No. 80

22nd December 1914.

GENERAL STAFF.

1. GRENADE COMPANIES – FORMATION OF.

It has become necessary for us to use Hand Grenades in the phase of operations with which we are confronted. That they may be used effectively, a proper understanding of their capabilities and a thorough training in their use is necessary.

It has therefore been decided to make a special organization in each Brigade to this end. In each Brigade a separate Company will be formed from specially selected men drawn from each battalion. The composition of the Company will be as follows:-

1 Officer, Commanding the Company.
1 Specially selected Non-commissioned officer as acting Sergeant Major and Q.M.Sergeant.
with 3 sections from each Battalion consisting of 1 N.C.O. and 9 men.

These Companies are to be formed immediately and their instruction by the R.E. Company affiliated to their Brigade is to be taken in hand without delay. They are to understand each pattern of bomb or grenade and the throwing of them.

When they have passed a satisfactory standard they will be entitled to wear a red cloth grenade on the sleeve of the great-coat and tunic.

During the period of instruction, and while the Brigades are stationary, they will be billeted and live with the R.E. affiliated to the Brigade. When on the march they will move as a Company, and a 2 wheeled cart will be allotted to the Company by the Brigade.

Adequate arrangements are to be made for the storage of the bombs in the trenches and the replenishment of the supply from the ammunition supply system.

It must be understood that if necessary all or any of these Brigade Companies are at the disposal of the Divisional Command for any special emergency.

It must be understood that the instruction under the R.E. which must commence immediately, must be thorough as far as our knowledge goes at present. One section from each battalion will undergo the first course of instruction under the R.E. Company affiliated, and this section will be followed by another from each unit until all three sections per Battalion are thoroughly instructed.

2. TELEPHONE LINES – CARE OF.

During the recent strong gales, telephone posts have been continually blown down. As the wire lying in the mud deteriorates rapidly, it is the duty of all ranks to assist in maintaining communications in good order by re-erecting any fallen posts that they may notice.

3. DOCUMENTS – CARE OF.

The greatest care must be taken by all officers and men when in the trenches or when going into action, that they have no papers maps or documents on their persons which could be of use to the enemy.

This must be impressed on all officers and men who join units from time to time.

A. R. Hoskins
Colonel
General Staff.

P. T. O.

7th D.O. No.80 dated 22/12/14.

ADMINISTRATIVE STAFF

4. INSTRUCTIONS RE COLLECTION OF MATERIAL THAT CANNOT BE CARRIED ON THE MARCH.

All fur undercoats when not actually required in the trenches should be collected and dried under Battalion arrangements and stored in the Divisional Store. When Commanding Officers consider the weather sufficiently severe they will be reissued and must be collected again and dried as soon as the weather becomes milder. It is most important that they should not be permitted to lie about in wet trenches.

(2) In the event of a sudden move Units will send a demand to the O.C. Train for sufficient transport to carry such articles as cannot be taken on the march, to Battalion Stores. Here they will be sorted, cleaned and dried, before being stored in the Divisional Store.

(3) Arrangements will be made for the removal of such stores to the Divisional Store either by wagons left behind for the purpose or by transport hired locally.

(4) No more should be kept in the Battalion Stores than is required for the immediate requirements of Units.

(5) The Factory near the Divisional Store is available as a drying room by arrangement with the Quartermaster, Scots Guards.

(6) O.C. Units are responsible that their Transport is not overloaded through the carriage of unauthorized loads.

(7) All spare tools surplus to establishment, loopholes, etc, not in use, should be collected and taken to Battalion Stores.

(8) Instructions as regards storemen have already been issued, until Battalion Stores are closed 1 man per Battalion must be left behind as storeman.

5. SENTRIES

Routine Order No.76 (2) of 18th December is cancelled and the following substituted.

Sentries will halt all persons, motors and mounted men approaching their posts between 4-30 p.m. and 7 a.m.

South of the railway line all civilians must be in possession of a white residential pass signed by the A.P.M. 7th Division.

North of the railway line civilians may pass up to 8 p.m. without a pass.

Both North and South of line, no civilian is allowed out between 8 p.m. and 6 a.m. without a special pass signed by an A.P.M. stating reasons for being out.

All Foreign Officers and British Officers travelling in Motor Cars should be in possession of a green pass signed by an A.P.M.

Whenever there is any doubt as to the bona-fides of any individual Civil or Military of whatever rank, the Sentry will detain the person concerned and refer the case to an officer who if not satisfied will send the suspect under escort to the office of the A.P.M. at SAILLY BRIDGE.

6. PRINCESS MARY'S XMAS PRESENT TO THE TROOPS AT THE FRONT.

Extracts from 4th Army Corps Order No.422 dated 10/12/14.

x x x x x x x x x

(3) Every Commanding Officer will give a receipt for the Boxes received for his units, and render a certificate to the Senior Supply Officer on the 27th that every Officer and man present with his Unit on the 25th or 26th received one box only. Any balance left over will be handed to the Senior Supply Officer with the Commanding Officer's Certificate.

x x x x x x x x x

(continued)

Sheet (2)

x x x x x x x x x
(5) Every man who entrains for the Front on the 23rd or 24th will receive his box from his unit. A supplementary demand being made on the Senior Supply Officer if necessary.

x x x x x x x x
(6) Every man who leaves his Unit or Hospital for the Base on the 23rd or 24th will receive his box on arrival at the Base.

x x x x x x x
(7) Any man who entrains for the Base on the 25th will receive his box from his unit before starting. Similarly, any man who entrains for the front on the 25th will receive his box before entrainment.

x x x x x x x x x
(9) It must be distinctly understood that, while every effort will be made to ensure that each Officer and Man receives one Box, should by accident anyone not receive it, the non-receipt is not to form the subject of subsequent official correspondence.

7. CHRISTMAS PUDDINGS.
The plum puddings which have been kindly provided for the 4th Corps by a Committee presided over by Lady Rawlinson will be issued with rations at the refilling point on the 24th instant, the allowance will be about 7/8 lb per man.

8. FORAGE.
There have been a number of complaints from Units that they are not receiving their full allowance of forage. On investigation it almost invariably transpires that the shortage is due to their representative not indenting for the full amount.
The following is the scale of forage ordered vide 7th Div. Routine Order No. 50 dated 22/11/14 and is available:-

HORSES	Oats	Hay	Bran
Riding or Draught	12	8	2
Heavy Draught	15	8	2
Clydesdale and Shire	19	8	2

When bran is not available 2 lbs Oats will be issued in lieu.
The balance of the hay ration will be made up in straw procured locally, or, if no local supply is available, arrangements will be made by the Senior Supply Officer.
In future the responsibility of asking for the correct amount will rest with the Unit, and the Indent (B.55) will show clearly, in the Column "Remarks" the strength of Animals under the following heads, viz:- Riding and Draught, Heavy Draught, Clydesdale or Shire.

9. SANITATION.
It has been noticed that many of the billets are in an insanitary condition, empty tins and vegetable refuse being thrown about outside the houses.
O.C. Units must see that all refuse is buried in proper refuse pits.

10 HORSES - MANGE
The restrictions contained in D.Os 66 (5) and 74 (6) are cancelled.

P.T.O.

11 SICK.

The following are the percentages of Sick and Wounded in the 7th Division for the 21st inst:-

20th Infantry Brigade.
Admitted to Hospital, sick, 1 Officer, 38 men, Wounded 1 Officer, 6 men.
Percentage of admissions to Brigade Strength = 1.05%

21st Infantry Brigade
Admitted to Hospital, sick 16 men, Wounded 3 men.
Percentage of admissions to Brigade Strength = .56%

22nd Infantry Brigade.
Admitted to Hospital, sick, 1 Officer, 10 men, Wounded 6 men.
Percentage of admissions to Brigade Strength = .39%

Royal Artillery.
Admitted to Hospital, sick 1 man, Wounded Nil.
Percentage of admissions to R.A. strength = .03%

Royal Engineers
Admitted to Hospital, sick, 1 man, Wounded Nil.
Percentage of admissions to R.E. Strength = .17%

R. A. M. C.
Admitted to Hospital, sick, 4 men, Wounded Nil.
Percentage of admissions to R.A.M.C. strength = .59%

Total admissions from 7th Division = Sick 2 Officers, 71 men (includes 1 man of Details)
Wounded 1 Officer, 15 Men.
Percentage of admissions to Division Strength = .5.

A. C. Daly   Major
A. A. & Q. M. G., 7th Division.

7th DIVISIONAL ROUTINE ORDERS.   No. 81

23rd December 1914

GENERAL STAFF.

1. COURSES - MACHINE GUN.

A second Machine Gun Course will commence at ST OMER on the 28th December 1914.

The following vacancies are allotted to Infantry Brigades.

	Officers	Other Ranks
20th Infantry Brigade	1	7
21st Infantry Brigade	1	7
22nd Infantry Brigade	1	6

Further instructions will be issued as regards the despatch of these parties to ST OMER.

A. R. Hoskins   Colonel
General Staff

ADMINISTRATIVE STAFF.

2. SICK.

The following are the percentages of sick and wounded in the 7th Division for 22nd instant.

20th Infantry Brigade
Admitted to Hospital, sick 2 Officers, 47 men, Wounded 5 men.
Percentage of admissions to Brigade Strength = 1.23%

21st Infantry Brigade.
Admitted to Hospital, sick 8 men, Wounded 1 man
Percentage of admissions to Brigade Strength = .27%

22nd Infantry Brigade.
Admitted to Hospital, sick 1 Officer, 14 men, Wounded 7 men.
Percentage of admissions to Brigade Strength = .5%

Northumberland Hussars
Admitted to Hospital, sick 1 man, Wounded Nil.
Percentage of admissions to Units strength = .23%

Royal Artillery.
Admitted to Hospital, sick 6 men, Wounded Nil.
Percentage of admissions to R.A. strength = .19%

Royal Engineers.
Admitted to Hospital, sick 1 man, Wounded Nil.
Percentage of admissions to R.E. Strength = .17%

R.A.M.C.
Admitted to Hospital, sick 1 Officer, 1 man, Wounded Nil.
Percentage of admissions to R.A.M.C. Strength = .3%

Total admissions from 7th Division = Sick 4 Officers, 78 men. Wounded 13 men.
Percentage of admissions to Division strength = .53%

3. COURTS MARTIAL

Attention is directed to Circular issued this day relating to completion of Columns & Schedules on A.F.'s A.3 by Convening Officers.

4. BATH HOUSE.

The Bath House is allotted as follows:-

26th December	21st Infantry Brigade
27th December	20th Infantry Brigade
28th December	22nd Infantry Brigade
29th December	Royal Artillery.
30th December	21st Infantry Brigade
31st December	20th Infantry Brigade
1st January	22nd Infantry Brigade.

5. CHRISTMAS PUDDINGS AND PRINCESS MARY'S GIFT.

French Interpreters and chauffeurs employed with the British Forces are eligible for a share in the issue of Christmas Puddings, but not for Princess Mary's Christmas Present.

A. C. Daly   Major
A. A. & Q. M. G., 7th Division.

7th DIVISIONAL ROUTINE ORDERS　　　　No. 82

24th December 1914

ADMINISTRATIVE STAFF.

1. SICK

The following are the percentages of Sick and Wounded in the 7th Division for 23rd inst.

20th Infantry Brigade.
Admitted to Hospital, sick 2 Officers, 28 men.   Wounded 5 men.
Percentage of admissions to Brigade Strength = .8%

21st Infantry Brigade.
Admitted to Hospital, sick, 14 men, Wounded 2 men.
Percentage of admissions to Brigade strength = .48%

22nd Infantry Brigade.
Admitted to Hospital, sick, 15 men, Wounded 2 men.
Percentage of admissions to Brigade strength = .39%

Royal Artillery.
Admitted to Hospital, sick 10 men, wounded Nil.
Percentage of admissions to R.A. Strength = .32%

Royal Engineers.
Admitted to Hospital, sick 1 man, Wounded 1 man.
Percentage of admissions to R.E. strength = .34%

Army Service Corps.
Admitted to Hospital, sick 1 man, wounded Nil.
Percentage of admissions to A.S.C. strength = .25%

Total admissions from 7th Division = Sick 2 Officers, 69 men.
　　　　　　　　　　　　　　　Wounded 1 Officer, 10 men
　　　　　　　　　　　　　　　　(Details)
Percentage of admission to Division Strength = .46%

2. DIVINE SERVICE & HOLY COMMUNION.

There will be a celebration of the Holy Communion at 7-30 a.m. tomorrow, Xmas Day, at the house next door to the C.R.E's office.
Voluntary services (C. of E.) will be held tomorrow in the waiting room at the Bath House, at 11 a.m. ~~and 11.35 a.m. to 12.5 p.m.~~
These Services will be held every Sunday whilst the Division is in this vicinity.

　　　　　　　　　　　　　　　A. C. Daly　　　　　　Major
　　　　　　　　A. A. & Q. M. G.　7th Division

7th DIVISIONAL ROUTINE ORDERS   No. 83.

25th December 1914

ADMINISTRATIVE STAFF.

1. SICK.

The following are the percentages of Sick and Wounded in the 7th Division for 24th inst:-

20th Infantry Brigade.
Admitted to Hospital, Sick, 1 Officer, 67 men, Wounded 1 man.
Percentage of admissions to Brigade Strength = 1.6%

21st Infantry Brigade.
Admitted to Hospital, sick 9 men, wounded 7 men.
Percentage of admissions to Brigade strength = .48%

22nd Infantry Brigade.
Admitted to Hospital, sick 23 men, wounded 2 men.
Percentage of admissions to Brigade strength = .57%

Northumberland Hussars
Admitted to Hospital, sick, 1 Officer, 1 man, Wounded Nil.
Percentage of admissions to Units strength = .45%

Royal Artillery.
Admitted to Hospital, sick, 5 men, Wounded Nil.
Percentage of admissions to R.A. strength = .09%

Royal Engineers.
Admitted to Hospital, sick 5 men, Wounded 1 Officer.
Percentage of admissions to R.E. strength = 1.01%

Total admissions from 7th Division = Sick 2 Officers, 108 men.
                                      Wounded 1 Officer, 10 men.
Percentage of admissions to Division strength = .68%

2. OPTICAL APPLIANCES

O. C. Infantry Units should put forward Indents at once for the number of periscopes required to complete their Units to 6 per Battalion.

3. RIFLE OIL.

O. C. Units should put forward Indents at once for the Tins and Funnels required vide Army Corps Routine Order No.258.

A. C. Daly   Major
A. A. & Q. M. G., 7th Division.

7th Divisional Routine Orders   No. 65

27th December 1914.

ADMINISTRATIVE STAFF.

1. SICK.

The following are the percentages of Sick and Wounded in the 7th Division, for 26th inst:-

20th Infantry Brigade.
Admitted to Hospital, sick 1 Officer, 20 men,   Wounded Nil.
Percentage of admissions to Brigade Strength = .53%

21st Infantry Brigade.
Admitted to Hospital, sick 1 Officer, 17 men,   Wounded 1 man.
Percentage of admissions to Brigade Strength = .56%

22nd Infantry Brigade.
Admitted to Hospital, sick 8 men,   Wounded 1 man.
Percentage of admissions to Brigade Strength = .19%

Royal Artillery.
Admitted to Hospital, sick, 9 men,   Wounded Nil.
Percentage of admissions to R.A. strength = .27%

Army Service Corps.
Admitted to Hospital, sick 1 man,   Wounded Nil.
Percentage of admissions to A.S.C. strength = .23%

Total admissions from 7th Division = Sick 2 Officers, 55 men.
                                     Wounded, 2 men.
Percentage of admissions to Division strength = .35%

2. COURTS MARTIAL.

Attention is directed to Circular issued this day relating to unnecessary delays in Courts Martial.

3. FROST SHOES.

Units will furnish a return by 10 a.m. on 30th inst shewing:-
(a) Number of horses shod with frost shoes fitted with cogs.
(b) Number of such shoes now in possession ready for filling.

4. INDENTS

Indents put forward on A. O. D., for Clothing and Equipment should be forwarded in duplicate.

5. PRELLER HIDES.

A quantity of Preller leather Hides will shortly be received and will be issued to Units for repair of Harness. Reports as to the suitability of this leather should be rendered to D.A.D.O.S., when called for.

A. C. Daly   Lt.Colonel

A. A. & Q. M. G., 7th Division

NOTICE

LOST:- Bicycle - number on handlebars 8 5 4 3 8.
This Bicycle was taken away from C.R.E. office yesterday between 7 p.m. and 8 p.m.

Issued with 7th Divisional Routine Orders dated 27/12/14.

Return of Horse Casualties for week ending 26th December 1914.

Unit	Died	Destroyed	Transferred to Mob.V Section	Cured	Remaining under Treatment	Total Strength
Div: Hdqrs	-	-	2	2	6	81
7/Signal Coy.	-	-	-	-	4	64
N.Hussars	1	-	2	10	22	475
7/Cyclist Coy.	-	-	-	-	-	2
Hdqrs R.A. & Pom-Pom-Sect:	-	-	-	-	-	29
14th Bde R.H.A.	-	-	1	2	-	891
22nd Bde R.F.A.	1	3	5	13	31	768
35th Bde R.F.A.	2	2	4	21	62	776
3rd Heavy Bde.	-	1	2	40	39	304
Div.Amm.Col.	1	1	7	24	25	490
Hdqrs R.E.	-	-	2	25	24	8
4th Coy R.E.	-	-	-	-	1	78
5th Coy R.E.	-	-	-	1	6	76
6th Inf.Bde.	-	-	-	2	1	317
1st Inf.Bde.	1	1	-	19	26	243
2nd Inf.Bde.	-	2	1	10	32	313
Div. Train.	4	1	-	10	18	496
1st Fd.Amb.	-	-	-	8	12	62
2nd Fd.Amb.	-	-	2	3	1	85
3rd Fd.Amb.	-	-	-	1	1	64
8th M.V.Sect.	-	-	-	1	-	18
TOTALS	10	12	26	191	311	5,620

7th Divisional Routine Orders.   No.86.

28th December 1914

ADMINISTRATIVE STAFF.

1. SICK.

The following are the percentages of sick and wounded in the 7th Division, for 27th inst:-

20th Infantry Brigade.
Admitted to Hospital, sick, 15 men.   Wounded 2 men.
Percentage of admissions to Brigade Strength = .43%

21st Infantry Brigade.
Admitted to Hospital, sick 11 men.   Wounded Nil.
Percentage of admissions to Brigade Strength = .32%

22nd Infantry Brigade.
Admitted to Hospital, sick 13 men.   Wounded Nil.
Percentage of admissions to Brigade Strength = .27%

Royal Artillery.
Admitted to Hospital, sick 9 men, Wounded Nil.
Percentage of admissions to R.A. strength = .27%

Royal Engineers
Admitted to Hospital, sick 1 man.   Wounded Nil.
Percentage of admissions to R.E. strength = .15%

Army Service Corps.
Admitted to Hospital sick, 3 men.   Wounded Nil.
Percentage of admissions to A.S.C. strength = .69%

R. A. M. C.
Admitted to Hospital, sick 1 man,   Wounded Nil.
Percentage of admissions to R.A.M.C. strength = .13%

Total admissions from 7th Division = Sick 53 men.   Wounded 2 men.
Percentage of admissions to Division strength = .3%

2. BATH HOUSE.

The Baths are allotted as under:-
2nd January - Royal Engineers (Including Infantry details
8 a.m. to 12 noon   attached to them)
12 noon to 3 p.m. - Royal Army Medical Corps.
3 p.m. to 6.30 p.m. Train and A.S.C. Drivers with Units.
    The hours mentioned above must be adhered to.
January 3rd -   20th Infantry Brigade.
January 4th -   21st Infantry Brigade.
January 5th -   22nd Infantry Brigade.
January 6th. -   20th Infantry Brigade.
January 7th -   21st Infantry Brigade.
January 8th -   22nd Infantry Brigade.
January 9th -   Royal Artillery.

A. C. Daly   Lt.Colonel

A. A. & Q. M. G., 7th Division.

NOTICE.
****

FOUND
at SAILLY a Rifle numbered S. W.F. 7 1 8, in case.
Application should be made for same to Hd.Qr.Office,
7th Division.

7th Divisional Routine Orders. No. 87.

ADMINISTRATIVE STAFF. 29th December 1914.

1. LEAVE.
   (a) Arrangements will be made as heretofore.
       See Routine Orders No. 7 of 27th November.
                            No. 3 of 6th December.
                            No. 2 of 8th December.
   (b) Special attention is called to the necessity for demanding Bus accommodation at MERVILLE at least 24 hours in advance.

2. BLANKETS, CLOTHING & EQUIPMENT.
   Every effort should be made to collect all blankets, articles of clothing and equipment lying about in the trenches that are not in use, also rifles and ammunition. These should be collected daily and handed over to the men leaving the trenches to draw rations to be returned in the carts which bring up the rations.
   There is a great shortage in blankets and it is presumed they must be lying about in the trenches.

3. HORSE RUGS.
   Units should put forward Indents for their requirements of Horse Rugs at once.

4. HORSES.
   The following horses surplus to establishment will be sent to O. C. Train for reissue:-
   4 riding horses and 2 draught   from   T. Battery R.H.A.
   1 Riding Horse   from   H.Q. 35th F.A. Brigade.
   3 Officers Chargers   from   2nd Border Regiment.
   2 Draught Horses   from   1st S/Staffordshire Regt.

5. MEDICAL.
   Sick of Baggage and Supply Sections and other details of regimental units billeting in SAILLY and BAC St MAUR will report for treatment at the Field Ambulance which is affiliated to their Brigade.

                    R. F. A. Hobbs   Captain
                    D. A. A. & Q. M. G., 7th Division.

NOTICE
---oOo---

The following officers valises are in possession of the S.S.O. and have been since arrival of the draft on the 23rd instant, will the officers concerned make arrangements for their removal.
   1 Brown Valise with name:- F. POWELL.
   1 Green Valise with name:- H. A. POLAND, WEST KENTS.
   1 Green Valise with name:- ASHMEAD-BARTLETT, BEDFORDS.

7th Divisional Routhine Orders   No. 88

30th December 1914

ADMINISTRATIVE STAFF.

1. **HELIOS AND LAMPS.**
It has been decided that in future the scale of Helios and Lamps Signalling "B", shall be as follows:-

Formations	Helios	Lamps Signal--ling "B".
Divisional Signal Squadron	3	3
Signal Troop.	4	4
Cavalry Regiment.	4	4
Artillery Brigade H.Q., R.H.A.	1	-
-:- Battery R.H.A.	1	2
-:- Brigade H.Q., R.F.A.	1	-
-:- Battery R.F.A.	1	2
-:- -:- 60 pdr R.G.A.	2	4
-:- -:- -:- Ammn. Col.	1	2
Divisional Signal Coy. H.Q.	2	2
-:- -:- -:- Nos 2, 3, & 4 Sections, each.	1	1
Infantry Battalion	2	2

(2) Lamps & Helios in possession of units surplus to this scale should be returned to the Base, there to be held for re-issue in the Spring should such a course be considered necessary.

                              R. F. A. Hobbs   Captain

                   D. A. A. & Q. M. G., 7th Division.

7th Divisional Routine Orders.   No. 89.

31st December 1914

ADMINISTRATIVE STAFF.

1. SICK.

The following are the percentages of Sick and Wounded in the 7th Division for 30th insr:-

20th Infantry Brigade.
Admitted to Hospital, sick 1 Officer 15 men.   Wounded Nil.
Percentage of admissions to Brigade Strength = .4%

21st Infantry Brigade.
Admitted to Hospital, sick 23 men.   Wounded 1 man.
Percentage of admissions to Brigade Strength = .7%

22nd Infantry Brigade.
Admitted to Hospital, sick 10 men, Wounded 1 Officer, 4 men.
Percentage of admissions to Brigade Strength = .31%

Royal Artillery.
Admitted to Hospital, sick 13 men.   Wounded Nil.
Percentage of admissions to R.A. strength = .39%

Royal Engineers.
Admitted to Hospital sick, Nil.   Wounded 1 man.
Percentage of admissions to R.E. strength = .15%

Army Service Corps.
Admitted to Hospital, sick 1 man.   Wounded Nil.
Percentage of admissions to A.S.C. strength = .23%

R. A. M. C.
Admitted to Hospital, sick 3 men.   Wounded Nil.
Percentage of admissions to R.A.M.C. strength = .39%

Total admissions from 7th Division = Sick 1 Officer, 65 men.
                                     Wounded 1 Officer, 6 men.
Percentage of admissions to Division strength = .4%

2. ORDNANCE.

The following having arrived today are available for issue.
1000 Blankets,   2160 Fur Under Coats,   Leather Coats for Motor Drivers.

3. FORAGE.

The following maximum scale of forage is published for information:-

Riding Horses.)   12 lbs hay.   12 lbs oats.
Draught Horses)
Heavy Draught   16   -do-   15 lbs oats
Shires & Clydesdales   15   -do-   19 lbs oats.

When bran is drawn 1½ lbs of bran is equivalent to 1 lb of oats and is drawn in lieu.

It must not be overlooked that this is the maximum scale and the amount is seldom available for issue at railhead.

When the forage is short it must be divided up according to scale. The S.S.O. will however endeavour to supplement from local resources for which purpose straw only appears to be available at present.

The daily ration for each class of horse can be ascertained at the enquiry office, and all officers responsible for the care of horses should assure themselves that those under their command are made acquainted with the amount each horse should receive.

R. F. A. Hobbs   Captain

D. A. A. & Q. M. G., 7th Division

A & Q
7th Division

Nominal Rolls. Casualties &c
1914

State of Infty Bdes.

20th Infantry Brigade

	OFFRS.	O.R
1st Grenadier Guards	6	405
2nd Scots Guards	8	456
2nd Border Regt.	11	432
2nd Gordon Hdrs	5	435
Total for Bde	30	1728

21st Infantry Brigade

2nd Bedford Regt.	9	550
2nd Yorks Regt.	6	451
2nd R. Scots Fus.	6	250
2nd Wilts Regt	3	355
Total for Bde	24	1606

22nd Infantry Brigade

2nd "Queens"	3	236
2nd R. War. Regt	2	257
1st R. Welsh Fus.	3	198
1st S. Staffs Regt.	2	230
Total for Bde	10	921

TOTAL FOR 3 INFANTRY BDES.	64	4255

Appendix A.

CASUALTIES, 7th DIVISION, 18th OCTOBER 1914 to 15th NOVEMBER 1914.

Units &c.	Officers.			Other Ranks.			
	K	W	M	K	W	M	
Divisional Headquarters.	-	4	-	5	6	-	
7th Signal Company.	-	-	-	3	14	8	
Northumberland Hussars.	-	6	-	3	17	1	
Cyclist Company.	-	-	1	1	20	9	
C.R.A. and Pom-Pom Detachment.	-	1	-	1	4	-	
14th Bde R.H.A. "F" Btty.	-	2	-	7	20	1	
22nd Bde R.F.A.	1	5	-	11	51	7	
35th Bde R.F.A.	2	5	-	11	84	16	
111th Heavy Battery, R.G.A.	-	-	-	1	4	-	
112th Heavy Battery, R.G.A.	-	-	-	-	15	-	
7th Divisional Ammn. Column.	-	-	-	-	7	-	
Divl Engineers, Headquarters.	-	-	-	-	-	-	
54th Field Coy, R.E.	2	1	-	3	32	1	
55th Field Coy, R.E.	1	-	-	5	16	2	
20th Infantry Brigade Hdqrs.	-	1	-	1	6	-	
1st Bn Grenadier Guards.	6	14	-	83	277	315	655
2nd Bn Scots Guards.	6	8	8	41	204	529	774
2nd Bn Border Regiment.	9	11	-	79	259	253	591
2nd Bn Gordon Highlanders.	7	21	2	88	289	161	538
21st Infantry Bde, Headquarters.	-	2	-	5	6	1	
2nd Bedford Regiment.	9	18	2	75	324	151	550
2nd Bn Yorks Regiment.	8	17	-	104	374	153	631
2nd Bn R.Scots Fusiliers.	3	15	8	91	288	488	867
2nd Bn Wilts Regiment.	5	2	19	53	116	574	743
22nd Infantry Bde, Hdqrs.	2	-	1	2	8	6	
2nd Bn "Queens"	3	25	-	75	441	283	799
2nd Bn R.Warwick Regiment.	7	9	12	88	357	342	787
1st Bn R.Welch Fusiliers.	7	15	15	72	228	724	1024
1st Bn S.Staff Regiment.	6	17	5	25	97	742	846
Divisional Train.	-	-	-	1	1	6	
21st Field Ambulance.	1	3	3	1	2	3	
22nd Field Ambulance.	-	-	-	-	-	3	
23rd Field Ambulance.	-	-	1	-	-	22	
TOTALS :-	85	202	77	935	3567	4801	
		364			9303.		

APPENDIX:- B.

7th Division

List of Casualties - Officers from 18th October 1914

To November 30th 1914.

Unit.	Rank & Name.	Date.	Casualty
Div: Hd Qrs.	Lt.Col.C.J.Perceval	22/10/14	Wounded.
	Captain J.V.Isacc	24/10/14	Wounded
	Captain W.S.Douglas	2/10/14	Wounded ✕
	Captain P.R.Butler	2/11/14	Wounded.

✕ Since died.

7th Div: Signal Coy.

Northumberland Hsrs.	Major L.Johnston	22/10/14	Wounded
	2/Lieut.C.M.Laing	22/10/14	Wounded
	Captain W.A.Kennard	24/10/14	Wounded
	Captain H.Sidney	25/10/14	Wounded
	2/Lieut.A.R.Pease	25/10/14	Wounded
	2/Lieut.S.Clayton	25/10/14	Wounded
7th Div: Cyclist Company.	Captain L.Peel (Yorks)	24/10/14	Missing.
Hd Qrs & Pom-Pom Dett: R.A.	Major H.C.Cavendish.	13/11/14	Wounded.
14th Bde,R.H.A.	Lt.Col.H.D.White-Thomson, D.S.O.	22/10/14	Wounded.
	Lieut.H.L.Davies	24/10/14	Wounded. (Died 27/10/14)

APPENDIX:- B

Unit	Rank & Name	Date	Casualty
22nd Bde R.F.A.	Major T.C.W.Malony, D.S.O,	21/10/14	Wounded
	Lieut.F.C.C.Hayter Chaytor	21/10/14	Wounded
	Major G.E.Bolster	23/10/14	Killed
	2/Lieut A.N.Coxe	2/11/14	Wounded
	2/Lieut.F.R.P.Curry	8/11/14	Wounded
	Lieut.G.Sumpter	13/11/14	Wounded.
35th Bde R.F.A.	Major H.R.Phipps	20/10/14	Wounded
	Lieut.J.C.C.Dennis	24/10/14	Killed
	Lieut.A.J.Woodhouse	30/10/14	Killed
	Lt.Col.E.P.Lambert	30/10/14	Wounded
	Major H.W.A.Christie	30/10/14	Wounded
	Lieut.E.CLayton	3/11/14	Wounded
	Lieut.H.N.H.Williamson	29/10/14	Wounded
	2/Lieut.R.W.Oldfield	20/11/14	Wounded
54y 111th Heavy Batty R.G.A.	—		
12th Heavy Batty R.G.A.	—		
7th Div.Ammn Column.	—		
Hd Qrs Div:Engineers	—		
54th Field Coy R.E.	Capt.J.A.McEnery	26/10/14	Killed
	2/Lieut M.Wynne-Jones (S.R.)	29/10/14	Killed
	Lieut.S.F.C.Sweeny	3/11/14	Wounded
	Lieut.C.A.West	20/11/14	Wounded
	Major D.S.McInnes	26/11/14	Wounded

APPENDIX:- B.

Unit.	Rank & Name	Date.	Casualty.
55th Field Coy R.E.	Lieut J.M.Smeathman	25/10/14	Killed
	Captain L.St.V.Rose	28/11/14	Killed
Hd Qrs 20th Inf:Bde.	Brig.Genl.Ruggles Brise	2/11/14	Wounded.
1st Bn Grenadier Gds.	Major L.R.V.Colby	25/10/14	Killed
	Lieut.E.Antrobus	25/10/14	Killed
	2/Lieut.N.A.H.Somerset	25/10/14	Killed
	2/Lieut.S.Walters	25/10/14n	Killed
	Capt.R.E.K.Leatham	25/10/14	Wounded
	Lieut.H.L.Aubrey-Fletcher	28/10/14	Wounded
	Major H.St.L.Stugley	29/10/14	Killed
	Capt.Lord R.Wellesley	29/10/14	Killed
	Capt.Hon.C.M.B.Ponsonby M.V.D.	29/10/14	Wounded
	2/Lieut R.S.Lambert	29/10/14	Wounded
	Major Hon.Weld Forester, M.V.O.	29/10/14	Wounded (Died)
	2/Lieut.R.O.R.Kenyon Slaney	29/10/14	Wounded
	Lt.Col.M.Earle,D.S.O.	31/10/14	Wounded & Missing.
	Captain G.Rennie	31/10/14	Wounded & Missing
	Lt.Hon.A.G.S.Douglas-Pennant	31/10/14	Wounded & Missing
	Lieut P.Van Neck	31/10/14	Wounded & Missing.
	Lieut.L.G.Ames	31/10/14	Wounded
	Lieut.Harcourt Powell	31/10/14	Wounded
	2/Lt.Sir G.H.J.Duckworth King	3/11/14	Wounded
	Lieut G.E.Hope	4/11/14	Wounded
	Lieut.E.S.Ward	15/11/14	Wounded

APPENDIX:- B.

Unit	Rank & Name	Date	Casualty
2nd Bn. Scots Guards	Maj.Lord E.C.Gordon-Lennox	22/10/14	Wounded
	Capt T.H.R.Bulkeley	22/10/14	Killed
	Capt.Hon D.A.Kinnaird	25/10/14	Killed
	Capt.C.F.P.Hamilton	27/10/14	Wounded
	Lieut W.H.Holbech	27/10/14	Wounded (Died)
	2/Lieut W.H.Wynne-Finch	27/10/14	Wounded
	Maj.Hon H.J.Fraser,M.V.O.	28/10/14	Killed
	Lieut A.R.Orr	28/10/14	Wounded
	Lt,Lord G.R.Grosvenor	28/10/14	Wounded
	Lt.Col.R.G.I.Bolton	28/10/14	Missing
	Major Visc.Darymple	28/10/14	Missing
	Capt C.V.Fox	28/10/14	Missing
	Capt Hon.J.S.Coke	28/10/14	Missing
	2/Lt.Lord Garlies	28/10/14	Missing
	Lieut.E.B.Trafford	28/10/14	missing
	Lt.R&Steuart Menzies	28/10/14	Missing
	Lt.R.F.H.Gladwin	28/10/14	Missing
	Lt.Earl of Dalhousie	29/10/14	Wounded
	Capt H.L.Kemble,M.V.O.		Wounded
	2/Lt Gibbs		Killed
	Lt,D.R.Drumond	3/11/14	Killed
	Capt Hon.R.Coke	30/11/14	Wounded.
	2/Lieut C.Cottrell Dormer	28/10/14	Killed
2nd Bn.Border Regt.	Lt.P.J.E.~~Gorton~~ Egerton.	17/10/14	Killed
	Major J.T.I.Besanquet	27/10/14	Wounded
	Lieut T.H.Beves	27/10/14	Wounded
	Capt.E.H.H.Lees	28/10/14	Killed
	Capt C.A.J.Cholmondeley	28/10/14	Killed
	Capt R.N.Gordon	28/10/14	Killed
	Major W.L.Allen, D.S.O.	28/10/14	Killed
	Capt.C.G.W.Andrews	28/10/14	Killed
	Lieut J.B.B.Warren	28/10/14	Killed
	2/Lt.C.V.G.Surtees	28/10/14	~~Killed~~ W + m.
	2/Lieut T.J.Clancey	28/10/14	Killed
	Lt.H.P.O.Sleigh	28/10/14	Wounded & Mis.
	2/Lieut C.H.Evans	28/10/14	Wounded & Mis.
	Lt.Col.L.L.Wood	29/10/14	Wounded
	Capt.L.E.H.Molyneux-Seel	29/10/14	Wounded & Mis
	Lieut.H.V.Gerrard	27-1/11/14	Killed
	Capt G.E.Warren		Wounded
	Lieut W.Watson		Wounded
	Lieut G.W.H.Hodgson		Wounded Died 7/11/14
	Lieut. A.P.Johnson		wounded.
	~~Lieut E.C.Clegg~~	28/10/14	S.

APPENDIX:- B

Unit	Rank & Name	Date	Casualty
2nd Bn.Gordon Highlanders			
	Capt.F.R.E.Sworder	28/10/14	Wounded
	Lieut T.H.O.Thistle	28/10/14	Wounded
	Lieut.L.Carr	30/10/14	Wounded
	Capt.C.D.G.Huggins	30/10/14b	Wounded
	2/Lt.W.Waring	30/10/14	Wounded
	Lt.Col.H.P.Uniacke	31/10/14	Wounded
	Lieut J.A.O.Brooke	29/10/14	Killed
	Lieut.C.K.Latta	29/10/14	Killed
	2/Lt.G.McAuliffe (Camerons)	29/10/14	Killed
	2/Lt.Hon.S.Fraser	29/10/14	Killed
	Lt.P.M.Mackenzie	29/10/14	Wounded
	2/Lt A.Mc Bride(H.L.I.)	29/10/14	Wounded
	Lt.J.H.Fraser	30/10/14	Killed
	2/Lt.G.F.Webster(Black W)	30/10/14	Killed
	2/Lt.D.G.F.Macbean	30/10/14	Wounded
	2/Lt.J.P.Boyd	30/10/14	Wounded
	2/Lt.J.Pringle (Camerons)	30/10/14	Wounded
	2/Lt.T.F.Murdoch(Black W)	30/10/14	Wounded
	2/Lt.J.H.Duguid	30/10/14	Wounded
	Capt J.L.G.Burnett	31/10/14	Wounded
	Capt B.G.R.Gordon	31/10/14	Wounded
	Capt K.H.Bruce	31/10/14	Wounded
	Lt.Hon.W.Fraser	31/10/14	Wounded
	Lt.C.E.Anderson	31/10/14	Wounded
	2/Lt.Q.D.Bell	31/10/14	Wounded
	Lt.A.S.Graham	31/10/14	Killed
	Capt C.N.McLean	31/10/14	Missing
	2/Lt.W.C.Robertson	31/10/14	Missing
	Major G.S.C.Crauford	1/11/14	Wounded
	Capt J.R.E.Stansfeld	2/11/14	wounded.
21st Inf.Bde.Hd.Qrs			
	Capt A.L.Godman (Staff Capt)	1/11/14	Wounded
	Capt A.S.Bruce (M.G.Offr)	1/11/14	Wounded
2nd Bedford Regt.	2/Lt.C.O.Bell	18/10/14	Killed
	Capt F.M.Bassett	18/10/14	Wounded
	Capt C.H.Woolfe	18/10/14	Wounded
	Lt.G.M.Hosford Horsford	18/10/14	Wounded
	Lt.D.G.C.Wright	25/10/14	Killed
	Lt.A.E.Hopkins	25/10/14	Wounded
	Capt A.J.Patron	24/10/14	Wounded
	Capt A.G.Hall	26/10/14	Killed
	Lt.W.Bastard	26/10/14	Killed
	Lt.E.E.Punchard	29/10/14	Killed
	Capt W.E.M.Wetherell	29/10/14	Wounded
	Lt.H.E.Huntriss	29/10/14	Wounded
	2/Lt.Innes	29/10/14	Wounded
	2/Lt.Inskip	29/10/14	Wounded
	2/Lt.Small	29/10/14	Wounded
	2/Lt.Kuhn	29/10/14	Wounded
	2/Lt.R.R.L.Thom	29/10/14	Wounded
	2/Lt.Whittemore	29/10/14	Wounded
	Major J.M.Traill	30/10/14	Killed
	Major R.P.Stares	30/10/14	Killed
	Lt.J.A.Paterson	30/10/14	Killed.

APPENDIX:- B

Unit.	Rank & Name	Date	Casualty
Bedford Regt (Continued)	Capt C.S.Garnett-Botfield	30/10/14	Wounded
	Capt.A.B.Lemon	30/10/14	Missing & Wounded.
	Lt,G.E.Gott	30/10/14	Wounded
	Lt.Dixon	30/10/14	Wounded
	Capt E.H.Lyddon	30/10/14	Wounded
	Lt.W.C.Anderson	30/10/14	Missing
	Lt.D.G.C.Thomson	31/10/14	Wounded & Missing.
	Lt.D.L.de T.Fernandes	23/10/14	Killed
2nd Bn.Yorks Regt	Lt.F.C.Ledgard	23/10/14	Killed
	Lt.R.Walmesley	23/10/14	Killed
	Capt C.G.Jeffery	23/10/14	Wounded
	Lt.C.G.Forsyth	23/10/14	Wounded
	Lt.W.F.I.Bell	23/10/14	Wounded
	Capt H.W.McCall	25/10/14	Wounded
	Capt.H.Levin	29/10/14	Wounded
	Major W.L.Alexander	29/10/14	Wounded
	Lt.A.T.Thorne	29/10/14	Wounded
	Capt.J.W.Stansfield	25/10/14	Wounded
	Major W.B.Walker	29/10/14	Killed
	2/Lt.M.T.Thwaites	29/10/14	Wounded
	2/Lt.L.Sykes	29/10/14	Wounded
	2/Lt.L.H.Marriage	29/10/14	Wounded
	Lt.Col.C.A.King	30/10/14	Killed
	Capt E.S.Broun	30/10/14	Killed
	2/Lt F.C.Hatton	30/10/14	Killed
	Lt W.H.Colley	30/10/14	Wounded
	2/Lt.D.C.Kidd	30/10/14	Wounded & Mis
	2/Lt.W.A.Worsley	30/10/14	Wounded & Mis
	2/Lt.R.H.Middleditch	30/10/14	Wounded & Mis
	Capt R.B.Corser	1/11/14	Wounded
	Lt.R.H.Phayre	26/10/14	Killed
	2/Lt.L.Studley	25/10/14	Killed
	2/Lt.H.G.Brooksbank	3/11/14	Wounded

APPENDIX:- B

Unit	Rank & Name	Date	Casualty
2nd Bn R.S.Fusiliers	Lt.J.E.Utterson-Kelso	22/10/14	Wounded
	Capt.F.Fairlie	23/10/14	Killed
	Capt A.C.Adair	23/10/14	Wounded
	2/Lt G.B.Bayley	25/10/14	Killed
	Lt.W.Tod	25/10/14	Wounded
	Lt.C.G.G.Mackenzie	25/10/14	Killed
	Lt.N.Kennedy	25/10/14	Wounded & Mis.
	2/Lt.C.Mc.C.Alston	25/10/14	Missing
	Capt.G.C.Fleetwood	26/10/14	Missing
	Lt.R.V.G.Horn	29/10/14	Wounded
	2/Lt.M.B.Buchanan	29/10/14	Wounded
	Maj.A.M.H.Forbes		Wounded
	Capt.J.G.Whigham		Wounded
	Lt.G.R.T.Kennedy		Wounded
	Lt.A.L.Thomson		Wounded
	2/Lt.Whitton		Wounded
	2/Lt.W.E.Clutterbuck		Wounded
	Major A.C.H.MacGregor		Missing
	Capt.A.G.L.E.Gallais		Missing
	Lt.H.W.V.Stewart		Missing
	2/Lt.E.P.O.Boyle		Missing
	2/Lt.J.L.Bowen		Missing
	2/Lt.Christie		Missing
	Lt.Col.Baird-Smith		Wounded & Mis.
	Capt.R.M.Burgoyne		Wounded & Mis.
	Lt.A.Ross Thomson		Wounded & Mis.
2ns Bn.Wilts Regt.	Capt A.C.Magor	17/10/14	Killed
	Capt C.G.M.Carter	23/10/14	Killed
	Lt.H.S.Grimston	23/10/14	Killed
	2/Lt.Burges (Ox.Uv.O.T.C.)	23/10/14	Killed
	Lt.E.Spencer	23/10/14	Killed
	2/Lt.F.L.D.Shelford	23/10/14	Wounded
	Lt.Col.J.F.Forbes	24/10/14	Missing
	Major J.R.Wyndham	24/10/14	Missing
	Major C.A.Law	24/10/14	Missing
	Capt E.L.W.Henslow	24/10/14	Missing
	Capt A.W.Timmis	24/10/14	Missing
	Capt.H.F.Coddington	24/10/14	Missing
	Capt C.H.E.Moore	24/10/14	Missing
	Capt G.LeHuquet	24/10/14	Missing
	Capt R.P.Culver	24/10/14	Missing
	Lt.R.Smith	24/10/14	Missing
	Lt A.S.Hooper	24/10/14	Missing
	Lt.A.H.Bleckley	24/10/14	Missing.
	Lt.D.A.Ansted.	24/10/14	Missing
	2/Lt.R.P.Rogers	24/10/14	Missing
	2/Lt.C.H.R.Barnes	24/10/14	Missing
	2/Lt.E.L.Betts	24/10/14	Missing
	2/Lt.G.P.Oldfield	24/10/14	Missing
	2/Lt.F.Rylands	24/10/14	Missing
	2/Lt.W.P.Campbell	24/10/14	Missing
	2/Lt.M.R.Fowle	24/10/14	Wounded.

APPENDIX:- B

Unit.	Rank & Name	Date	Casualty.
Hd Qrs 22nd Inf.Bde.	Lt.F.V.Thicke (Int Corps)	31/10/14	Missing
	Capt G.M.James (Bde Major)	4/11/14	Killed
	Capt R.V.Barker(S.Capt)	32/10/14	Killed
	Lt C.B.Adams (Bde M.G.O)	30/10/14	Missing.
2nd Bn "Queens"	Capt H.F.Lewis	19/10/14	Wounded & Mis.
	2/Lt.C.S.Ingram	21/10/14	Killed
	Lt.R.I.G.Heath	21/10/14	Wounded
	Lt H.C.Williams	21/10/14	Wounded
	2/Lt G.M.Cabb	21/10/14	Wounded
	Capt H.C.Whinfield	21/10/14	Wounded
	2/Lt.D.Ive	21/10/14	Killed
	Lt.E.W.Bethell	25/10/14	Wounded
	Capt H.F.H.Master	20-22/10/14	Wounded & Mis
	Capt P.C.Esdaile	" "	Wounded
	2/Lt.J.G.H.Bird	25-27/10/14	Killed
	Lt.A.D.Brown	26/10/14	Wounded
	Lt.Col.M.C.Coles	29- 2/11/14	Wounded
	Maj.L.M.Crofts	" "	" "
	Maj.H.R.Bottomley	" "	" "
	Capt.T.Weeding	" "	" "
	Lt.D.R.Wilson	" "	" "
	2/Lt.R.H.Philpot	" "	" "
	Lt.A.C.Thomas	6/11/14	Wounded
	Lt.E.K.B.Furze	6/11/14	Wounded
	Capt W.H.Alleyne	7/11/14	Wounded & Mis.
	Lt.C.R.Haig	7/11/14	Killed
	Capt A.N.S.Roberts	7/11/14	~~Killed~~ Wounded
	Lt.J.A.L.Brown	7/11/14	Wounded
	2/Lt.J.G.Collis	7/11/14	Wounded
	Lt.G.A.White	5/11/14	Wounded
	2/Lt.Smith	5/11/14	Wounded
	2/Lt.C.Pascoe	7/11/14	Wounded
	2/Lt.J.D.Burrows	22/11/14	Wounded
2nd Bn.R.Warwick Regt.	Lt,J.E.Ratcliff	19/10/14	Killed
	Lt.R.T.Stainforth.	19/10/14	Killed
	Maj.G.N.B.Forster	19/10/14	Wounded
	Capt G.R.Taylour	19/10/14	Wounded
	Lt.J.H.G.McCormack	19/10/14	Missing
	Capt.C.O.B.H.Methuen	21/10/14	Killed
	Capt.T.Whaley	21/10/14	Wounded
	Lt.N.B.F.Collins	20-21/10/14	Missing
	Lt.G.H.R.B.Somerville	" " "	~~Wounded & Mis.~~
	2/Lt.J.E.Medcalfe	" " "	Missing
	Lt.Col.W.L.Loring	25/10/14	Killed
	2/Lt.Deane	25/10/14	Killed
	Lt.J.P.Duke	25/10/14	Wounded
	Lt,J.S.Knyvett	25/10/14	Wounded
	2/Lt.N.H.L.Matear	29/10/14	Wounded
	Capt.F.B.Follett	31/10/14	Wounded
	Capt A.J.Peck	21/10/14	Missing
	Capt E.G.Sydenham (Sydenham)	31/10/14	Missing
	Capt P.J.Foster	31/10/14	Missing
	Lt.E.M.Onslow	31/10/14	Missing
	Lt.H.W.Ozanne	31/10/14	Missing
	Lt.I.A.Brown	31/10/14	Missing

APPENDIX:- B

Unit	Rank & Name	Date	Casualty
2nd Bn.R.Warwick Regt. (Continued)	Lt.J.Lucas	31/10/14	Missing
	2/Lt.Harrison (Sher For.)	2/11/14	Killed
	2/Lt.P.J.Burn (Leicester R)	7/11/14	Wounded
	2/Lt.R.Hutton -do-	7/11/14	Missing
	Capt.E.C.Schooling	20-7/11/14	Wounded
	2/Lt.Vacher	29/11/14	Killed
1st Bn.R.Welsh Fusiliers	Capt.E.O.Skaife	20/10/14	Wounded & Mis.
	Capt J.H.Brennan	20/10/14	Killed
	Lt.G.O.de P.Chance	20/10/14	Killed
	Capt.W.Harris-St-John	20/10/14	Wounded
	Capt.S.Jones	20/10/14	Wounded
	Capt.W.G.Vyvyan	20/10/14	Wounded
	2/Lt.R.E.Naylor	20/10/14	Wounded
	Capt.W.M.Kington, D.S.O.	21/10/14	Killed
	Capt M.E.Lloyd	21/10/14	Killed
	Lt.E.C.L.Hoskyns	21/10/14	Killed
	2/Lt.G.P.J.Snead-Cox	21/10/14	Killed
	2/Lt.C.G.H.Peppe	21/10/14	Wounded & Mis.
	Lt.J.M.Courage	21/10/14	Wounded & Mis.
	Lt.L.A.A.Alston	21/10/14	Wounded
	2/Lt.J.M.J.Evans	21/10/14	Wounded
	Capt J.G.Smyth-Osbourne	21/10/14	Missing
	Lt.D.M.Barchard	21/10/14	Missing
	2/Lt Bingham	21/10/14	Missing
	2/Lt.A.Walmsley	21/10/14	Wounded
	2/Lt.H.T.Ackland-Allen	23/10/14	Killed
	Lt.R.E.Hudson	23/10/14	Missing
	2/Lt.S.Williams	27/10/14	Wounded
	Capt D.J.Burk (D.C.L.I.)	29/10/14	Wounded
	Lt.Col H.D.S.Cadogan	30/10/14	Missing
	Lt.A.E.C.T.Dooner	30/10/14	Missing
	Lt.B.C.H.Poole	30/10/14	Missing
	2/Lt.E.Woodhouse	30/10/14	Missing
	2/Lt.R.L.B.Egerton	30/10/14	Missing
	2/Lt.A.M.G.Evans	30/10/14	Missing
	Capt T.H.Disney (5/Essex)	30/10/14	Missing
	Capt.E.E.Barrow (3/D.C.L.I.)	30/10/14	Missing
	Capt.W.Vincent -do-	30/10/14	Missing
	2/Lt.N.Pynn -do-	30/10/14	Missing
	Lt.C.V.de G.Elyde(2/D.C.L.I.)	30/10/14	Missing
	2/Lt.Proctor	27/10/14	Wounded
	2/Lt.F.R.Orme	7/11/14	Wounded & Mis
	Major R.E.P.Gabbett	17/11/14	Wounded

APPENDIX:- B

Unit.	Rank & Name	Date.	Casualty.
1st Bn. S Staffs Regt.	Capt.C.G.Ransford	20-21/10/14	Wounded
	Lieut.C.W.Evans	20-21/10/14	Wounded
	Lieut E.L.Holmes	23/10/14	Killed
	Capt.J.S.S.Dunlop	25/10/14	Killed
	Major S.C.Welchman	27/10/14	Wounded
	Capt.C.H.Green	27/10/14	Wounded
	2/Lieut.H.R.S.Bower	27/10/14	Wounded
	Capt.S.Bonner	29/10/14	Wounded
	Maj.J.E.Loder-Symons	31/10/14	Killed
	Lieut C.F.Crousaz	31/10/14	Killed
	Lt.Col.R.M.Ovens	31/10/14	Wounded
	Major A.C.Buckle	31/10/14	Wounded
	Lieut Archer Shee	31/10/14	Wounded & Mis
	Lieut H.Willoughby	31/10/14	Wounded & Mis
	Lieut W.A.P.Foster	31/10/14 died	Missing
	Lieut.C.Adams (Bde M.G. Offr)	31/10/14	Missing
	Capt.J.F.Vallentin	7/11/14	Killed
	Capt O de Trafford	20-7/11/14	Wounded & Mis
	Lieut H.W.McGeorge	" "	Wounded
	Lieut C.R.C.Bean	" "	Wounded
	Lieut C.E.C.Bartlett	" "	Wounded
	Lieut D.G.Twiss	" "	Wounded
	Lieut I.H.K.Shore	" "	Wounded
	Lieut C.G.Hume	" "	Killed
	2/Lieut.R.R.Riley	" "	Missing
	2/Lieut G.E.Parker	" "	Missing
	2/Lieut Burke	" "	Missing
	2/Lieut.Tomlinson	" "	Wounded.
7th Divisional Train	~~Capt.C.O.Hay~~	~~24/10/14~~	~~Wounded~~
~~21st Field Ambulance~~ R.A.M.C.	Lieut F.G.Thatcher	27/10/14	Wounded
	Capt.H.S.Dickson	28/10/14	Wounded
	Lieut.Butt	29/10/14	Missing
	Lieut.H.L.Shore	2/11/14	Wounded
	Capt.H.Robertson	30/10/14	Missing
	Lieut H.B.Winter	1/11/14	Missing
	Lieut S.W.Richardson	4/11/14	Killed
	Capt.T.Mc C.Phillips	4/11/14	Wounded
	Capt.K.Comyn	3/11/14	Wounded
23rd Field Ambulance	Lieut.S.R.Hayman	23/10/14	Missing
8th Bn. Royal Scots	Capt.J.A.Todd	20/11/14	Wounded & Mis
	~~2/Lieut D.M.Stewart~~	~~1/12/14~~	~~Wounded~~
1st Medium Siege Battery	Capt C.L.Evans	8/11/14	Wounded
	2/Lieut E.C.Scott (5th Battery)	21/11/14	Killed

Appendix C   Reinforcements received.   7th Division

		Officers.	men
October 26th.	2nd Bn. Warwickshire Regt.	1	56
	1st Bn. Royal Welsh Fus.	1	90
	22nd F. A. Brigade		6
October 29th.	2nd Bn. Bedfordshire Regt.	1	20
	2nd Bn. R.S. Fusiliers	1	20
	2nd Bn. "Queens".	1	—
	1st Bn. Royal Welsh Fus.	7	—
October 30th.	2nd Bn. Bedfordshire Regt.	2	—
	22nd F. A. Brigade.	—	3
November 1st.	2nd Bn. Bedfordshire Regt.	2	96
	2nd Bn. R.S. Fusiliers	1	30
	22nd F. A. Brigade	—	2
November 3rd.	1st Bn. Grenadier Guards	1	96
	2nd Bn. Scots Guards	1	99
	2nd Bn. Border Regt.	1	96
	2nd Gordons.	1	93
	2nd Bn. Yorkshire Regt.	1	88
	2nd Bn. R.S. Fusiliers	1	50
	2nd Bn. Wiltshire Regt	1	96
	2nd Bn. "Queens".	1	112
	2nd Bn. Warwickshire Regt.	2	96
	1st Bn. S. Staffordshire Regt.	1	100
	Divisional Head Quarters	1	—
	3rd Heavy Brigade	—	3
November 6th	Divisional Head Quarters	1	—
	7th Signal Company	—	3
	2nd Bn. Bedfordshire Regt.	1	—
	1st Bn. Royal Welsh Fus.	1	109
November 7th	Divisional Head Quarters.	1	—
	2nd Bn. Bedfordshire Regt.	1	20
	2nd Bn. R.S. Fusiliers	—	30
	2nd Bn. Wiltshire Regt.	—	32
November 8th	Northumberland Hussars	4	—
	35th F.A. Brigade.	2	15
	1st Bn. Royal Welsh Fusiliers	2	99
November 9th	7th Signal Company	—	12
	2nd Bn. "Queens"	—	20
	1st Bn. S. Staffordshire Regt.	1	30

Appendix C

Reinforcements received 7th Division.

Date	Unit	Officers	men
10th November	35th F.A.Brigade	–	44
	21st Field Ambulance	2	--
November 11th	Div H.Q.	1	–
	35th F.A.Brigade	–	7
	3rd Heavy Brigade	–	10
	1st Bn Grenadier Guards	4	401
	2nd Bn.Scots Guards	7	250
	2nd Bn.Gordon Highlanders	1	91
	2nd Bn.Bedfordshire Regt	1	119
	2nd Bn.Wilts Regt	1	--
	2nd Bn."Queens	2	207
	2nd Bn.Warwickshire Regt	–	160
	1st Bn.R.Welsh Fusiliers	2	303
	21st Field Ambulance	1	--
	23rd Field Ambulance	1	--
November 12th	Divisional Hd Qrs.	1	--
	35th F.A.Brigade	1	1
	1st Bn.Grenadier Guards	2	133
	2nd Bn.Scots Guards	5	285
	2nd Bn.Wiltshire Regt	1	60
	2nd Bn."Queens	3	247
	2nd Bn.Warwickshire Regtz	–	250
	1st Bn.R.Welsh Fusiliers	–	151
	21st Field Ambulance	1	--
November 13th	35th F.A.Brigade	–	11
	2nd Bn.Gordon Highlanders	4	--
	22nd Infantry Brigade	1	--
	1st Bn.S.Staffordshire Regt	–	20
November 14th	35th F.A.Brigade	–	40
	7th Div.Ammn Column	1	4
	20th Infantry Brigade	1	–
	1st Bn.Grenadier Guards	4	–
	21st Infantry Brigade	1	–
November 15th	7th Signal Company	–	13
	2nd Bn.Bedfordshire Regt	–	100
	2nd Bn "Queens"	1	12
	22nd F.A. Brigade	–	12
November 16th	7th Signal Company	–	11
	7th Division Ammn Column	–	3
	2nd Bn.Yorkshire Regt	5	510
	22nd F.A.Brigade	–	45
November 17th	7th Signal Company	–	5
	14th Brigade R.H.A.	1	32
	35th F.A.Brigade	1	25
	7th Division Ammn Column	–	24
	1st Bn.Grenadier Guards	1	--
	1st Bn.R.Welsh Fusiliers	1	5
	22nd F.A.Brigade	–	7
November 18th	22nd F.A.Brigade	–	11
	35th F.A.Brigade	1	–
	7th Division Ammn Column	–	26
	1st Bn.Grenadier Guards	1	2
	2nd Bn.Bedfordshire Regt	1	–
	7th Division Train	–	34

Appendix G   Reinforcements received 7th Division

		Officers	men
November 19th	1st Bn. Grenadier Guards	5	100
	2nd Bn. Border Regt	-	17
	2nd Bn. Gordon Highlanders	-	16
	2nd Bn. Bedfordshire Regt	3	100
	2nd Bn. R.S. Fusiliers	-	100
	2nd Bn. Wiltshire Regt	3	155
	2nd Bn. Warwickshire Regt	-	7
	R.A.M.C.	-	38
November 20th	54th Field Coy, R.E.	-	44
	55th Field Coy R.E.	1	32
	22nd Infantry Brigade H.Q.	1	1
	2nd Bn. Warwickshire Regt	2	98
	R.A.M.C.	-	16
	22nd F.A. Brigade	-	3
November 22nd	2nd Bn. Gordon Highlanders	1	89
	2nd Bn. Bedfordshire Regt	1	94
	2nd Bn. R.S. Fusiliers	-	65
	2nd Bn. Wiltshire Regt	1	9
	2nd Bn. R. Welsh Fusiliers	1	96
November 24th	R.A., H.Q.	-	1
	14th H.A. Brigade	-	35
	3rd Heavy Brigade	-	20
	22nd F.A. Brigade	-	6
	1st Bn. Grenadier Guards	1	-
November 26th	H.Q. R.A.	-	1
	22nd F.A. Brigade	-	2
	3rd Heavy Brigade	-	7
	2nd Bn. Border Regt	3	11
	2nd Bn. Gordon Highlanders	-	13
	2nd Bn. R.S. Fusiliers	4	5
	2nd Bn. Wiltshire Regt	4	1
	2nd Bn. "Queens"	2	120
	2nd Bn. R. Welsh Fusiliers	3	--
	R.A.M.C.	1	--
November 29th	7th Signal Company	1	2
	54th Field Coy, R.E.	1	-
	1st Bn. Grenadier Guards	1	-
	22nd Infantry Brigade H.Q.	-	1
November 30th	22nd F.A. Brigade	-	10
	54th Field Coy R.E.	1	1

1st Battalion, Grenadier Guards.

Roll of Officers present with above Unit at 12 noon on 18th Nov: 1914.

Rank.	Name.	Remarks.
Major	Duberly, G.W.	Reserve of Officers.
Captain	Lygon, M.V.O., The Hon.R.	Reserve of Officers.
Lieut:	Mitchell, C.	Reserve Of Officers.
Lieut:	Sykes, C.	Reserve of Officers.
Lieut:	Rowley, J. Sick 27%	Special Reserve Officer.
Lieut:	Blundell, C.L.	Reserve of Officers.
2/Lieut:	Darby, M.A.A.	Regular Officer.
2/Lieut:	Fisher-Rowe, C.	Special Reserve Officer.
Lieut & Q.M.	Teece, J.	Regular Officer.
	ATTACHED.	
Lieut:	McCutcheon, A.M.	R.A.M.C. Medical Officer.
2/Lieut:	Miller, A.A.	Territorial. Attached from 'Artists' Rifles on probation for tempy 2/Lieutenant.
2/Lieut:	Drake, R.	- do -
2/Lieut:	Eldmann, F.J.F.	- do -
2/Lieut:	Crisp, F.E.F.	- do -

Captain	Stanhope, Earl.	Reserve of Officers.
Captain	Morrison, J.A.	- do -
2/Lieut:	Brabourne, Lord, W.W.	Special Reserve.
2/Lieut:	Percy, Lord W.	- do -
2/Lieut:	Rhys Williams.	
Major	Trotter, E.H.	Regular Officer. Joined 25/11/14.

2nd Battalion, Scots Guards.

Roll of Officers present with above Unit at 12 noon on 18th Nov: 1914.

Rank	Name.	Remarks.
Captain	Paynter, G.C.B.	Regular Officer.
Captain	x Romer, M.	- do -
Captain	Coke, R.	Reserve of Officers.
Captain	Coke, Viscount.	Special Reserve.
Captain	Bagot Chester, G.J.N.	Reserve of Officers. Sick
Lieut:	Loder, G.H.	Regular Officer.
Lieut:	Warner, E.C.T.	Regular Officer.
Lieut:	Hulse, Sir E.H. Bt.	Regular Officer.
2/Lieut:	Swinton, A.H.C.	Regular Officer.
Lieut:	Fitz-Wygram, Sir F.L.Bt.	Regular Officer.
Lieutenant.	Hanbury Tracey, Hon.C.H.	Reserve of Officers.
2/Lieut:	Lisburne, Earl of.	Reserve of Officers.
Lieut:	Cator, C.A.M.	Reserve of Officers.
2/Lieut:	Clive, Visct.	Regular Officer.
2/Lieut:	Liddell Granger, H.H.	Reserve of Officers.
Lieut:	Saumarez, Hon.J.St.V.	Special Reserve Officer.
2/Lieut:	Ottley, G.C.L.	Regular Officer.
Lieut:	Massey, C.	Reserve of Officers.
Lieut:	Taylor, H.	Regular Offr.(Machine Gun Offr.(Bde).)
Lieut:	Barry.	R. of Offrs. (Machine Gun Officer.)
Lieut: & Q.M.	Ross, T.	Regular Officer.
	ATTACHED.	
Captain	Davies, T.H.T.	R.A.M.C. Medical Officer.
Lieut	Nugent, R.F.	R. of Offrs.

8th Battalion, Royal Scots.

Roll of Officers of above unit present at 12 noon on 18th November 1914.

Rank & Name.		Remarks.
Major.	Brook, A.	Territorial Officer.
Captain	Gemmill, W.	,, ,,
Captain	Tait, J.	,, ,,
Captain	Todrick, T.	,, ,,
Captain	McEwen, B.	,, ,,
Captain	Ballantyne, G.H.	,, ,,
Captain	Todd, J.A.	,, ,, 6th Bn Royal Scots.
Captain	McRae, W.A.R.M.	,, ,,
Captain	Rowbotham, J.	,, ,, 8th Bn H.Light Infty.
Lieut:	Mitchell, T.B.	,, ,,
Lieut:	Watson, T.W.	,, ,,
Lieut:	Burt, A.	,, ,,
Lieut:	Kerr, R.B.	,, ,,
Lieut:	Plew, F.G.	,, ,,
Lieut:	Richardson, J.	,, ,,
Lieut:	Turner, J.A.L.	,, ,, 6th Bn Royal Scots.
Lieut:	Greenshields, J.B.	,, ,, 8th Bn H.Light Infty.
2/Lieut:	Stewart, D.M.	,, ,,
2/Lieut:	Young, J.	,, ,,
2/Lieut:	Pringle, J.S.	,, ,,
2/Lieut:	Kemp, J.G.	,, ,,
2/Lieut:	Thorburn, R.M.	,, ,,
2/Lieut:	Nicol J.L.	,, ,, 6th Bn Royal Scots.
2/Lieut:	Elder, J.H.	Sick 2 12/1. ,, ,,
2/Lieut:	Wallace, W.E.	,, ,,
2/Lieut:	Maxwell, R.	,, ,,
2/Lieut:	Martin, J.	,, ,, 8th Bn H.Light Infty.
Captain	Grant-Suttie, G.D.	Regular Officer (Black Watch) Adjutant.
Lieut & Qr:Mr.	Clark, F.	Territorial Officer. 8th Bn R.Scots.
Major	Crombie, J.F.	,, ,, R.A.M.C.

2nd Battalion, Border Regiment.

Roll of Officers present with above Unit at 12 noon on 18th Nov: 1914.

Rank	Name.	Remarks.
Captain	Warren, G.E.	Regular Officer.
Captain	Askew, H.A.	- do -, a/Adjutant.
Captain	Jenkins, N.F.	Special Reserve Officer.
Lieut:	Watson, W.	Regular Officer. Machine-Gun Officer.
Lieut:	Kennedy, M.S.N.	Special Reserve Officer.
2/Lieut:	Hutton, B.	Regular Officer. Promoted from ranks.
2/Lieut:	Kerr, W.	Regular Officer. Promoted from ranks.
Lieut & Qr. Mr.	Mitchell, F.W.	Regular Officer (Qr.Mr. & Tpt Officer.)
	Attached.	
Lieut.	Ormsby. W.	R.A.M.C. Medical Officer.
2/Lieut:	Wornum T.H.	Territorial. Attached from "Artists" Rifles on probation for tempy 2/Lieut:.
2/Lieut:	Closey, M.A.	- do -
2/Lieut:	Cuthbertson, F.J.	- do -
2/Lieut:	Sampson, H.F.	- do -

2nd Battalion, Gordon Highlanders.

Roll of Officers present with above Unit at 12 noon on 18th Nov: 1914.

Rank	Name	Remarks
Lieut:	Hamilton, J.M.	Regular Officer.
Lieut:	Sprot, H.M.	- do -
2/Lieut:	Graham, W.J.	- do -
Capt: & Qr. Mr.	Mackie, J.	- do -
2/Lieut:	Letters, T.A.	Special Reserve Officer.
2/Lieut:	Gibb, W.H.	Special Reserve Officer. Black Watch.
	ATTACHED.	
Lieut:	Cowtan, F.C.	R.A.M.C. Medical Officer.
2/Lieut:	Mullock, E.R.	Territorial. Attached from "Artists" Rifles on probation for tempy 2/Lieutenant.
2/Lieut:	Chater, A.D.	- do -
2/Lieut:	Horsley, S.	- do -
2/Lieut:	Horsley, O.	- do -

Capt. B.G.R. Gordon.

2nd Battalion, Bedfordshire Regiment.

Roll of Officers present with the above Unit at 12 noon on 18th Nov: 1914.

Rank	& Name.	Remarks.
Captain	Cumberlege, C.B.	Regular Officer.
Captain	Foss, C.C.	- do -
Lieut:	Shearman, C.E.G.	- do -
Lieut:	Mills, S.D.	- do -
Cpt & Q.M.	Cressingham, H.	- do -
Lieut:	Goudie, W.D.	R.A.M.C.
Captain	Collings-Wells, J.S.	Special Reserve, 4/Bedfords.
2/Lieut:	William Wilson G.	sick - do - 5/Middlesex Regt.
2/Lieut:	Waddy, G.H.	- do - Gloucester Regt.
2/Lieut:	Carstake, W.B.	- do - R.W.Surrey Regt.
2/Lieut:	Dabbell, H.V.	Territorial, attached from 'Artists' Rifles on probation for tempy 2/Lieut.
2/Lieut:	Brewer, C.H.	- do -
2/Lieut:	Williams, H.	- do -
2/Lieut:	de Buriatle, F.	- do -

2/Lieut: J.W.Wyld, S.R. Hampshire Regiment.

2nd Battalion, Yorkshire Regiment.

Roll of Officers present with above Units at 12 noon on 18th Nov: 1914.

Rank &	Name,	Remarks.
Captain	Moss-Blundell, B.S.	Regular Officer.
Lieut:	Kreyer, H.S.	- do -
2nd Lieut:	Chauncy, W.A.A.	- do -
Lieut: & : Mr:	Pickard, E.	- do -
Major	Southey, E.	Special Reserve, 3rd S.W.Borderers.
Captain	Milnes, H.R.	- do - 3rd Lincoln Regt.
2nd Lieut:	Payton, D.	- do - 3rd W.Riding Regt.
2nd Lieut:	Burbury, J.F.	- do - 3rd R.W.Kent Regt.
2nd Lieut:	Montesole, H.S.R.	- do - 3rd R.Sussex Regt.
	ATTACHED.	
2nd Lieut:	Hollis, H.L.	Territorial, attached from 'Artists' Rifles on probation for tempy 2/Lt.
2nd Lieut:	Crosse, M.E.B.	- do -
2nd Lieut:	Pickup, A.J.	- do -
2nd Lieut:	Cuttle, G.	- do -
Lieut:	Laud, D.A.	R.A.M.C. Medical Officer.

(S.R.)

2nd Battaluon, Royal Scots Fusiliers

Roll of Officers present with the above Unit at 12 noon on 18th Nov: 1914.

Rank & Name.	Remarks.
Captain Traill, T.B.	Regular Officer.
Lieut: Thomson, K.C.	- do -
- Benson, T.B.	From retired list, holding commission for period of the War.
/Lieut: Clutterbuck, W.E.	Regular Officer.
2/Lieut: Kennedy. C.N.J.	- do -
Lt: & Q.M. Spence, A.	- do -
ATTACHED.	
Lieut: Ingram, W.W.	R.A.M.C. Medical Officer.
2/Lieut: Wallace, J.A. Sick 2%	Territorial, attached from 'Artists' Rifles on probation for tempy 2/Lieutenant.
2/Lieut: Stewart, J.	- do -
2/Lieut: Raymond Barker, C.L.	- do -
2/Lieut: White, L.S.	- do -

```
Lieut:   M.W.Parr.          S.R. 3/H.L.I.
2/Lieut: W.M.Dickenson,     Regular. 2/H.L.I.
2/Lieut: R.M.Graham.        Regular, 2/Essex Regt.
2/Lieut: A.C.G.Lansdale,    S.R., 3/K.R.R.
```

2nd Battalion, Wilts Regiment.

Roll of Officers present with above unit at 12 noon on 18th Nov: 1914.

Rank	& Name.	Remarks.
Lieut:	Beaver, D.S.L.	Regular.
2/Lieut:	Waylen, ...	Regular.
Lt:& Q.M.	Hewitt, S.	Regular.
	ATTACHED.	
2/Lieut:	Strawson, F.M.	Territorial, attached from 'Artists' Rifles on probation for tempy 2/Lieut.
2/Lieut:	Shepherd, W.S.	- do -
2/Lieut:	Kitcat, A.J.	- do -
2/Lieut:	Carden, R.H.	- do -
Lieut:	Beaumont, E.	R.A.M.C. Medical Officer.

2nd Battalion "Queens".

Roll of Officers present with above Unit at 12 noon on 18th Nov: 1914.

Rank	Name.	Remarks.
Lieut:	Ross, R.K.	Regular Officer.
2/Lieut:	Allan, A.M.	Regular Officer.
Capt & Q.M.	Wort, C.H.J.	Regular Officer.
	ATTACHED.	
Captain.	Montague Bates, F.S.	Regular Offr. E.Surrey Regiment. ✓
Captain	Hewitt, A.S.	Regular Offr. R.W.Kent Regiment. ✓
Lieut:	Buchanan, J.S.	R.A.M.C. Medical Officer.
2/Lieut:	Burrows, J.D. W.22/11/14	Regular Offr. R.W.Kent Regiment. ✓
2/Lieut:	Wort, P.C.	Regular Offr. East Kent Regiment. ✓
2/Lieut:	Ramsay, D.G.	Regular Offr. Royal Sussex Regiment. ✓
2/Lieut:	Humphreys, D.F.	Territorial. Attached from "Artists" Rifles on probation for tempy 2/Lieutenant.
2/Lieut:	Masson, H.	- do -
2/Lieut:	Austin, C.F.	- do -
2/Lieut:	Rought, C.G.	- do -

2/Lieut:	Butterworth, H.	Special Reserve.
Lieut:	Gripper, W.V.T.	Special Reserve 3/East Surrey R.
Capt.	Fearon, P.J.	3/Queens. 5/12/14.

2nd Battalion, Royal Warwickshire Regiment.

Roll of Officers present with the above Unit at 12 noon on 18th Nov: 1914.

Rank	& Name.	Remarks.
Major	Brewis, R.H.W.	Regular Officer.
Lieut:	Swinhoe, L.R.	Regular Officer.
2nd Lieut:	Strevens, H.	Regular Officer. (Promoted from Ranks.)
2nd Lieut:	Richardson, R.F.	Regular Officer.
Lieut & Qr: Mr:	Hyde, W.N.	Regular Officer.
	ATTACHED.	
2/Lieut:	Herbage, G.F.W.	Territorial, attached from 'Artists' Rifles on probation for 2nd Lieutenant (tempy).
2/Lieut:	Pearce, G.V.	-do-
2/Lieut:	Monk, G.B.	- do -
2/Lieut:	Standring, B.A.	- do -
Major	Browne, M.	Attached from 10th (S) Bn L.N.Lancs Regiment.
Captain	Wright, A.R.	R.A.M.C. Medical Officer.
Captain	~~Stone, P.V.P.~~	To 1st Norfolk 23.11.14. Norfolk Regiment (attd) Arrived 19/11/14.
Lieutenant	Burnard, B.F.P.	2/R.Warwick Regiment. - do -

1st Battalion, Royal Welsh Fusiliers.

Roll of Officers present with above Unit at 12 noon on 18th Nov: 1914.

Rank & Name.		Remarks.
Major	Habbett, R.E.P.	Regular Officer.
Captain	Garnett, W.B.	Regular Officer.
Captain	Minshull Ford, J.R.M.	Regular Officer.
Captain	Wood, C.E.	Regular Officer.
Cpt & Q.M.	Parker, A.E.	Regular Offr.(attd: Hdqrs,7th Division.)
2/Lieut:	Cottrell, J.	Regular Officer (a/Quartermaster).
2/Lieut:	Gore, G.R.	Special Reserve Officer.
2/Lieut:	John, S.B.	Regular Offr, S.W.Bdrs (unposted).
	Attached.	
2/Lieut:	Rees, J.T.	Territorial.Attached from 'Artists' Rifles on probation for tempy 2/Lieutenant.
2/Lieut:	Winters, J.W.	- do -
2/Lieut:	Jones, L.	- do -
2/Lieut:	Parkes, H.F.	- do -

2/Lieut:	A. Walmsley.	Regular Officer. Joined 22/11/14.
2/Lieut :	I.H.Austin,	S.R., 3/Devons.
2/Lieut:	R.B.Ledgen.	S.R. Rif.Bde.
2/Lieut:	H.M.Heyland,	S.R. K.R.R.C.

7th Division

Commissions
    Artists Rifles

M.S.to C-in-C.No: 1878.   115.(A).

Headquarters,
    Fourth Corps.

1.   X   X   X

2.   The granting of commissions to those candidates (Pearce, Monk, Standring and Rought) who have become casualties is the subject of correspondence with the War Office. They have all been recommended for commissions.

3.   Private Herbage, who is still on sick leave or serving in England, was recommended for a commission under my No: 510/285/3 of 5th instant to War Office, and will no doubt be gazetted in due course.

4.   Second Lieutenant Silcock has been gazetted evidently, as his name appears on page 2678a of the Army List for February.

General Headquarters.   (Signed) W. Lambton, Brig:General,
25th February 1915.   Military Secretary to Commander-in-C.

4th A.C.No: 1315(a).   (2)

General Officer Commanding,
    7th Division.

        To note and return.

D.H.Q.   (Signed) J. Doyle, Lieutenant-Colonel,
27/2/1915.   D. A. A. & Q. M. G., 4th Corps.

(3)   115(A).

Headquarters,
    22nd Infantry Brigade.

    Forwarded for your information and retention, with
reference to your minute of the 17th instant, No: I/332.

                        Sgd:R.F.A.Hobbs.
                                    Major,
                            D.A.A.& Q.M.G.,
28/2/1915   7th Division.

                        (3)
Headquarters,
    Fourth Corps./

    Noted, communicated and returned.

                        Sgd:R.F.A.Hobbs, Major,
28/2/15.   D. A. A. & Q. M. G., 7th Division.

115.(A).

Headquarters,
20th Infantry Brigade.

With reference to your minute of the 15th instant,
No: 20/177, relative to the antedating of the commission
of Second Lieutenant F.T.Cuthbertson, 2nd Battalion,
Border Regiment (ex-Artists' Rifles), this matter will
be taken up.

It is however pointed out that Second Lieutenant F.T.
Cuthbertson has made an error in stating he joined on
probation on the 9th November 1914. He actually joined
on the 13th November 1914.

Please see attached g return

17/2/1915.

Lieutenant-Colonel,
A. A. G. & Q. M. G., 7th Divn.

Remarks

Endeavours are being made to
obtain full infn.
Invalided home - wounded.

- Prisoner of War

Endeavours are being made to
obtain full infn.
Missing
Killed
Wounded - died of wounds.

Regt No.	Present Rank	Name in full	Attached To	Whether Temporary or Permanent Commission.
		Archer		
1186	Pte	Albert Appleby Mellor	1/ Green	P
1076	"	Edward FitzJohn Crisp	-:-	T.
997	L/Cpl	Edward Ronald Mullock	2/ Gordons	Temp.
691	Cpl	Arthur Dougan Chaler	-:-	T.
1436	Pte	Sewadd Myles Horsley	-:-	T.
1434	"	Oswald Horsley	-:-	T.
1614	Pte	Frank Tetter Cuthbertson	2/ Borders	Tempy.
1551	"	Harold Tetison Sampson	-:-	Perm.
1030	Pte	Harry Williams	2/ Bedf/p	Tempy
1260	"	Charles Herbert Brewer	-:-	T.
1929	"	Norman Kicker Dabell	-:-	T.
1038	L/Cpl	Harold de Buriasse	-:-	T.
1968	Pte	Jack Stewart	2 R.S.F.	T.
		J. A. Wallace	at present in Hosp.	
Number unknown	Pte	Alfred James Pickup	2/ Yorks	P.
2255	"	Henry Lewis Hollis	-:-	P.
2220	"	Marlburg Evelyn Bedford Crosse	-:-	P
1167	"	Geoffry Castle	-:-	T.
1725	Pte	Frank Merlin Strawson	2/ Wilts	Perm.
1823	"	Ronald Hugh Carden	-:-	P.
1138	"	Alfred James Kitcat	-:-	P.T
1536	"	Walter Scott Shepherd	-:-	P.
1259	Pte	John Trevor Rees	1/ R.W.F.	P.
608	L/Cpl	Harry Frederick Parkes	-:-	T.
954	Cpl	Leonard Jones	-:-	T.
1934	Pte	Jesse William Winters	-:-	T.
1087	L/c	Arnold Silcock	1/ S. Staffs	P.
1744	Cpl	Harold Keith Mackintosh	-:-	P.
693	Sgt	Cyril Frederick Austin	Queens	T.
1390	Cpl	Harold Messon	-:-	T.
not known	Pte	Charles Gardner Rought	-:-	T.
1372	Pte	Dudley Francis Humphreys	-:-	T.

Prisoners of War — Herbage, Pearce, Money, Standring — at present in Hospital

No information from Warwicks (put them in)

T. Temporary. P. Permanent.

7th Division

Roll of men of Artist's Rifles granted commissions as Second Lieutenants.

Regt No	Present Rank	Name	Attached to	Whether Temp: or Permt: Commis:	Remarks.
1186	Private	Arthur Appleby Moller	1/Gren Gd.	Permanent	
1076	Private	Edward Fitzjohn Crisp	-do-	Temp:	
997	L/Cpl.	Edward Ronald Mullock	2/Gordons	Temp:	
691	Corpl.	Arthur Dougan Chater	-do-	Temp:	
1426	Private	Sewadd Myles Horsley	-do-	Temp:	
1437	Private	Oswald Horsley	-do-	Temp:	
1614	Private	Frank Tebbet Cuthbertson	2/Border R.	Temp:	
1551	Private	Harold Fehrson Sampson	-do-	Permt.	
1030	Private	Harry Williams	2/Bedf:R:	Temp:	
1260	Private	Charles Herbert Brewer	-do-	Temp:	
1929	Private	Norman Vicker Dabell	-do-	Temp:	
1033	L/Cpl.	Harold de Burlatte	-do-	Temp.	
1758	Private	Jack Stewart	2/R. S. F.	Temp.	
		J.A.Wallace (In Hospital)			Endeavours are being made to obtain full information Invalided home wounded
	Private	Alfred James Pickup	2/Yorks R.	Permt:	
2255	Private	Henry Lewis Hollis	-do-	Permt:	
2220	Private	Marlbury Evelyn Bedford Crosse	-do-	Permt:	
1167	Private	Geoffry Cuttle	-do-	Temp:	
1725	Private	Frank Merlin Strawson	2/Wilts R.	Permt:	
1823	Private.	Ronald Hugh Carden	-do-	Permt.	
1138	Private.	Alfred James Kitcat	-do-	Permt.	
1536	Private	Walter Scott Shepherd	-do-	Permt.	
1259	Private	John Trevor Rees	1/R.W.Fus.	Permt.	
608	L/Corpl.	Horace Frederick Parkes	-do-	Temp:	
954	Corpl.	Leonard Jones	-do-	Temp:	
1934	Private	Jesse William Winters	-do-	Temp:	
1087	L/Corpl.	Arnold Silcock	1/S.Staff:	Permt.	
1744	Corpl.	Harold Leith Mackintosh	-do-	Permt.	
693	Sergt.	Cyril Frederick Austin	2/Queens	Temp:	
1590	Corpl.	Harold Messon.	-do-	Temp.	
	Private	Charles Gardner Rought	-do-	Temp:	Pris:of War.
1372	Private	Dudley Francis Humphreys	-do-	Temp.	

2/Warwicks:
- Herbage (In Hospital
- Pearce (Missing)
- Monk (Killed)
- Standring (Wounded - died of Wounds)

(Endeavours are being made to obtain full information)

24/12/14

Major General

Commanding 7th Division.

Head Quarters,
    4th Army Corps.

Herewith rolls (in duplicate) showing the information as far as possible, relating to the probationers of the Artist's Rifles, as requested under your No.588/A dated 18/12/14.

The present Officer Commanding 2nd Bn.Royal Warwickshire Regiment, reports that he can offer no information on these probationers, as the correspondence was kept by the late Major Brewis, 2nd Bn.Royal Warwickshire Regiment.

24/12/14.   Major General
                                    Commanding 7th Division

Headquarters,
    4th Army Corps.
———————————

I forward herewith nominal roll of men of Artists' Rifles who have been attached as probationary Second Lieutenants to Battalions of the 7th Division (as shown), since the 15th November 1914. They have all been well reported on by their respective Commanding Officers who certify that they are fit to hold commissions.

In the event of Commissions being given them, I recommend that their appointment as Second Lieutenants should be antedated as from 15th November 1914.

A few, who were found not entirely suitable, have returned to their Regt. The majority have been most satisfactory, & it seems that this & similar sources of Supply can well be exploited for reinforcing the number of offrs

Sd T Capper
Major-General,

7th December 1914.   Commanding 7th Division.

Note - A letter has been written to O.C. Artists Rifles on this subject

(2)

Military Secretary,
    G.H.Q.
        These young officers have been most satisfactory, & in cases where young officers are urgently required I am sure the experiment could be repeated with success. Only four have been returned to the Regiment as unsuitable.

MERVILLE.   Signed H. RAWLINSON, Lieutenant General,
10/12/14.   Commanding 4th Corps.

STATEMENT SHOWING DISTRIBUTION AND RETURN OF PROBATIONARY OFFICERS FROM
ARTISTS' RIFLES.

Name	Date of Joining	Unit to which attached	Remarks
Arthur Appleby Mellor	15/11/14	1st Bn. Gren. Gds.	
Edward Fitzjohn Crisp	15/11/14	1st Bn. Gren. Gds.	
Frank Tebbot Cuthbertson	15/11/14	2nd Bn. Border Regt.	
Harold Fohrson Sampson	15/11/14	2nd Bn. Border Regt.	
Edward Ronald Mulock	15/11/14	2nd Bn. Gordon Hrs.	
Alfred Dougan Chater	15/11/14	2nd Bn. Gordon Hrs.	
Sewadd Myles Horsley	15/11/14	2nd Bn. Gordon Hrs.	
Oswald Horsley	15/11/14	2nd Bn. Gordon Hrs.	
Harold De Buriatto	15/11/14	2nd Bn. Bedford R.	
Harry Willans	15/11/14	2nd Bn. Bedford R.	
Charles Herbert Brewer	15/11/14	2nd Bn. Bedford R.	
Norman Vickor Babell	15/11/14	2nd Bn. Bedford R.	
Wallace *	15/11/14	2nd Bn. R.S. Fusiliers	
Jack Stewart	15/11/14	2nd Bn. R.S. Fusiliers	
Alfred James Pickup	15/11/14	2nd Bn. Yorks R.	
Henry Lewis Hollis	15/11/14	2nd Bn. Yorks R.	
Marlbury Evelyn Bedford Crosse	15/11/14	2nd Bn. Yorks R.	
Geoffry Cuttle	15/11/14	2nd Bn. Yorks R.	
Frank Merlin Strawson	15/11/14	2nd Bn. Wilts R.	
Walter Scott Shepperd	15/11/14	2nd Bn. Wilts R.	
Ronald Hugh Carden	15/11/14	2nd Bn. Wilts R.	
Alfred James Kitcat	15/11/14	2nd Bn. Wilts R.	
Cyril Frederic Austin	15/11/14	2nd Bn "Queens"	
Harold Hesson	15/11/14	2nd Bn "Queens"	
Charles Gardner Rought	15/11/14	2nd Bn "Queens"	
Dudley Francis Humphreys	15/11/14	2nd Bn "Queens"	
John Trevor Rees	15/11/14	1st Bn. R. Welch F.	
Horace Frederick Parkes	15/11/14	1st Bn. R. Welch F.	
Jesse William Winter	15/11/14	1st Bn. R. Welch F.	
Leonard Jones	15/11/14	1st Bn. R. Welch F.	
Percy Frederick William Herbage	15/11/14	2nd Bn R. Warwick R.	
Geoffrey Vincent Pearce	15/11/14	2nd Bn R. Warwick R.	
George Bertram Monk	15/11/14	2nd Bn R. Warwick R.	
Benjamin Arthur Standring	15/11/14	2nd Bn R. Warwick R.	
Arnold Silcock	15/11/14	1st Bn. S. Staffs R.	
Harry Leith Mackintosh	15/11/14	1st Bn. S. Staffs R.	

* In Hospital.

M.S. to C.-in-C. No: 510/26/8.

4th A.C. No: 388(A).

Headquarters,
    4th Army Corps.

       Approval is given for commissions as Second Lieutenants to be granted to all those mentioned on the attached roll. These commissions will be notified at an early date, and the Officers will be posted to the battalion to which they are now attached.

       Will you please cause the roll to be completed in following respects:-

(i). Regimental number, present rank, and full name of each
    candidate.
(ii). Whether a temporary commission for duration of war or a permanent commission is desired.

       Please return as early as possible.

G.H.Q.   Signed W. LAMBERTON,   Brigadier General,
17/12/14.   Military Secretary to Commander-in-Chief.

                (2)

Headquarters,
    7th Division.

       For information and necessary action.
       The completed rolls should be forwarded to this Office in duplicate, as early as possible.
       Please return.

D.H.Q.   Sgd: H. P. SHEKLETON,   Colonel,
18/12/1914.   A. A. & Q. M. G., 4th Corps.

                (3)

4th Corps.

       Noted and returned. Completed rolls will follow.

       Signed T. CAPPER, Major General,
19/12/14.   Commanding 7th Division.

115.(A).

Headquarters,

3   Infantry Brigade.'s

With reference to the temporary commissions which have been granted to N.C.Os and Men of the Artists' Rifles who were attached to various Battalions of the Division from the 13th November 1914, please note that the following is a copy of a G.H.Q. decision given in reply to applications for these Commissions to be antedated to 13th November 1914. Further applications in this respect should, therefore, not be submitted :-

"   It is regretted that the request for an antedate "cannot be granted.
"   The matter of the promotion of the members of the "Artists Rifles attached to Units of the 7th Division was "carefully considered at the time and the date then "determined.
"   All these candidates should have drawn the pay of "their former rank up to date of promotion."

(Signed) R. F. A. Hobbs.,
Major,
D. A. A. & Q. M. G.,
7th Division.

26th February 1915.

List of Men of Artists Rifles for commissions as Second Lieut.

Name	Remarks
1/Grenadier Guards.	
A. A. Moller	Granted, 1st S.L.I.
E. F. Crisp	— ״ — 2/Suffolk Rgt (since killed)
2/Gordons	
E. R. Mullock	Granted. 2/G.H.
A. D. Chater	— do —
S. M. Horsley	— do —
O. Horsley	— do —
2/Bedford R.	
H. Williams	Granted. 2/Beds Rgt
C. H. Brewer	— do —
N. V. Babell	— do —
H de Buriatte	— do —
2/Border R.	
F. T. Cuthbertson	Granted. 2/Border Rgt
H. F. Sampson	— do —
2/R.S.F.	
J. Stewart	Granted 2/R.S.Fus.
J. A. Wallace (Hosp)	At home sick. Commn. being dealt with by W.O.
2/Yorks	
A. J. Pickup	Being dealt with by W.O.
H. L. Hollis	Granted 2/Yorks
M. E. B. Crosse	— ״ —
C. Cuttle	— ״ —
2/Wilts R.	
F. M. Strawson	Granted 2/Wilts
R. H. Carden	— ״ —
A. J. Kitcat	— ״ —
W. S. Shepherd	— ״ —
1/R.W.Fusiliers	
J. T. Rees	Granted 1st RWFus
H. F. Parkes	— ״ —
L. Jones	— ״ —

List of men of Artists Rifles for commissions as Second Lieut.

Name	Remarks
J.W.Winters.	Granted 1st R.W.Fus.
1/S.Staff R.	
A.Silcock	Further report required when discharged from H.P.
H.L.Mackintosh	Granted 1st S.Staffs
2/Queens	
C.F.Austin ✓	Granted 2/Queens
H.Messon ✓	— do —
C.G.Rought	P. of W.
D.F.Humphreys ✓	Granted 2/Queens.
2/Warwicks	
Herbage	Sick. Further report required
Pearce	Killed
Monk	— " —
Standring.	— " —

www.ingramcontent.com/pod-product-compliance
Lightning Source LLC
Chambersburg PA
CBHW080843010526
44114CB00017B/2363